Becoming a School Consultant

Most consultation courses in school psychology focus heavily on theoretical models of consultation and associated intervention procedures. Little time is devoted to developing communication and process skills. Yet these process skills are key to properly identifying student problems and selecting appropriate interventions. Without skillfully conducted consultations, the implementation and evaluation of an intervention can be minimal. This book is designed to help students develop the process skills needed to become effective school consultants in consultee-centered consultation, with special emphasis on the instructional consultation model. The authors address specific skills and issues faced by novice consultants and document how they worked through particular issues that are likely to occur in school consultation practice.

Distinguishing Features

Field Tested—All the cases have been completed by students in a consultation course and are presented in the students' voice.

Chapter Structure—All chapters address specific skills and issues faced by novice consultants and document the skills they used to work through the issues. Each chapter begins with a set of advance organizer questions that frame the experience and ends with a set of questions that support the readers' self-reflection on their own work.

Sylvia Rosenfield (Ph.D. U. of Wisconsin-Madison) is Professor Emerita of the Counseling and Personnel Services Department at the University of Maryland. She is a Fellow of APA and AERA and a past president of APA Division 16 (School Psychology). Her awards include the National Association of School Psychologists Legends Award and the American Psychological Association's Distinguished Contributions to Education and Training Award. Her research has focused on training and practice in indirect services, particularly consultee-centered and instructional consultation. She has multiple publications and presentations on consultation and other topics as well as three previous books.

Becoming a School Consultant

Lessons Learned

Edited by

Sylvia Rosenfield

NEW YORK AND LONDON

First published 2012
by Routledge
711 Third Avenue, New York, NY 10017

Simultaneously published in the UK
by Routledge
2 Park Square, Milton Park, Abingdon, Oxon OX14 4RN

Routledge is an imprint of the Taylor & Francis Group, an informa business

Library of Congress Cataloging in Publication Data
Rosenfield, Sylvia A.
Becoming a school consultant : lessons learned / Sylvia Rosenfield.
p. cm.
Includes bibliographical references and index.
1. Educational consultants. I. Title.
LB2799.R67 2012
371.2—dc23 2011036140

ISBN: 978-0-415-88343-6 (hbk)
ISBN: 978-0-415-88344-3 (pbk)
ISBN: 978-0-203-81858-9 (ebk)

Typeset in Minion
by RefineCatch Limited, Bungay, Suffolk, UK

The SFI label applies to the text stock.

Printed and bound in the United States of America by
Walsworth Publishing Company, Marceline, MO.

Dedication

To the students in consultation courses from whom I have learned so much and to the future generation of school consultants.

Contents

Reviewer Acknowledgments

The authors gratefully acknowledge the contributions of the chapter reviewers for this volume: Wendy Cochrane, Kate Cramer, Heather Drumm, Pamela Fenning, Jorge Gonzalez, Meaghan Guiney, Lauren Kaiser, Cris Lauback, Deborah Nelson, Markeda Newell, Elise T. Pas, Ethan Schwer, and Kimberly Watche.

Contributors

Courtenay Barrett is a school psychology intern in the Anne Arundel County (MD) Public Schools and is completing her doctorate in school psychology at the University of Maryland. Her research/practice interests include multicultural issues and program evaluation.

Jill Berger is a school psychology intern with the Howard County (MD) Public School System, and is completing her doctorate in school psychology at the University of Maryland. Her research and practice interests include effective teaching practices and classroom management, school crisis response, and the influence of social media on young people.

Katie Burkhouse is completing her school psychology doctoral degree at the University of Maryland and working as a substitute school psychologist for the Howard County (MD) Public Schools. Her research interest is in consultation training of pre-service school psychologists.

Emily Gustafson is a school psychologist with the Olympic Educational Service District 114 (WA). She completed her doctoral degree in the school psychology program at the University of Maryland. Her interests include implementation of RTI and problem solving teams, prevention, and counseling connected to drug and alcohol use among teenagers.

Kathleen Gifford is a school psychology intern in the Anne Arundel County (MD) Public Schools and is working on her doctoral degree in school psychology at the University of Maryland. Her research/practice interests include early childhood intervention, social skills interventions, crisis response, and consultee-centered consultation.

Daniel Newman is an assistant professor at National Louis University in Chicago, having earned his doctoral degree in the school psychology program at the University of Maryland. His research interests focus on school consultation, consultation training, and supervision, and he co-chairs the NASP Interest Group for Consultee-Centered Consultation, and the TSP Consultation Training Interest Group.

Elise T. Pas is an assistant scientist at the Johns Hopkins Bloomberg School of Public Health. She earned her doctoral degree in the school psychology program at the University of Maryland. Her research interests include school consultation, coaching models and preventive interventions.

Cyril Pickering earned his masters degree in the school psychology program at the University of Maryland. He has research and professional interests in truancy and school attachment, and academic self-concept.

Sylvia Rosenfield is professor emerita at the University of Maryland. Her research and writing interests include consultation (training and practice) and the study of implementation.

Laura Schussler is a school psychology intern in the Fairfax County (VA) Public Schools, and is working on her doctorate in school psychology at the University of Maryland. Her research/practice interests are in preschooler's temperament and social-emotional competence.

Erica Sherry is Director of Young Adult Autism Services at Chimes International in Maryland, having earned her masters degree in the school psychology program at the University of Maryland. Her research and practice interests include academic, behavioral ad communication-based interventions for children and young adults with autism.

Elizabeth Tsakiris is a practicing school psychologist and a member of the faculty of the Interdisciplinary Council for Developmental and Learning Disorders. She earned her doctoral degree in the school psychology program at the University of Maryland. She specializes in research, assessment and interventions for children with autism and other complex learning challenges.

Megan Vaganek is a school psychology intern in the Arlington (VA) Public School District, and is working on her doctorate in school psychology at the University of Maryland. Her interests are in team functioning, team leadership and consultation.

Preface

When the great Fred Astaire had his first screen test, the comments were: "Can't act. Can't sing ... Can dance a little." Just as Astaire developed his skill over time, learning to be a consultant requires practice with feedback, persistence, and support through the novice and early competence stages. While not everyone will become an expert professional dancer (or even ready for *Dancing with the Stars*) or consultant, consultation is a learnable set of skills for most students in training for school practice. But as Gutkin and Conoley (1990) remind us, it should not be assumed "that psychologists who are adequately prepared to provide direct service are also adequately prepared to provide indirect service" (p. 205). It is our hope that this book will provide both information and a growing sense of confidence to the next generation of school consultants.

Recently, a consortium of faculty members in school psychology came together to discuss consultation training. A consistent theme among these faculty members, who are concerned about the state of consultation training, is the lack of materials to support the skill development of their students. It is, of course, essential to educate students about data, interventions and outcomes, and many courses in consultation focus on those aspects. However, research on consultation training has also documented the lack of emphasis on processes, communication, and relationships—it is the intent of this volume to address concerns of novice consultants in these areas. Additionally, exploring how to apply knowledge about consultation in school practice has also received scant attention. This book is designed to support the process of training in school consultation by demonstrating how novice consultants integrate knowledge and skill in doing consultation in the schools.

The authors of these chapter narratives provide a broad overview of the concerns of novice consultants at the pre-service level, that is, prior to completing their graduate level training. All but one was a full-time graduate student in the school psychology program at the University of Maryland at the time; one of the authors was a practicing school psychologist finishing her doctoral degree. They have had the courage to share in these narratives their personal and professional challenges, victories, and struggles as they completed their first or an early case while they were enrolled in the consultation courses or a third-year fieldwork in the program. As they continued their training and practice, they have come to respect what they learned, and believe it is important to share that learning with others. They each have my full respect and appreciation for their willingness to collaborate on this book.

Multiple acknowledgments are surely due here, too. We thank with heartfelt gratitude the site supervisors, the administrators, and the staff of the schools in which these authors learned the basics of consultation practice. In addition, we thank the reviewers for their insightful comments. Every chapter was reviewed by an individual who is currently involved in teaching consultation at the graduate level; in several cases, their graduate assistants and students in their consultation class also had the opportunity to comment. Finally, it should be acknowledged that the authors also shared their work with one another, an example of collaboration within the group.

On a personal note, I wish to acknowledge with gratitude, all of the school psychology students in the consultation classes that I have taught over nearly four decades at Fordham University, Temple University, and the University of Maryland. They have enriched my learning beyond measure. In addition, I thank the school psychologists and, in one case, the Instructional Consultation Team Facilitator, who took on the responsibility of supporting the students on site—helping them to learn the school culture, ensuring that they received referrals, modeling best practice, and dealing with crises that arose. No names are listed here to maximize confidentiality. The majority of the intensive supervision on the consultation process was done on campus by advanced graduate students and by me in my role as instructor, and I have had the privilege of working with outstanding assistants, three of whom are authors of chapters in this volume. My thanks also to Lane Akers, the editor at Routledge, who has been so supportive of the consultation book series over many years. To Julie Ganz, the editorial assistant at Routledge who was responsible for getting the book into production, a very special additional thanks for her patience with all the multiple changes and the thoroughness of her attention to detail. And a heartfelt thank you to my husband, Marvin Feuerberg, who provides an island of support and love in my life.

Because this is a work that represents so many individuals, any royalties from this book will be used to support graduate students in doing and presenting consultation research. There is much work still to be done on teaching and supervising consultation. It is my hope that this book will stimulate additional research in that domain along with supporting future novice consultants along the journey to competence as school consultants.

Sylvia Rosenfield

Reference

Gutkin, T.B., & Conoley, J.C. (1990). Reconceptualizing school psychology from a service delivery perspective: Implications for practice, training, and research. *Journal of School Psychology, 28*, 203–223.

Introduction: Becoming a School Consultant

Sylvia Rosenfield

> Alone we can do so little, together we can do so much.
>
> (Helen Keller)

Working together in the schools is a value across the education professions. In recent surveys, two-thirds of teachers and over three-quarters of principals concur that creating school environments that facilitate educators working together across disciplines impacts major outcomes, including student success and teacher learning (MetLife, 2010). Research confirms that staff collaboration is a key to student achievement (Little, 2007).

But although belief in collaboration is high among many educators and research supports this activity, practice is more variable, and training to make collaboration effective remains elusive. This book is designed to support school professionals, especially school psychologists and school counselors, who are in the process of learning to become consultee-centered consultants, one form of collaboration. It was created to provide concrete examples of consultation skill application and reflection by novice consultants in the context of school practice.

Consultee-Centered Consultation

Consultee-centered consultation provides the opportunity to engage with educators in collaborative problem solving. In his classic work, Caplan (1970) differentiated between consultee-centered and client-centered consultation approaches. According to Caplan, consultee-centered consultation focuses on the consultee's professional functioning, such that,

> improvement in the client is a side effect, welcome though it may be; the primary goal is to improve the consultee's capacity to function effectively in the category of case, in order to benefit many similar clients in the future.
>
> (Caplan, 1970, p. 101)

The types of problems that consultees bring to the table, according to Caplan, fall into four categories: lack of knowledge, lack of skill, lack of objectivity, and lack of self-confidence.

A more recent definition of consultee-centered consultation, developed by an international consortium (Lambert, 2004), still assumes the triad of consultant, consultee and client, and a work related problem:

> The work problem is a topic of concern for the consultee who has a direct responsibility for the learning, development, or productivity of the client.
>
> The primary task … is to choose and reframe knowledge about … effectiveness appropriate to the consultee's work setting.
>
> The goal of the consultation process is the joint development of a new way of conceptualizing the work problem so that the repertoire of the consultee is expanded and the professional relationship between the consultee and the client is restored or improved.
>
> (Lambert, 2004, pp. 11–12)

On the other hand, client-centered consultation occurs when a specialist (i.e., the consultant) is called in for help with a client where the primary focus is on helping the client. It is only a secondary goal, although not unimportant, that:

> the consultee should learn something from the encounter with the consultant that will increase his ability to handle similar cases better in the future. The secondary goal is limited … most of the consultant's time is spent with the client.
>
> (Caplan, 1970, p. 86)

Such consultation occurs even when the consultant does not see the client, as, for example, when reviewing files or diagnostic findings.

The authors in this volume implement a consultee-centered model, most often the Instructional Consultation model (Rosenfield, 1987, 2008); this model clearly represents the framework in their courses. Even when the processes described in the chapters stray, they are congruent with a systemic and ecological perspective to support services delivered in schools (e.g., Ysseldyke et al., 2006). Whether the client is a single student or a classroom of students, the work is centered on the teacher. The outcome of consultee-centered consultation "when effective, goes beyond changes in the client's presenting problem. The consultation process promotes conceptual changes in the consultee" (Lambert, 2004, p. 17). According to Hylander (2004), the conceptual shift or, in her words, the *turning*, occurs when "the consultee claims that the problem he or she brought to consultation is now solved or can be handled. He or she has framed the problem in another way" (p. 45). That does not mean, of course, that the outcomes for the client are ignored, and use of data is incorporated as well.

Research on Consultation Training

It should not be assumed that professionals "who are adequately prepared to provide direct service are also adequately prepared to provide indirect service" (Gutkin & Conoley, 1990, p. 205). Yet, there is a relative silence about consultation training in applied psychology fields, including school psychology (Rosenfield, Levinsohn-Klyap, & Cramer, 2010). In the introduction to a special issue on training in the *Journal of Educational and Psychological Consultation*, Alpert and Taufique (2002) reflect on "the lack of research and writing in consultation training" (p. 8), and the need to evaluate and describe consultation training. While there is a modest literature on training, largely about behavioral consultation skills, there is much to learn about the initial application of skills in practice settings by consultants-in-training (CITs).

Truscott and Albritton (2011) summarize the research on training school-based consultants (SBC): "multiple calls for research on training have produced little research ... The research that is available suggests that SBC may not be covered adequately in existing school specialist training programs, even in doctoral school psychology programs" (p. 172). In particular, research on training in school psychology programs has documented a lack of application of skills, especially with supervision, for CITs. For example, Anton-Lahart and Rosenfield (2004), in a survey of consultation courses in school psychology programs, found that most programs taught more than one model, with a focus on breadth rather than depth. In addition, relatively little time was devoted to communication and process skills during training, in comparison to theory and intervention development skills. Even when a program offered two courses, the second course typically focused largely on theoretical issues and intervention development. Hazel, Laviolette, and Lineman (2010) similarly documented the lack of supervised experience requirements in school psychology consultation course syllabi. While there are several textbooks (e.g., Brown, Pryzwansky, & Schulte, 2006, now in its sixth edition), less available are case studies and a literature on methods to develop competence as novice consultants engage in their initial fieldwork experiences.

Purpose of this Book

How does one learn to become a school consultant? Consultation, as other similar practice domains, can be described as "an art, science, craft and profession" (Thomas, 2004, p. 136), and development as a skilled consultant needs to be viewed as a complex interpersonal process that unfolds over time (Rosenfield, 2002). A good start is the didactic knowledge learned in a university classroom or reading materials about models, research, and skills, as well as content such as evidence-based interventions. However, as Confucius observed, *I hear, and I forget. I see and I remember. I do and I understand.* To become a competent school consultant, doing consultation under supervision in the context of school settings is also required. For example, Newell (in press) explored the differences between what school psychology students believed they knew about consultation based on didactic course work and minimal experience, to their lack of skill in doing consultation even in simulated contexts.

In teaching consultation courses over the years, I recognized the importance of experience applying consultation skills in the schools, but these opportunities were most useful when combined with CIT reflection and feedback in the form of quality supervision. In addition, it became clear that many issues and concerns occurred repeatedly to new consultants, such as their recognition that they found it difficult to match their thoughts and feelings to their words in consultation sessions. Unfortunately, there is not always sufficient time in training to demonstrate to the CITs that they are not alone in their concerns; nor is it always easy to provide examples of how these common issues can be understood and addressed.

Thus, in collaboration with the other authors, we created this book. We will explore together a set of major competencies that need to be mastered on the path to competence in school-based consultation. We will also seek to make the early experiences less formidable by knowing what to expect, what strategies support productive reflection, and what can be done to improve the quality of the experience for consultant and consultee alike.

Given the nature of skill development, the purpose of graduate level consultation coursework should be to help CITs not only to gain and organize the central knowledge base of consultation and its role in practice, but also be able to apply that knowledge and skill set in the school context. Professional education in any domain requires the individual move from acclimation or awareness of a domain, to early competence in skill use, and in time, to a higher level of competence; finally, some individuals will acquire expertise (Alexander, 1997). Blueprint III (Ysseldyke et al., 2006) articulates the importance of moving from knowledge of skills to the "ability to apply and integrate these skills fluently in everyday practice" (p. 14). To move along that continuum to at least early competence in consultation, CITs require different activities and strategies, culminating in consulting experiences in school settings under supervision. Table I.1 (Rosenfield et al., 2010) provides a description of how instructional methods move the CIT through the learning process to application.

Table I.1 Training from Awareness to Application

Training Method	*Level of Impact*	*Evidence of Impact*
Didactic Presentation of Theory and Concepts	**Awareness**	Participant can articulate general concepts and identify problem
Modeling and Demonstration (i.e. live, video, etc.)	**Conceptual Understanding**	Participant can articulate concepts clearly and describe appropriate actions required
Practice in Simulated Situations with Feedback (i.e. role play, written exercises, etc.)	**Skill Acquisition**	Participant can begin to use skills in structured or simulated situations
Coaching and Supervision During Application	**Application of Skills**	Participants can use skills flexibly in actual situation

The importance of this continuum is reinforced by Mintzberg (2004), who cautions that techniques and tools must be tied to context; they become most powerful when applied "with nuance by people immersed in a specific situation" (p. 39). He views programs as too often pushing "theories, concepts, models, tools, techniques in a disconnected classroom ... practice, however, is about *pull* [italics in original]—what is needed in a particular situation" (p. 39). As such, novice consultants need the opportunity to engage in consultation at the school site, have the opportunity to reflect on the experience, and receive skillful supervision and feedback. The chapters in this book provide the opportunity to see how 10 CITs applied the skills they were learning under those conditions, and the lessons they learned that they considered important to share with other novice consultants. The issues raised here are ones that have reappeared multiple times for novice consultants, documented in part by Newman (Chapter 2, this volume).

Essential Elements of Consultation

Many consultation courses focus on different models of consultation, for example, behavioral, mental health, instructional, organizational (Anton-Lahart & Rosenfield, 2004). However, no matter the specific model, several parameters of consultation are essential for consultee-centered consultation, and likely for client-centered models as well. First, consultation involves a consultant, a consultee, and a client or clients. Second, there is largely agreement, either implicitly or explicitly, that consultation also is based on a set of critical components, although there are subtle differences among models on how these components might be operationalized. We live in a world that "increasingly emphasizes relationship building, clear communication and a strong sense of community" (Silverman, 2006, p. xxvii), and consultation elements must reflect those realities. These components include:

1. an understanding of the context in which the participants reside;
2. the working relationship between the consultant and the consultee;
3. the communication skills that serve as a core tool in developing the relationship; and
4. a systematic approach to addressing the concerns that the consultee brings to the table.

These competencies are ones that novice consultants can learn and practice in a course, but generally find problematic to apply in actual cases in the schools. As Newman (Chapter 2, this volume) found in his research, most concerns were related to "the problem-solving process as a whole; the individual problem-solving stages; communication processes; use of data and relationships." Before reading the case narratives, it is important to review the domains of competence required by school based consultants.

Understanding School Culture

School consultation does not take place in a vacuum. The larger organizational context needs to be understood by the consultant to be an effective school based consultant. No one makes a clearer case for the importance of understanding school culture than Sarason (1996), who, in his classic volume on school culture, describes the complexity of the school context. In order to step back from a context in which we have been participants, he suggests we take the perspective of a "being from outer space" (Sarason, 1996, p. 96) that is trying to understand everything going on in an elementary school. He uses this perspective to introduce the concept of programmatic and behavioral regularities, the way things are, sometimes representing "the weight of custom" whether or not these regularities serve the goals of the school (Fried, 2003, p. 91). Commenting on the value of Sarason's concept of school culture, Fried states that "school culture is so evident, so pervasive, yet so invisible" (p. 6), but it is "so important that the main features of that culture be identified, examined, challenged, and changed" (p. 6).

In the chapters that follow, you will see the authors struggle with the school regularities that are perceived as barriers to the consultation process. Novice school consultants benefit from identifying the regularities within the culture that impact their consultation work. While not all are modifiable by CITs in their early experiences in the schools, awareness is the first step toward identifying potential strategies to reduce them or to minimize their impact on the consultation process.

AN INDIVIDUAL VERSUS AN ECOLOGICAL ORIENTATION

One regularity that impacts consultee-centered consultation is recognizing the tendency to focus on individual rather than context as the source of a problem. Sarason (1981) comments that psychology has been "a study of the individual organism unrelated to the history, structure and unverbalized world views of the social order" (p. ix). Thus, consultants in most mental health professions often require support in making a shift from a focus on the individual to a social and ecological framework. As one student stated in a reflection on her work:

> Both my undergraduate and graduate work focused on the identification, classification, and testing aspects of psychology, in addition to clinical skills and theory.… my … training emphasized the individual and the importance of identification and classification of personality variables, traits, and disorders. The consultation class first opened up a whole new way of looking at my school with the readings and discussion on school culture, and then opened up a new way of looking at students and the match between the learner and their environment.

All the authors in this volume discuss the impact of school culture on their work as consultants.

TYPES OF COLLABORATION

Fullan and Hargreaves' insight into school culture can also be useful to novice consultants. They provide a substantive definition of the often-vague concept of collaboration, including a warning about less effective collaboration structure:

> Mere existence of collaboration should not be mistaken for a thoroughgoing *culture* [italics in original] of it. Some kinds of collaboration are best avoided. Others are wastes of time and limited in their impact. Still others should be regarded only as way-stations to be surpassed in the pursuit of more ambitious forms.
>
> (1991, p. 52)

They describe four types of collaboration in school cultures:

1. Balkanized, in which there are "separate and sometimes competing groups, jockeying for position and supremacy" (p. 52).
2. Comfortable Collaboration, which gets "stuck with the more comfortable business of advice-giving, trick-trading and material-sharing of a more immediate, specific and technical nature … and does not embrace the principles of systematic reflective practice" (pp. 55–56).
3. Contrived Collegiality, which is a form of collaboration controlled by the administrators of the building, and "characterized by a set of formal, specific, bureaucratic procedures … to encourage greater association among teachers and to foster more sharing, learning and improvement" (p. 58). However, it does not ensure that what happens during the collaboration is productive, although it can be an essential first step in bringing staff together.
4. Interactive Professionalism, similar to Little's (1990) concept of joint work. Little describes joint work as "shared responsibility for the work of teaching (interdependence) … Collegiality *as* collaboration … anticipates truly collective action" (p. 519). For consultants, schools in which there is a culture of interactive professionalism provide a rich context for their work.

It is helpful to examine the culture of the school with respect to how much collaboration is valued and what types of collaboration are supported. It is not that one cannot or should not do consultee-centered consultation in schools that have low levels of collaboration; rather, novice consultants need to become aware of the barriers that will often be in place in schools with low levels of productive collaboration. In several of the consultation cases presented here, even in these relatively collaborative school settings, there were issues raised related to the culture of collaboration. Developing collaborative cultures can often begin with one teacher or a small group of teachers, if the consultant has the skills to address the barriers.

DEMOGRAPHICS, DIVERSITY, AND RESOURCES

Knowledge of school culture requires a clear understanding of the demographics of the school community, student and staff population. A map of the school can be helpful, as well as diagrams that illustrate relationships, priorities, and hierarchies. A list of programmatic resources within and external to the school, and the interrelationships of school staff with one another and the students enable the consultant to have a stronger grasp of the school culture.

How school staff integrate cultural diversity within their building is essential to understanding the school's culture. Wyner (1991) describes how an examination of the location of bilingual classes and the relative isolation of the bilingual educators in a school reflected a lack of diversity integration within the building. She examines the space and resource allocation for the bilingual educators and staff, specifically the bilingual teachers' isolation in the teacher's lounge, the placement of the classes, and the lack of books and materials. The Elementary ESL teacher commented:

> No room, books or materials during the first 3 months in the building. Eventually, the school's coal bin was petitioned. As an ESL teacher, I occupied one side; a special ed. teacher was on the other side.
>
> (p. 99)

Isolation of kindergarten classes, which Sarason (1996) comments on and which is reflected in Sherry's chapter (Chapter 5), or the isolation in Tsakaris' special education program (Chapter 12) reflect cultural patterns in a school.

According to Newell (in press), consultants need a broader conceptualization of multiculturalism beyond addressing bias, racism, and oppression. Consultants need to be proactive in understanding multiple dimensions of clients, including how factors such as their racial identity, socioeconomic status, gender, language, and religion actually influence their functioning or not (see, e.g., Chapter 8, this volume, where the same vocabulary issue was relevant for many students in the same classroom). She concludes that understanding these dimensions of your clients is actually a strengths-based, comprehensive approach to knowing your client. In acquiring this information, consultants can engage in a consultative process that aligns with the client's perspective and beliefs to maximize the effectiveness of the process as well as outcomes. Being aware of these same factors in yourself and your consultee is part of consultee-centered consultation.

ROLE OF PRINCIPAL

Finally, the role of the principal in the culture of the school is a critical element. Sarason (1996) devotes considerable attention to this role, examining the ability of the principal to lead the school rather than focus on bureaucratic rules. Fullan (2001), after reviewing the literature on principal leadership, comments that:

> I know of no improving school that doesn't have a principal who is good at leading improvement … it should be absolutely clear that school improvement is an organizational phenomenon and therefore the principal, as leader, is the key for better or for worse.
>
> (pp. 145–146)

In a school in which the principal supports the collaborative environment, consultee-centered consultation has more potential to flourish. Learning to work with principals to develop collaborative environments is beyond the scope of this book, but should be one aspect of the development of school consultants as they move beyond the basic consultation skills to those in organizational development and change (e.g., Rosenfield & Gravois, 1996). Being comfortable with authority figures such as the principal is critical to functioning at the systems level in a school.

The Working Relationship

The second critical element is the working relationship. Building a working relationship with the consultee is key to consultee-centered consultation because of the focus on the consultee rather than on directly working with the client. Strong working relationships are the foundation for collaboration, teamwork (Sanborn, 2004) and problem solving. As Sanborn (2004) reminds us, people don't care how much you know until they know how much you care. Developing a relationship with the consultee is one of the most important components of effective consultation.

Since outcomes in consultation are created by and through our interactions with others, every interaction is an opportunity and a potential intervention. One of the prime principles that Schein (1999) proposes for process consultation is that "Everything You Do Is an Intervention" (p. 17). Acknowledging that principle requires consultants to take responsibility for all their actions to be sure they fit the goal of creating a helping relationship. It is through the relationship that the consultee is able to "perceive, understand, and act on the process events that occur in the … internal and external environment in order to improve the situation as defined" by the consultee (p. 20). In several of the chapters, this principle became apparent to the authors (e.g., Vaganek, Chapter 10, this volume), as they recognized the impact of their interactions. The working relationship is the forum in which the concern, whatever the consultee's lack of skill, knowledge, objectivity or self-confidence, can be engaged.

In a collaborative consultee-centered consultation, the consultee and the consultant work shoulder-to-shoulder, rather than the consultant shouldering the problem. Moreover, a strong working relationship provides an opportunity for consultees to be supported in the process of reflecting on their practice. Teachers often comment on the benefit of their consultation experience in reframing how they viewed the problem and their own contribution to creating and then resolving the concern (e.g., Chapter 3, this volume). A solid working relationship is one that can be sustained through the problem-solving process, allowing the consultant and consultee dyad to address potential differences that are likely to arise in case conceptualization (see, e.g., Chapters 6 and 9, this volume); it also allows the consultation dyad to work through the common issues of intervention implementation in the busy world of the classroom (see, e.g., Chapters 7 and 12, this volume), increasing the likelihood of treatment integrity.

One of the tasks of the consultant is to monitor the quality of that relationship over time. CITs need to develop the capacity to be authentic in the relationship without damaging it, to be trustworthy, and to develop the skill of establishing an alliance with the teacher (e.g., ensuring that they trust you understand their perspective even if you do not fully agree with it). Certainly trust at the operational level involves consultant behaviors such as showing up for sessions and completing what the consultant agreed to do, even if the teacher does not. At the more conceptual level, trust involves confidence in another, and perhaps most importantly, "an expectancy that the word, promise, and actions of another … can be relied on and that the trusted party will act in the best interests of the consultee and client" (Forsyth, Adams, & Hoy, 2011, p. 4).

The working relationship is first discussed and negotiated in the contracting stage of problem solving, which will be described in a later section of this chapter. Consultants need to clarify with their consultee the nature of the consultation model that will be conducted, and obtain informed consent to engage in the process. That is recommended no matter the model of consultation that is employed.

Communication Skills

A primary tool to building a working relationship is the effective use of communication skills. As one of Faulkner's characters says, "words don't ever fit even what they are trying to say at." How we use our words makes a huge difference, given that consultation is largely conducted through verbal exchange between consultant and consultee. Wachtel (1980) makes the same case for therapy, which is also conducted through words: "Surprisingly little has been written about just how therapists should word their comments to patients … there are questions of technique with regard to the selection, focus, and wording of … comments that are important to consider in their own right" (p. 183). According to Johnston (2004), language "actually creates realities and invites identities … Language works to position people in relation to one another" (p. 9). Language also positions people in relationship to what they are doing and learning.

A SOCIAL PSYCHOLOGICAL PERSPECTIVE

The work of Higgins (1999) is instructive in furthering our understanding of the effect of language in a consultation session. First, he defines audience tuning as the process by which we tailor a message to the audience. So, if the consultee believes that your questions or your profession as a psychologist means you want to talk about deficits and diagnoses, the teacher will frame her comments to meet the implicit expectation. Second, he describes the "saying is believing" phenomenon, in which how we talk about a problem shapes our beliefs about it. Thus, the more we talk about a student as disabled, the more likely that the teacher will come to believe that is a valid assumption. In some problem-solving teams, the discussion can shift a teacher uncertain about the cause of the student's behavior into believing the deficit is in the student, and make her less willing to try a classroom intervention (Benn, 2004). Similarly, Higgins describes a concept he terms shared reality, that as we talk with others, our individual experiences become more valid and reliably true to us. As a result, teachers in problem-solving teams may become even more certain of a concern being out of their capacity to intervene effectively in the classroom. In several of the chapters in this volume, you will see reference to these phenomena.

APPLICATION OF COMMUNICATION SKILLS IN PRACTICE

A skillful consultant is highly aware of the communication skills that facilitate the process, as well as when to use them. While learning about the different communication skills builds awareness and conceptual understanding, their application in practice requires reflection and feedback based on listening to oneself in tapes of consultation sessions. Under such conditions, novice consultants come to see how verbal exchanges in consultation sessions are critical and how their own verbal behavior can be transformed to obtain more positive outcomes. In terms of positioning the consultant in building a collaborative relationship to the consultee, for example, you will find authors in this volume talking about using "we" rather than "I" language.

USING SPECIFIC COMMUNICATION SKILLS SKILLFULLY

Several specific communication skills can be used individually and together. For example, the helping skills of clarifying, perception checking, and paraphrasing, used alone, can support relationship building and problem solving (Rosenfield, 2004). But combining communication skills can be even more powerful. In a strategy I have called "bond and move," it is recommended that consultants first demonstrate that they have heard the consultee, either through paraphrasing or perception checking, before moving on into another communication strategy, such as clarifying, which would move the problem-solving process forward. That enables the teacher to feel heard and not dismissed, before moving on to another topic. Increasing the use of clarification rather than asking relevant questions is also recommended. In the case studies, you will find multiple examples of how using clarifying statement or questions ("Can you give me an example?" or "Tell me more about what you mean by lack of attention") enabled consultees to reflect on their lived experiences in the classroom rather than the labels they had assigned to the student's behavior.

Helping teachers to move down the "ladder of inference" (Argyris, 1993) from broad general labels to specific behaviors is an important part of problem solving (Rosenfield, 2004). Argyris emphasizes the importance of making "inferences explicit" (p. 57) and testing their validity. The ladder of inference is his metaphor that illustrates movement from an experience or observation to an inference:

1. an observable behavior, say a student not attending to class work;
2. an inference, often in milliseconds, about the meaning of the behavior;
3. attribution about the meaning or reason for the behavior, such as a willful refusal to attend or a deficit such as ADHD; and
4. an action based on the attribution.

By using clarification, it is possible to "walk the teacher down the ladder" back to the original behavior and develop a way to evaluate the meaning of the behavior rather than inferring a reason without checking on its validity (e.g., exploring the possibility that the student finds the work too difficult, rather than having an ADHD or motivational problem; see, e.g., Chapters 4 and 9, this volume).

But, as you will see from the case narratives, using words wisely is a skill that develops with supervised experience. At first, novice consultants may find it irritating to focus on communication skills other than asking the direct questions that they believe will gain them a better picture of the problem (e.g., see Chapter 6, this volume). Asking the right kind of question can support teacher reflection, enable the teacher to focus and stretch, get a better or different perspective on the situation, and lead to breakthrough thinking (Marquardt, 2005).

Knowing exactly what the CIT said in the session is critical. In listening to tapes, students often find that they had asked questions they didn't remember they had asked, shared emotions they didn't know they shared, and used tone and volume they didn't know they had used. For example, one consultant was very worried about how assertive she had been in a session, when the tape revealed she had spoken in such a soft voice that she could hardly be heard. Others have had little memory of discussing interventions during the problem identification stage, and are surprised when they listen to their tapes.

With practice and feedback, automaticity in the skills develops. There is some evidence that skilled instructional consultants use more clarifying communication strategies than novices, but the quality of their communication skills is an even better indication of expertise (Benn, Jones, & Rosenfield, 2008). Moving from simply counting the types of communication strategies used, a technique at the beginning of learning these skills, to understanding how to enhance the quality of the verbal exchanges, is a sign of development. Further, as the reader will find in the cases presented in this volume, the value of skillful communication becomes apparent over time to CITs.

Problem-Solving Process

While problems and concerns brought by consultees to the consultant differ widely, a structured problem-solving framework enables the consultant, especially a novice, to be sure that critical steps are completed. Depending upon the consultation model, different tasks may be assigned to the stages. The set of problem-solving stages used by the CITs in this volume is based on behavioral and instructional consultation (IC) models (Rosenfield, 1987, 2008), since that is the problem-solving structure that was taught in the courses. The chapter authors refer to the Student Documentation Form (SDF) in the case narratives. This form is used to document progress through the instructional consultation process. A copy of page 1 and 2 of the form are found in Figures I.1 and I.2. Training on the use of the SDF is required as part of the consultation coursework.

Each stage has essential elements to be completed and is sequential, although sometimes it is necessary to cycle back through the stages. Figure I.3 presents the sequence of the stages. A brief description of the stages follows (see, e.g., Rosenfield, 1987, 2008 for further detail).

1. *Contracting*, to ensure that the consultee has been given enough information to make an informed decision to engage in the process
2. *Problem Identification*, in which the concern brought by the teacher is identified in observable and measurable terms. In this stage, the concern of the teacher is co-constructed with the consultant into the problem to be addressed. Often the CIT learns that the original concern brought by the teacher might not be the one that needs to be addressed (e.g., see Chapters 4 and 11, this volume). In the IC process, all classroom concerns are assessed to determine whether the student has an instructional match in the curriculum. Data on the match are gathered most often through the use of an Instructional Assessment (IA; Gravois & Gickling, 2008).

   Before leaving this stage all of the following tasks need to be completed: (a) specify the teacher's concerns in observable and measurable terms, defined as a *gap* between current and expected performance; (b) select a data collection method and establish a baseline with at least three data points; (c) identify the context of the problem within the instructional triangle; (d) decide if the gap is significant and requires intervention; and (e) establish short, intermediate, and long-term goals for the student. (Rosenfield, 2008).
3. *Intervention Design and Planning*, the stage in which the intervention is selected and implementation details considered. The consultant and consultee together plan the intervention, based on the identified problem. The specific details include: who, what, when, where, and what materials,

Instructional Consultation Student Documentation Form

Student's Name ______________ Grade ______ Date of Birth ______ Date Started ______

Teacher's Name ______________ Case Manager ______________ School ______________

Goal Attainment Scale (GAS)

Step 1: Initial description of concern				
Step 2: Prioritize	**Importance 1 2 3 4** (student at instructional level? Y N)	**Importance 1 2 3 4** (student at instructional level? Y N)	**Importance 1 2 3 4** (student at instructional level? Y N)	**Importance 1 2 3 4** (student at instructional level? Y N)
Step 3: Observable/measurable statement of current performance (following baseline)	Date collected ______	Date collected ______	Date collected ______	Date collected ______
Step 4: Short-term goal: Expected performance in ____ weeks (4–6 weeks)	Date consistently attained ________	Date consistently attained ________	Date consistently attained ________	Date consistently attained ________
Step 5: Interim goal: Expected behavior in ____ weeks	Date consistently attained ________	Date consistently attained ________	Date consistently attained ________	Date consistently attained ________
Step 6: Long-term goal: Expected behavior in ____ weeks	Date consistently attained ________	Date consistently attained ________	Date consistently attained ________	Date consistently attained ________

Figure I.1 The Student Documentation Form (SDF): Front Cover.

Operational Definition of Academic/Behavioral Performance: Priority #____ on GAS

KEY

☐ __________

☐ __________

☐ __________

What specific academic / behaviors will be recorded? ____________________

When will the behavior be recorded? ____________________

Where will the behavior be recorded? ____________________

Baseline (Step 3)

End Baseline

Describe intervention design and materials	When and how often?	Persons responsible?	Motivational strategies?

Figure I.2 The Student Documentation Form (SDF): Inside Form.

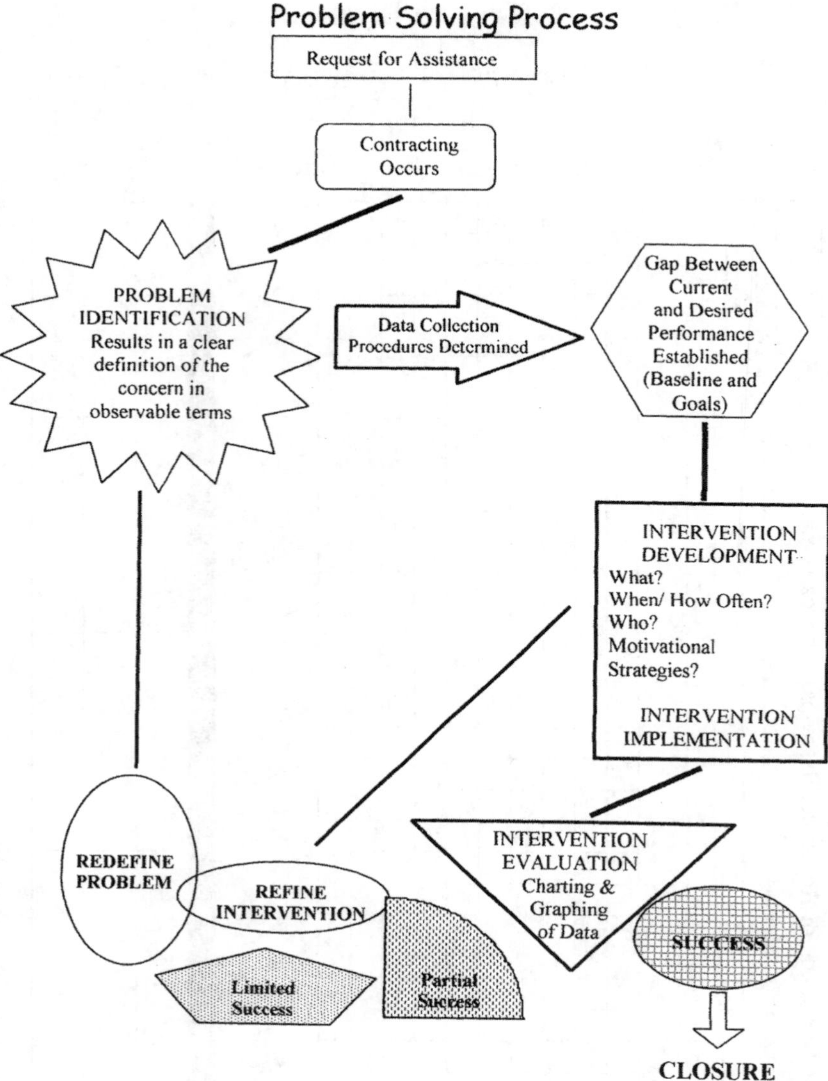

Figure I.3 Sequence of the Problem-Solving Process.

as well as how the implementation and outcomes will be evaluated. Not only must these details be completed, but, in addition, the consultee must consider the intervention do-able. When possible, the intervention should be one with some empirical support, but in all cases, plans must also be made to evaluate the outcomes. No intervention works for everyone and the details of an intervention often require some flexibility.

4. *Intervention Implementation*, the stage in which the intervention is delivered. Because of the complexity of classroom settings, consultation support during implementation is required, as often the intervention needs to be tweaked. Data are collected for that purpose, and progress toward goals is monitored as part of the Evaluation stage. Lack of progress is addressed by changes in intervention, or sometimes recycling through earlier stages. Treatment integrity is monitored.
5. *Evaluation*, as part of implementation, to ensure that progress is occurring.
6. *Closure*, which represents the formal conclusion of the problem-solving process. There is a decision to continue or terminate working together, based on outcomes: celebration of progress; or development of an alternate source of support for the student and teacher when progress is not satisfactory. An open door for future consultation is also extended. At this stage, necessary documentation of the decision and data is completed in line with school procedures.

The Tools for Learning

Several tools were available for reflection and support to the authors of these narratives, and they are frequently referred to in the chapters. A full description of these tools and the rationale for their use is available in Chapter 1.

Taping

Each CIT was required to tape each session and listen to the tape prior to the following session. The supervisor at different points in the learning process suggested transcription of parts or entire tapes, and examples of how transcription and analysis were used are found in the chapters.

Process Log

CITs completed a log after listening to each session tape. The log format was provided electronically (a copy of the log is found in Chapter 1) and asked the CIT to address the following:

1. problem-solving stage of the case;
2. working relationship;
3. communication skills (often with a request for partial or full transcript of the session); and
4. request for feedback during supervision.

Supervision

The CIT submitted both the tape and the session log to the supervisor, who reviewed them prior to the supervision session; typically this was done prior to the next consultation session. Chapter 2 details the supervision process and typical issues that have been found important in supporting CIT learning.

Using the Book

The chapters in this book are designed to supplement your initial consulting experiences as you begin to develop from novice to early competence. Each chapter opens with a set of advanced organizing questions to consider as you read the chapter. At the end of the chapter, there is another set of questions for reflection, asking you to consider how the issues presented might be relevant to your own experiences and professional growth.

Supporting the Novice Consultant

The two chapters in the first section provide a framework for supporting and evaluating novice consultants. The methods for reflecting on and obtaining feedback about their meetings with the consultees are described in detail in Chapter 1 and the supervision process is detailed in Chapter 2; it is helpful to read these chapters first. The learning tools described in these chapters are frequently referenced in the rest of the book.

The Case Narratives

The remaining chapters form a set of consultation narratives, each from the perspective of the consultant-authors who lived them. The authors provide a narrative about how the consultation and supervision process unfolded. Although the authors were preoccupied, as any novice would be, during the consultation "with their performing selves, with matters of technique, of knowledge" (Coles, 1989, p. 118), they are reflecting here on how they came to understand what transpired. The structure includes sections devoted to:

1. the school culture as it impacted their work;
2. their working relationship and communication skills;
3. the problem-solving process that they used; and
4. the lessons they took away from the experience and which they hope will be of value to the novice consultant reader.

Essentially they are presenting their perspective on how the essential elements of consultation worked in their experiences.

The CITs did their work in four different school systems. The names and other identifying information on the consultee and client(s) have been altered along characteristics common in case literature to protect their confidentiality (Kantrowitz, 2006); the consultee and client perspectives on the cases are not represented here. All the CIT authors had moved through the stages of awareness, conceptual understanding, and skill acquisition of the consultee-centered model of instructional consultation prior to or concurrent with placement in a school setting. The authors had received training in academic assessment and behavioral interventions prior to the consultation fieldwork, and had basic knowledge of several other consultation models (behavioral, mental health, and organizational). But the focus here is on their application of their knowledge and skills in the schools.

KINDERGARTEN READING CONCERNS

The first four narratives (Chapters 3–6) are conducted with kindergarten teachers. But each case raises a different set of issues for the consultation process—the concern itself is not as complex, as it will become with later grades, so the bones of the process are more easily identified. While there may be a similarity of grade and concern, the consultation process issues are different.

INSTRUCTIONAL MATCH

Chapter 7 is a case study about a second grade teacher's concern about reading, and documents a creative approach for constructing a method for evaluation of the instructional match.

CONSULTING ABOUT A CONCERN RELATED TO AN ENGLISH LANGUAGE LEARNER

Chapter 8 involves a fourth grade case with an English Language Learner (ELL), where the confusion between language and learning in social studies and science is clarified for the classroom teacher.

CLASS-WIDE CONCERNS

Chapters 9 and 10 describe cases in which there are classroom behavior concerns at grades three and four, one on homework and one on bullying, each with a consultee-centered focus.

CONSULTING WITH SPECIAL EDUCATION TEACHERS

The final two chapters reinforce the conclusion that an Individual Education Plan (IEP) does not remove the need for consultee-centered consultation for the special education teacher. As Tskaris (Chapter 13) reports in her informal survey of special education teachers, few received consultee-centered consultation services, in spite of their perceived need. Both narratives involve special education teachers in self-contained classrooms.

Final Thoughts for Novice Consultants

Coles (1989), in his discussion of how stories can facilitate learning, reminds us that stories possess an immediacy that "connects so persuasively with human experience" (p. 205). We have framed these experiences as narratives, recognizing that stories "breathe life into issues that otherwise might seem too remote to solve anytime soon" (Silverman, 2006, p. xxvi). The authors of the case narratives provide a window into their lived experience of school consulting that they have been willing to share with you. We hope that these cases will increase your persistence as a CIT in the face of the complexities and struggles faced by consultants, and support you in knowing that you are not alone. We hope that this book will help you to see learning to be a school consultant as a rich and rewarding, if not a simple, experience.

References

Alexander, P.A. (1997). Mapping the multidimensional nature of domain learning: The interplay of cognitive, motivational and strategic forces. *Advances in Motivation and Achievement, 10*, 213–250.

Alpert, J.L., & Taufique, S.R. (2002). Consultation training: A field in need of review, revision, and research. *Journal of Educational and Psychological Consultation, 13*, 7–11.

Anton-Lahart, J., & Rosenfield, S. (2004). A survey of preservice consultation training in school psychology programs. *Journal of Educational and Psychological Consultation, 15*, 41–62.

Argyris, C. (1993). *Knowledge for action: A guide to overcoming barriers to organizational change*. San Francisco: Jossey-Bass.

Benn, A. (2004). Communities of practice: Study of one school's first year of implementation of a new problem-solving model (Unpublished doctoral dissertation). University of Maryland, College Park, MD.

Benn, A., Jones, G., & Rosenfield, S. (2008). Analysis of instructional consultants' questions and alternatives to questions during the problem identification interview. *Journal of Educational and Psychological Consultation, 19*, 54–80.

Brown, D., Pryzwansky, W.B., & Schulte, A.C. (2006). *Psychological consultation and collaboration* (6th ed.). Boston: Allyn & Bacon.

Caplan, G. (1970). *Theory and practice of mental health consultation*. New York: Basic Books.

Coles, R. (1989). *The call of stories*. Boston, MA: Houghton Mifflin.

Forsyth, P.B., Adams, C.M., & Hoy, W.K. (2011). *Collective trust: Why schools can't improve without it*. New York: Teachers College Press.

Fried, R.L. (Ed.). (2003). *The skeptical visionary: A Seymour Sarason education reader*. Philadelphia: Temple University Press.

Fullan, M. (2001). *The new meaning of educational change* (3rd ed.). New York: Teachers College Press.

Fullan, M. (2008). *The six secrets of change*. San Francisco: Jossey-Bass.

Fullan, M., & Hargreaves, A. (1991). *What's worth fighting for? Working together for your school*. Andover, MA: Regional Laboratory for Educational Improvement of the Northeast and Islands.

Gravois, T.A., & Gickling, E.E. (2008). Best practices in curriculum-based assessment. In A. Thomas & J. Grimes (Eds.). *Best practices in school psychology V* (pp. 503–518). Washington, DC: National Association of School Psychologists.

Gutkin, T.B., & Conoley, J.C. (1990). Reconceptualizing school psychology from a service delivery perspective: Implications for practice, training, and research. *Journal of School Psychology, 28*, 203–223.

Hazel, C.E., Laviolette, G.T., & Lineman, J.M. (2010). Training professional psychologists in school-based consultation: What the syllabi suggest. *Training and Education in Professional Psychology, 4*, 235–244.

Higgins, E.T. (1999). "Saying is believing" effects. In L.L. Thompson, J.M. Levine, & D.M. Messick (Eds.). *Shared cognition in organizations* (pp. 33–48). Mahwah, NJ: LEA.

Hylander, I. (2004). Analysis of conceptual change in consultee-centered consultation. In N.M. Lambert, I. Hylander, & J. Sandoval (Eds.). *Consultee-centered consultation: Improving the quality of professional services in schools and community organizations* (pp. 45–61). Hillsdale, NJ: Lawrence Erlbaum Associates.

Johnston, P. (2004). *Choice words: How our language affects children's learning*. Portland, ME: Stenhouse Publishers.

Kantrowitz, J.L. (2006). *Writing about patients: Responsibilities, risks, and ramifications*. New York: Other Press.

Lambert, N.M. (2004). Consultee-centered consultation: An international perspective on goals, process, and theory. In N.M. Lambert, I. Hylander, & J. Sandoval (Eds.). *Consultee-centered consultation: Improving the quality of professional services in schools and community organizations* (pp. 3–20). Hillsdale, NJ: Lawrence Erlbaum Associates.

Little, J.W. (1990). The persistence of privacy: Autonomy and initiative in teachers' professional relations. *Teachers College Press, 91*, 509–539.

Little, J. W. (2007). Professional communication and collaboration. In W. Hawley (Ed.). *The keys to effective schools* (pp. 51–65). Thousand Oaks, CA: Corwin Press.

Marquardt, M. (2005). *Leading with questions*. San Francisco: Jossey-Bass.

MetLife (2010). *The MetLife survey of the American teacher*. New York: Metropolitan Life Insurance Company.

Mintzberg, H. (2004). *Managers not MBAs: A hard look at the soft practice of managing and management development*. San Francisco: Berrett-Koehler.

Newell, M.L (in press). Tranforming knowledge to skill. Evaluating the consultation competence of novice school-based consultants. *Consulting Psychology Journal*.

Rosenfield, S. (1987). *Instructional consultation*. Hillsdale, NJ: Lawrence Erlbaum Associates.

Rosenfield, S. (2002). Developing instructional consultants: From novice to competent to expert. *Journal of Educational and Psychological Consultation, 13*, 93–107.

Rosenfield, S. (2004). Consultation as dialogue: The right words at the right time. In N. Lambert, I. Hylander, & J. Sandoval (Eds.). *Consultee-centered consultation: Improving the quality of professional services in schools and community organizations* (pp. 337–347). Hillsdale, NJ: Lawrence Erlbaum Associates.

Rosenfield, S. (2008). Best practices in instructional consultation. In A. Thomas & J. Grimes (Eds.). *Best practices in school psychology V* (pp. 1645–1660). Washington, DC: National Association of School Psychologists.

Rosenfield, S., & Gravois, T.A. (1996). *Instructional consultation teams: Collaborating for change*. New York: Guilford Press.

Rosenfield, S., Levinsohn-Klyap, M., & Cramer, K. (2010). Educating consultants for practice in the schools. In E. Garcia-Vasquez, T. Crespi, & C. Riccio (Eds.). *Handbook of education, training and supervision of school psychologists in school and community volume 1: Foundations of professional practice* (pp. 259–278). New York: Routledge.

Sanborn, M. (2004). *The Fred factor*. Colorado Springs, CO: Waterbrook Press.

Sarason, S.B. (1981). *Psychology misdirected*. New York: The Free Press.

Sarason, S.B. (1996). *The culture of the school and the problem of change* (2nd ed.). Boston, MA: Allyn & Bacon.

Schein, E.H. (1999). *Process consultation revisited: Building the helping relationship.* Reading, MA: Addison-Wesley.

Silverman, L. (2006). *Wake me up when the data is over*. San Francisco: Jossey-Bass.

Thomas, G. (2004). A typology of approaches to facilitator education. *Journal of Experiential Education, 27*, 123–140.

Truscott, S.D., & Albritton, K. (2011). Addressing pediatric health concerns through school-based consultation. *Journal of Educational and Psychological Consultation, 21*, 169–174.

Wachtel, P. L. (1980). What should we say to our patients? On the wording of therapists' comments. *Psychotherapy: Theory, Research and Practice, 17*, 183–188.

Wyner, N.B. (1991). Unlocking cultures of teaching: Working with diversity. In N.B. Wyner (Ed.). *Current perspectives on the culture of schools* (pp. 95–107). Brookline, MA: Brookline Books.

Ysseldyke, J.E., Burns, M.K., Dawson, M., Kelly, B., Morrison, D., Ortiz, S., Rosenfield, S., & Telzrow, C. (2006). *School psychology: A blueprint for training and practice III.* Bethesda, MD: National Association of School Psychologists.

Part I
Supporting the Novice Consultant

Moving into the application stage of a skill is key to becoming competent. However, to maximize development in the chaos of the application stage, it is essential to have the opportunity to reflect upon those experiences and to receive support. Katie Burkhouse details how consultation skills can be monitored and measured over time, with tools for reflection and evaluation. Daniel Newman provides an overview of common concerns of consultants-in-training and how supervision is supportive of working through these issues. Reading these chapters will set the stage for understanding the reflective process of the case narrative authors.

1
Educating a Reflective School Consultant: Multi-Faceted Techniques

Katie Sutton Burkhouse

Advance Organizer Questions

- **What are the differences between evaluating didactic knowledge and skill growth?**
- **How can we engage in critical self-reflection and evaluation to understand our own skill growth and areas of need?**

School psychology training programs must impart both knowledge and skills to prepare competent professionals ready for practice or academia. Evaluation of knowledge comes in many forms; e.g., traditional tests, oral exams, and class participation. Evaluation of skill growth presents more challenges for school psychology trainers and for their students, who are learning new skills. It is not always explicit how to measure the growth of practice skills. Although, students start at varying levels of skill with different background experiences upon entering training programs, it seems likely that there is a threshold or minimum level of skill attainment necessary for all students regardless of their prior experience, in order to produce competent practitioners. Truly it is difficult to ensure that students leave graduate school with the skills necessary to be professional psychologists.

Consultation, one main component of most school psychology training programs, is an area where evaluation is especially challenging. Consultation requires the attainment of a broad knowledge base as well as growth in interpersonal and problem-solving skills. Not only is it difficult to measure consultant skill growth for the aforementioned reasons, consultation has additional challenges because there is such variety in the competencies that are taught (Anton-LaHart & Rosenfield, 2004; Hazel, Laviolette, & Lineman, 2010). The field of school consultation lacks both a consensus and research that would indicate the necessary skills and knowledge to be taught, leading to a diversity of training approaches. The purpose and focus of this chapter is three-fold:

1. to encourage students to become reflective practitioners and learn how to monitor their own skill growth in the area of consultation;

2. to provide trainers with additional tools for their consultation training toolbox to help evaluate student skill growth; and
3. to demonstrate how evaluation can fulfill multiple purposes.

Unlike other chapters in this book, this chapter is not a case study per se but a guide on evaluation of consultation cases. The recommendations in this chapter are the product of my own experience, taking and peer supervising over 20 consultation cases in schools, as well as the guidance of my instructor, an expert in the area of school consultation. Further, the recommendations in this chapter are the result of engaging in a process of critical self-reflection and, through coursework and supervision, helping other students to engage in such a process for their own growth and development.

Assumptions

Due to the dearth of research in consultation training, I want to share some of the basic assumptions that help to guide my approach. Because this chapter is intended to be applicable for students and trainers from a variety of consultation perspectives, I hope that outlining the following assumptions will not only aid in understanding my approach, but also allow readers to reflect on some of their own assumptions. In addition, it may help students and trainers to reflect upon how to tweak the recommendations in this chapter to match their own assumptions about consultation in schools.

First, coursework in consultation must have a practical, in-school component, in which students are taking consultation cases and receiving supervision and support through university and/or school based supervisors. In order to build skills, students need *in vivo* experience with extensive reflection. Without application, it is very difficult, maybe even impossible, to know one's own level of competence and skill when applying consultation principles. Further, many people believe consultation skills are intuitive. With application, it becomes clear that consultation is not as easy as it looks.

Second, learning about consultation involves learning about other important topics, such as:

1. how the culture of schools impact service delivery;
2. how systems work and how to affect system change; and
3. how to become a reflective practitioner.

This last point is salient because practitioners report that they have difficulty building consultation skills in the field because of a lack of supervision and support (Hall, 2002). In fact, once school psychologists complete their pre-service training and internship, it becomes very difficult to gain additional skill and knowledge in consultation. Therefore, for psychologists who choose to consult as part of their service delivery, it is vital that they are able to reflect in productive ways upon their own practice.

Finally, trainers should have a variety of tools in their toolboxes for evaluating students. There are different approaches for evaluating didactic knowledge and skill growth. While most faculty members are comfortable evaluating the growth of knowledge through a variety of different approaches, it is less clear how to evaluate discrete skill growth and determine attainment of acceptable skill levels. With an increasing focus on accountability for accredited training programs and new training guidelines from NASP and APA, it is necessary to think more about how to go about evaluating practical skill growth.

Components of an Evaluation System

Didactic Components

Training in school consultation involves learning in a variety of knowledge domains regardless of the training program's approach to or model of consultation. Although traditional criterion-referenced tests may have their place in a comprehensive evaluation system, graduate students benefit from evaluation that involves a variety of approaches to measuring knowledge gained. In addition to helping instructors determine if their goals have been accomplished, evaluation of didactic knowledge can also be targeted toward helping students to reflect on their own knowledge and how they will apply this knowledge in schools. Table 1.1 includes some possible examples to use to evaluate consultation knowledge.

JOURNALING

Reflective journals are one way to integrate and synthesize course readings and experiences. They provide a venue for communication between instructor/

Table 1.1 Examples for Evaluating Didactic Consultation Knowledge

Component	*Description*
Reflective Journals	Thoughts shared between student and instructor on a regular predicted interval that synthesize knowledge and help the student derive individual meaning
School Culture Analysis	Formal analysis of school characteristics and culture of practicum placement with reference to applicable readings
Case Summaries	Thorough account of case progressions, reviewing problem solving process, relationship building, interpersonal communication, supervision, etc.
Class Participation/ Reflection on Readings	Structured (outlining) and unstructured reflection on course readings as well as participation in class discussion through individual or group work
Exams	Formal measures of knowledge with rubrics for evaluating answer applicability, accuracy, and completeness

supervisor and student to meet a variety of purposes. Consultants-in-training (CIT) should be encouraged to view journaling as an opportunity to go beyond the readings. Students may be instructed to pose questions, infer broader concepts, tie together different readings, and/or reflect on how the information will impact their practices. Journals also provide the course instructor with a way of determining if CITs are deriving the intended messages from the reading and to ensure adequate preparation for in-class discussions.

CITs should be instructed on the expected timeline for turning in journals and an approximate amount of reflection expected by the instructor. While instructors can offer some additional guidelines, they should do so with the consideration that guidelines may result in the stifling of journal material. In the end, what goes into each journal may be different for each CIT and different throughout the course. I have included in Appendix A an example of a journal I wrote during my second consultation course. This journal provides an example of relating course reading to my current experience in a school and trying to fit the readings into my growing conceptual framework for the practice of school psychology.

SCHOOL CULTURE ANALYSIS

Each CIT should do a thorough analysis of the culture of the school(s) they are placed in for practicum work. Students can begin by reflecting on the demographics of the school and try to understand how these demographics impact the people in the school. Also, students can reflect on the leadership and school administration, integrating readings on school culture. Some examples are: Fullan and Hargreaves (1991), Fried (2003), Horn and Little (2010), Little (1990, 2007), Sarason (1996), and Wyner (1991).

Other potential topics of reflection include school meetings, high stakes testing, school teaming, response to intervention, and system level school programs such as positive behavioral supports and pre-referral services. CITs should pay careful consideration to the relationships and collaboration among and between teachers and other staff at their particular school, exploring relational challenges presented in the work of Sarason (1996) and collaboration presented in the work of Little (1990), as two possible examples. While it is beyond the scope of this chapter to outline all aspects of culture to be investigated, it is important for CITs to have spent time reflecting on the context of their consultation activities to understand the types of collaboration, teaming, leadership, and relationships that exist in their school.

CASE STUDIES

Case studies are a crossover between didactic and practical knowledge gained through consultation training. In other words, they provide CITs with an opportunity to reflect on their own practice by integrating relevant research and course materials. Further, case studies can provide a forum for self-reflection that goes beyond just what was done and involves critical reflection on what could be done differently in the future. Generally speaking, case studies can be summative in that they are the result of the culmination of consultation experiences throughout the course(s) and formative in the sense that cases can be presented in milieu to obtain feedback from instructors and peers. Format for these studies should match expectations of each unique training program and can coincide with the format for case logs (described below).

CLASS PARTICIPATION/REFLECTION ON READINGS

An important part of any consultation course is the in-class discussion. Graduate students rely on in-class discussions to make connections and sense of numerous readings and to understand how the knowledge they are gaining has practical application. One way to minimize the load on students is to divide up readings. CITs can outline and present information for their fellow classmates in a way that is accessible because they are on a similar developmental level. Student presentations combined with knowledgeable input by the instructor is a way to present essential didactic material in a consultation course. Additionally, students can work in groups to help synthesize and critically evaluate knowledge obtained through coursework. Group projects can illustrate the complexities of working with teams to give students first-hand knowledge to predict the challenges of teamwork.

TRADITIONAL TESTS

Traditional tests can have a place in consultation training to allow students to demonstrate knowledge gained from the coursework. Essay and short-answer tests seem particularly appropriate for this topic area but will differ depending on the training program. Additionally, mock transcripts can be used to demonstrate knowledge of communication skills. As a student, I find it particularly helpful when an instructor has created a rubric for grading such tests. Then, it is possible to understand why certain grades are assigned and also cues CITs into important pieces that they may not have included in their responses.

SUMMARY

There are multiple ways of accessing the growth of consultation knowledge. Some are straightforward (e.g. class participation and traditional tests). However, some ways of measuring knowledge are more involved and provide the opportunity for additional insight into individual growth. One important overview point is that students, through coursework and class discussions, should be challenged to expand upon higher-order thinking skills, such as complex integration of ideas and critical self-reflection, to benefit them in their professional careers.

Skill Growth Components

Unlike didactic knowledge, evaluating the growth of applied consultation skills involves establishing minimum levels of competence for CITs. In other words, training programs must challenge themselves to establish criteria for determining whether a student has met the threshold for competence expected for his or her experience level. Further, each step in the learning process should involve evaluation to ensure adequate understanding and application of key consultation principles. Table 1.2 provides examples of some ways to developmentally evaluate consultation skill growth.

SIMULATIONS

Simulations provide a way of gaining performance feedback in a safe environment. Prior to work in schools, CITs can practice simulations of different steps of the problem-solving process, which may allow for more realization about the complexities of consulting. Through simulations, students are challenged to apply skills *in vivo* and find it is often difficult to know what to say next. In the UMD training program, CITs do a simulation of problem identification, developed by a former student (Jones, 1999). Supervisors take on the role of teacher and read from a script of common concerns expressed by teachers. The CIT's job is to use active listening and communication skills to help the teacher

Table 1.2 Examples for Evaluating Consultation Skill Growth

Component	*Description*
Simulations	Practice for different steps of problem-solving process in safe, structured environment with audio- or video-taping and reflection, evaluation guided by rubric
Analysis of Tapes	Critical review of audiotaped consultation sessions, paying specific attention to interpersonal communication styles, problem-solving approaches, areas of supervision need
Logs	Combined with tape review, critical self-evaluation of tapes and consultation progress paying specific attention to relationship issues, communication techniques, problem-solving steps, and supervision requests
Self-Assessment of Skills	Self-evaluation of skills prior to practicum, mid practicum experience, and after practicum experience, as well as a reflective comparison of skills at the beginning and end of course
Supervisor(s) Assessment of Skills	Evaluation of skill level at end of course (as well as other critical time points) to help determine whether the student has mastered skills to an acceptable pre-internship level (could also be used on internship)

identify concerns in an observable and measurable way by breaking down high inference statements. The script ensures that all CITs get a comparable experience; however, subsequent research showed that consultants with more experience used techniques that arrived at more observable and measurable behaviors (Benn, Jones, & Rosenfield, 2008). Specifically, novice consultants used less clarification and more offering of opinions than more experienced consultants. As a result, less experienced consultants did not always get the same degree of concern specificity during simulation.

An integral part of the simulation process is the videotaping and critical reflection done by both student and supervisor. Students do not receive supervisor feedback until after they have engaged in their own critical reflection. CITs view their own video after completing the simulation to analyze their use of skills and the outcome of the problem identification process. Then, CITs create a report of their analysis specifically addressing different skills and language choices that would have furthered their effort. Supervisors also watch the videos to provide constructive feedback and highlight strength areas. A rubric can be designed to help evaluate the students based on competencies valued by different consultation models or faculty can develop their own simulations to match their course competencies.

While problem identification lends itself to simulation because it requires the use of advanced interpersonal communication and relationship building skills, any stage of the problem-solving process could be simulated as part of a consultation course. There is truly nothing like watching yourself on video to highlight areas that you want to address. Simulations are an invaluable way to provide students with interpersonal feedback and challenge students to start identifying growth areas. Also, students appreciate the opportunity to practice new skills in a safe environment prior to a first case. Of course, simulations could be developed to evaluate competencies as a summative activity.

ANALYSIS OF TAPES

Like simulations, taping allows for the critical reflection of actual consultation practices as well as communication and interpersonal skill development for early consultants. Instead of relying on what you think or remember happened in a consultation session, video- or audio-taping provides the opportunity to analyze and reflect on what occurred. Students consistently are surprised at what they actually said during the consultation session. Listening to tapes, as part of a supervision process, allows for analysis in the moment and provides opportunities to role-play different skills. Especially for novice consultants who have multiple foci, it is critical to be able to analyze actual performance as a foundation to build on for future consultation practice.

Analyzing tapes can take multiple forms. One way to reflect is to create a transcript of all or portions of the consultation session. This transcript provides the data to evaluate independently and in supervision. At least at the beginning, it is helpful to transcribe entire sessions so that the content as well as the process issues can be discussed. As CITs gain experience, they may choose to only transcribe portions that they want to reflect upon more or portions to discuss with their supervisor. As CITs gain experience, transcription can provide a valuable way to think about what could be done differently, and to practice communication skills.

Analyzing tapes and transcriptions has the added bonus of being completely relevant to the case at hand. Instead of practicing skills on a simulation or hypothetical scenario, CITs and their supervisors can explore skill growth in the context of actual cases. Therefore, scenarios role played or practiced in supervision can be immediately applied in subsequent consultation sessions. In my experience, CITs often replicate the words we have co-constructed through modeling and/or rehearsal in supervision during their actual cases, and their positive response to supervision is obvious in the tape of the following session.

LOGS

Tapes and transcriptions are the starting point for creating reflective logs of each consultation session. After careful listening to and transcription of taped sessions, students should create logs to guide their weekly supervision. Logs can take many forms but should include reflection on all major areas of the consultation process. For example, logs might contain the following information: Name, Date, Target Teacher, Grade Level, Session #, Stage of Problem-Solving Process, Reflection on Working Relationship, Reflection on Communication Skills, and Requests for Feedback or Supervision (see Appendix B for an example).

In the Stage of the Problem-Solving Process section, the CIT discusses the current content and progress thus far in problem solving. A quick summary of what has been done, what is currently happening, and any future directions that are already apparent are included. It is also the place to describe any assessments or data collection that has occurred, or background information about the client that is pertinent to the case (e.g., history of absences).

The Working Relationship section is a place for the CIT to reflect on how he or she is working with the consultee. In the Instructional Consultation model (Rosenfield, 1987, 2008), building a strong working relationship in a consultation setting is different than the rapport building done in counseling or traditional assessment. Working relationships should be ones in which ideas can be challenged and conflicts resolved in a collaborative manner. In order to share the problem fully and engage in a collaborative, consultee-centered approach, consultants and consultees must feel comfortable sharing ideas, critically evaluating possible solutions, and compromising throughout the process to make sure it is consultee led. In other models of consultation, developing a working relationship is also essential, yet it may take different forms.

Regardless of approach to consultation, after each session, CITs should reflect on their language, nonverbal messages, and teacher's reaction to them to monitor the working relationship. With nearly every CIT I have supervised (and as a CIT, myself), listening to a session highlighted something the teacher/consultee said that the CIT completely missed. For example, one of my supervisees reflected that as she was completing the documentation form the teacher mentioned an additional concern that she missed hearing during the session and only picked up on after listening to the tape. Upon reflection, she decided that she needed to address and clarify this concern in the next consultation session. Careful listening to tape, discussion in supervision, and then revisiting in the next session can positively impact a working relationship and the progress of the case.

The Communication Skills section is the place where transcription is arguably the most helpful. By carefully transcribing and analyzing the use of communication, it is possible to find areas of strength and areas on which work is needed. By reflecting on these prior to supervision, the CIT and supervisor can make best use of the supervision time and engage in role play or practice alternate communication techniques. Without prior reflection captured on the logs, supervision time may have to be devoted to finding or remembering communication skills used.

Communication skills employed may also vary as a result of the consultation model presented but evaluating what is said is critically important regardless of model. Just listening to your work and hearing the tone of your voice is instructive. In nearly every supervision session, I recall hearing phrases like, "I can't believe I said that" or "I didn't remember saying that" or "That's not at all what I meant." Reflecting on communication skills and how we communicate is invaluable beyond consultation training. Taking my own cases and then supervising nine of my peers meant I was challenged on a regular basis to hear how I communicate and how I am perceived. I was able to set personal goals to work on and reflect on areas I wanted to improve upon throughout this process. I will take these lessons with me into my life, not just as a consultant, but also as a psychologist, a co-worker, a mother, a friend, and a family member.

Finally, logs provide a place for CITs to request assistance or discussion about a particular part of the consultation session. From a supervisor's point of view, I knew what the CIT really wanted to get out of supervision by reading this portion of his or her log. Also, it allowed for pattern analysis to see if there were any areas that needed to be addressed as a class because the concern was universal. For students, requesting supervision allows for some control in what occurs in supervision as well as a place to begin answering their own questions. As students gain more experience, students are able to pose questions that they begin answering themselves. In fact, often as a supervisor, I challenged students to answer their own questions prior to our discussion. As the year progressed, students were encouraged and expected to become more autonomous in addressing their reflections. Newman (Chapter 2, this volume) provides additional discussion on supervision in consultation training.

Additional sections to add may include Plan for Next Session and/or Happenings Outside of Consultation Session. Logs may take a variety of forms but careful reflection on what happened in a consultation session and planning for what will happen in the future are critical components.

SELF-ASSESSMENT OF CONSULTATION SKILLS

The course instructor and I created a self-assessment to coincide with the skills targeted by our training program. While some of these skills are unique to *Instructional Consultation* (Rosenfield, 1987, 2008), the model of consultation in my training program, other skills on this assessment are probably applicable to any school-based consultants. Consultation skills are organized into seven broad categories: Collaborative and Consultative Skills, Interpersonal Communication Skills, Problem-Solving Process, Assessment, Intervention Design, Professional Interaction Skills, and Systems Change. CITs were asked to rate the level of skill based on Joyce and Showers' (2002) adult-learning principles: NA = No prior knowledge or skill in this area (1), AW = Awareness: able to generally articulate concept (2), CU = Conceptual Understanding: able to clearly articulate concept and describe appropriate actions (3), SA = Skill Acquisition: able to demonstrate skill or knowledge in structured or simulated settings (4), AP = Application of Skills: able to use skill or knowledge flexibly in actual setting (5). See Appendix C for the self-assessment template.

Self-assessment encourages careful reflection on current skill level. Not only does it challenge CITs to think critically about their present levels, it also challenges them to look into the future to think about what they hope to accomplish. However, self-assessment has a variety of challenges in that sometimes it is very difficult to evaluate one's ability without a lot of knowledge about a domain. Said plainly, it is difficult to approximate what we can do when we have never done it and know very little about it, especially if the skills sound similar to other ones we have. As a result, self-assessments of skill growth have been traditionally problematic, sometimes showing little to no growth after training (and sometimes even diminished skill levels as raters come to understand more precisely their level of pre-training knowledge). One cause may be *response-shift bias*, or the change in perception of the phenomenon being measured between pre-test and post-test (Howard & Dailey, 1979). One way to help correct for *response-shift bias* is to have CITs complete retrospective pre-test after a post-test (e.g., Drennan & Hyde, 2008; Pratt, McGuigan, & Katsev, 2000).

During my supervision and co-teaching experience in pre-service consultation training, we administered self-assessments at multiple points to help document skill growth. As expected, we saw initial overestimation of skill level followed by levels dropping off when students began taking consultation

Table 1.3 Class-wide Self-Assessment Results: Pre-, Mid- Post- and Retrospective Pre-tests

Skill Area	*Pre*	*Mid*	*Post*	*Retro-Pre*
1 Collaboration and Consultative Skills	3.43	2.02	4.43	1.37
2 Interpersonal Communication Skills	3.54	2.61	4.36	1.59
3 Problem-Solving Process	3.28	2.27	4.61	1.69
4 Assessment	2.9	2.47	3.68	2.2
5 Intervention Design	2.92	2.38	4.28	1.8
6 Professional Interaction Skills	4.02	2.65	4.65	2.2
7 Systems Change	1.5	1.66	4.04	1.21

cases under supervision. We administered pre-assessments prior to the CITs taking consultation cases (September), mid-assessments at the end of the first consultation course (December), post-assessments near the end of the second consultation course (May), and retrospective pre-assessments after the post-assessments (also in May). Results of these assessments (by broad consultation skill category) are found in Table 1.3. Figure 1.1 illustrates pictorially the *response-shift bias* and subsequent correction by retrospective pre-testing. As illustrated in Table 1.3 and Figure 1.1, pre-assessment scores in almost every consultation skill area were elevated, higher than mid-assessment scores. But

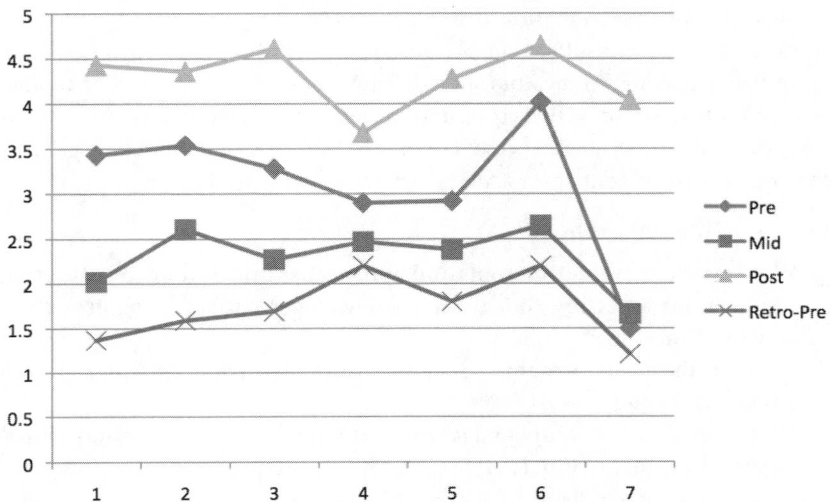

Figure 1.1 Class-wide Self-Assessment Results Demonstrating *Response-Shift Bias.*

when students were asked to recall their starting levels, via a retrospective pre-assessment, these numbers are more in line with novice consultants.

SUPERVISOR ASSESSMENT OF SKILLS

Finally, at the end of the training course sequence, it is helpful to have additional perspectives about skill levels. In-school supervisors and/or on-campus supervisors may each be able to contribute to any overall picture of the CIT's final skill level and areas of strength and weakness. In addition to the self-assessment, we designed a supervisor assessment based on the same skills, but with a different scaling system and some changes based on the piloting of the assessment. The supervisors' assessment is scaled to represent preparation level, from novice to proficient. For the purpose of our training program, we also included an acceptability scale to determine if the CIT's skill level was at the level expected in each domain. Thus, this tool is also more versatile and can be used to determine skill level after fieldwork, advanced practicum, or internship. See Appendix D for this tool.

Summary

The purpose of this chapter was to provide some ideas for formative and summative evaluations of the knowledge and skills gained through consultation training. Throughout this chapter, I have tried to address how to support school psychology students to engage in critical self-reflection. Through careful self-reflection, advanced CITs should be able to identify target concerns, determine what they would do differently, and then act on this reflection in subsequent sessions. In addition, instructor and supervisor evaluation at formative and summative stages have been presented. One of the difficulties in evaluating school consultation is the lack of clear and defined competencies needed to be a consultant in schools. Once universal competencies are identified, behavioral indicators and additional evaluation tools can be created to help unite the field. While consultation training models may value different competencies, the strategies presented in this chapter should have utility across programs and different approaches to school-based consultation.

Questions for Reflection

1. **What types of evaluation tools and approaches are used in your training program for assessing consultation knowledge? For assessing growth of consultation skills?**
2. **How do the ideas presented relate to your own training program and consultation coursework?**
3. **What consultation competencies do you believe extend beyond individual approaches and are universal for school consultants?**
4. **How can you challenge yourself to engage in critical self-reflection throughout your career?**

References

Anton-LaHart, J., & Rosenfield, S. (2004). A survey of preservice consultation training in school psychology programs. *Journal of Educational and Psychological Consultation, 15*, 41–62.

Benn, A.E., Jones, G.W., & Rosenfield, S. (2008). Analysis of Instructional Consultants' questions and alternatives to questions during the Problem Identification interview. *Journal of Educational and Psychological Consultation, 18*, 54–80.

Drennan, J., & Hyde, A. (2008). Controlling response shift bias: The use of the retrospective pre-test design in the evaluation of a master's programme. *Assessment & Evaluation in Higher Education, 33*, 699–709.

Fried, R.L. (2003). *The skeptical visionary: A Seymour Sarason education reader.* Philadelphia, PA: Temple University Press.

Fullan, M.G., & Hargreaves, A. (1991). Total Schools. In *What's worth fighting for? Working together for your school* (pp. 37–62). Andover, MA: Regional Laboratory for Educational Improvement.

Hall, J.D. (2002). Contemporary practices in school psychology: A national survey of roles and referral problems. *Psychology in the Schools, 39*, 327–335.

Hazel, C.E., Laviolette, G.T., & Lineman, J.M. (2010). Training professional psychologists in school based consultation: What the syllabi suggest. *Training and Education in Professional Psychology, 4*, 235–243.

Horn, I.S., & Little, J.W. (2010). Attending to problems of practice: Routines and resources for professional learning in teachers' workplace interactions. *American Educational Research Journal, 47*, 181–217.

Howard, G., & Dailey, P. (1979). Response shift bias: A source of contamination of self-report measures. *Journal of Applied Psychology, 64*, 144–150.

Jones, G.W. (1999). Validation of a simulation to evaluate instructional consultation problem identification skill competence. *Dissertation Abstracts International, 60* (12A), 4317.

Joyce, B., & Showers, B. (2002). *Student achievement through staff development* (3rd ed.). Alexandria, VA: ASCD.

Lentz, F.E., Jr., Allen, S.J., & Ehrhardt, K.E. (1996). The conceptual elements of strong interventions in school settings. *School Psychology Quarterly, 11*(2), 118–136.

Little, J.W. (1990). The persistence of privacy: Autonomy and initiative in teachers' professional relations. *Teachers College Record, 91*, 509–536.

Little, J.W. (2007). Teachers' accounts of classroom experience as a resource for professional learning and instructional decision making. In P.A. Moss (Ed.). *Evidence and decision making* (pp. 217–240). Malden, MA: Blackwell Publishing.

Pratt, C.C., McGuigan, W.M., & Katsev, A.R. (2000). Measuring program outcomes: Using retrospective pretest methodology. *American Journal of Evaluation,* 21, 341–349.

Rosenfield, S. (1987). *Instructional consultation.* Hillsdale, NJ: Erlbaum.

Rosenfield, S. (2008). Best practices in instructional consultation. In A. Thomas & J. Grimes (Eds.). *Best practices in school psychology V* (pp. 1645–1660). Washington, DC: National Association of School Psychologists.

Sarason, S. (1996). *Revisiting "The culture of the school and the problem of change"*. New York: Teachers College Press.

Wyner, N.B. (1991). Unlocking cultures of teaching: Working with diversity. In N.B. Wyner (Ed.). *Current perspectives on the* culture *of schools* (pp. 95–107). Brookline, MA: Brookline Books.

APPENDIX A

Supervision Log

Session #4
J./3rd grade

1. IC Stage

We are still in the problem identification and analysis stage. During this session, we decided to review what happened during the reading IA, discuss whether we wanted to do another reading IA or do the math IA next, revisit the SDF, discuss the teacher's concerns with absenteeism, and plan a math IA. First, we reviewed the reading IA because we did not have enough time to discuss it after we conducted it last session. The teacher and I both agreed that J. is a very good reader, and we discussed some concerns that she had with J.'s comprehension after the first snapshot. However, the second snapshot minimized some of the teacher's concerns with comprehension. She thought that J. did a great job relating his personal experiences to what he read which is one of her expectations for her students and finds it to be an important skill. The teacher also pointed out that she wants to know more about his skills in pulling out a clearly definable main idea. Eventually we decided that she would like to conduct another reading IA with a more challenging, realistic fiction text at the fourth grade level to get more information on comprehension and his ability to pull out the main idea, but she would rather conduct a math IA first.

Second, we revisited the SDF together because I realized that many of the concerns written were not what we were focusing on in our meetings together. She agreed and told me which concerns she would like to leave on the SDF and we could erase, re-word, and add. The concerns we have on the SDF now are:

1. not focused, asking unrelated questions, concerns with comprehension;
2. math: number sense, what an equation is, how to add together after decomposing (add and regroup, three-digit numbers), reasoning, problem-solving, strategies, understanding);
3. getting work started, materials out;
4. reading comprehension, missing main idea.

This brought us to the discussion of absenteeism. I asked her if she wanted to consider adding this to the SDF. The teacher said that J. is usually about 1–2 hours tardy, but not necessarily absent. We discovered together that language arts is the first subject of the day and that his ability to work in his reading group is often affected as a result. However, the teacher noted that she spoke with his parents about this, and that it has improved recently, so she does not want to focus on this issue right now. She does not want to ignore it entirely, but she does not want to focus on it right now.

Third, we discussed her math concerns and began planning a math IA. The teacher wants to know more about J.'s understanding of what an equation is, his number sense in terms of ones, tens, and hundreds, and his strategies for adding and subtracting (specifically, three-digit numbers). After we looked at the math domains hexagon, she pointed out that her concerns fall mainly into the reasoning and problem-solving domains. We looked over some of J.'s work samples and began constructing our math IA problems based on these samples. We had a great work session and decided to use the following method for our math IA:

1. quiz J. on addition and subtraction using flashcards and making piles based on what he knows and what he does not know;
2. play the math game "Go Collecting" that asks J. to add two- and three-digit numbers together;
3. ask J. to do four story problems (i.e.: If x and y are added together, how many are there in all? Write an equation, solve the problem, and show your solution) that we constructed based off of "Go Collecting" which asks him to add two- and three-digit numbers both with and without regrouping (i.e.: 82+36, 58+46, 176+123, and 154+247).

Last, I had the teacher summarize and we decided that we have quite a few concerns on the SDF, but the math IA and perhaps another reading IA will help us to narrow these down. She also wants to pay attention to how many times we have to redirect J. back on topic, and if he asks relevant questions during the math IA.

2. Consultant-Teacher Working Relationship

My teacher and I had a great session together that was very productive. After this session, I feel like I really understand her math concerns a lot more clearly, and I feel comfortable and ready to do the math IA with her. We worked very well together and we both gave each other new information that helped us collaborate and plan the math IA. I was a little nervous describing the math IA process to her because I did not want to seem like an expert. However, it went well and I did not feel that way at all by the end of the session. I was also nervous because I have never planned a math IA before, and knew much less about this compared to reading. Again, I think this went well and was not a problem because I was honest with her about this and we figured it out together. I felt great about our working relationship after this session!

3. Communication Skills

I used a clarifying statement, "Tell me about absenteeism," to help me understand that the teacher meant that he is actually tardy in the mornings, not absent for the entire day. This also helped me understand that his tardiness affects his performance in his reading group because he misses language arts every time he is late. I also used some relevant questions, such as, "Does your class have the same schedule everyday?" to help me get to this point. I used other clarifying statements such as, "Tell me more about what you mean by number sense" to help me understand that she meant the ones, tens, and hundreds place, and using them to add multiple digit numbers. I now realize that J. can decompose numbers, but has trouble putting them back together, which is different from what I previously understood regarding the teacher's math concerns. Finally, the teacher said, "His social skills aren't where they should be either" but went back to discussing the math IA. I tried not to say "ok" or "yeah" when she said this to give the impression that I agreed with her, but she made it easier for me because she went back to discussing the math IA on her own with a response from me.

4. Requests for Feedback During Supervision

- Does our plan for the math IA sound reasonable and effective?
- Are there still concerns on our SDF that should be removed (such as numbers 1 and 4)?
- Should I just wait to do this until after the IA?
- Is it ok to keep track of how many times we have to redirect J. back on topic/how many relevant questions he asks during the math IA like the teacher suggests at the end of the session?

APPENDIX B

Journal 10
Katie Sutton (Burkhouse)
EDCP 635

I think one of the major points I took away from the Lentz, Allen, and Ehrhardt (1996) article was that weak interventions are costly. Sometimes I think educators believe that if they put something in place then they are doing something positive. Often I feel this is how some people view psychoeducational assessments, as well. Doing something is sufficient. Unfortunately, that is not the case with interventions or assessments. There can be loss of instructional time, forming of bad habits, and more unsuccessful experiences for both teacher and student. I feel we have a responsibility to the people we work with to not waste time and resources and not expose them to bad interventions.

Unfortunately, we don't necessarily know if a particular intervention will work for a particular student. But if we choose from a bank of research-supported interventions and tailor these to the particular classroom and the particular student, we can increase our chances of success. I also thought it was useful to read more about the logistics of managing intervention requests. This reminded me of some of the conversations I've had with [in-school supervisor]. [School] has a referral sheet for the [consultation] process and mandates some steps prior to a referral. One of his (and others) biggest frustrations was teachers using [consultation] as a replacement for special education. Prior to these referral sheets, teachers did not take the time to do a record review or explore the students' strengths. Though this is certainly a part of the problem ID process in the IC model, this was incorporated as a beginning step to set the tone for this process. The different routine helped to facilitate this change process.

Some of the points made by this article were straightforward but a different way of thinking about interventions. For example, we often get caught up in the how of an intervention and fail to appreciate the fact the student must be engaged to truly benefit from this experience. Then quality interventions may be cast aside and consultation may break down. It was clear to me after reading this article that part of the intervention process is ensuring that the target student and teacher were focused and engaged in the chosen intervention. It also made sense to me that if a classroom teacher is having a problem the intervention should take place in the classroom with the teacher "taking the reigns" so to speak. I don't think this is always the mindset of a teacher in need of assistance. Treatment integrity relates to the previous two points. If the teacher is not engaged and the student is not engaged in the intervention or the intervention is only partially implemented, it is difficult to assess that interventions capacity for success. Also, if a classroom teacher feels that she can not help the particular student or expects the student to receive help outside the classroom, treatment integrity for classroom interventions may suffer. The advice giving in this section is valuable for helping to ensure treatment integrity (copy of procedures, etc).

The other two articles were very beneficial. I heard someone mention that there may be a class about reading added to our program requirements (don't remember who was saying this). Since over 80% of referrals are for reading concerns, I think this would be a very valuable addition to our curriculum. The breaking down of reading phases and components in the two articles was helpful. I especially enjoyed the reference about the physicist explaining that teaching reading was actually much harder than rocket science. I agree with Ehri that teachers probably aren't given enough training in the basic processes of learning and reading, how to assess these processes, and how to teach them. However, I also don't think as a society we give teachers enough credit. Teaching should be more than a four year program with one year of student teaching.

Further, if we respect our educational system we should offer teachers comparable salaries to other professionals (especially if greater educational requirements are mandated, as I think they probably should be). However, that is probably a discussion for another time.

APPENDIX C

University of Maryland

School Psychology Consultation Practicum Evaluation
Self-Assessment

Name: Date:
PRE MID POST RETRO-PRE (circle one)

Key:
NA = No prior knowledge or skill in this area
AW = Awareness: able to generally articulate concept
CU = Conceptual Understanding: able to clearly articulate concept and describe appropriate actions
SA = Skill Acquisition: able to demonstrate skill or knowledge in structured or simulated settings
AP = Application of Skills: able to use skill or knowledge flexibly in actual setting

Consultation Skill Area	*NA*	*AW*	*CU*	*SA*	*AP*
Collaboration and Consultative Skills					
Form working relationships with diverse consultees					
Understand consultee's strengths and needs					
Flexibly adhere to problem-solving process					
Successfully address difficulties that arise in consultation					
Use Student Documentation Form (SDF) to facilitate consultation process					
Interpersonal Communication Skills					
Clarify consultee's concerns through use of paraphrasing, summarizing, and asking questions					
Reflect feelings of consultee					
Adapt communication to meet needs of consultee					
Respond to non-verbal cues of consultee					
Reflect on thoughts and ideas of consultee					
Use clarifying questions appropriately					
Acknowledge differences of opinions and resolve conflicts					

Consultation Skill Area	*NA*	*AW*	*CU*	*SA*	*AP*
Problem-Solving Process					
Address all areas of contracting					
Create a shared understanding of consultee's concerns					
Conceptualize consultee's concerns in observable and measurable terms					
Gather data based on curriculum expectations to aid in problem-solving process					
Assess student's instructional match					
Prioritize concerns of consultee					
Set measurable goals with consultee					
Elicit teacher's ideas for strategies					
Discuss intervention plans related to assessment goals					
Anticipate potential barriers to implementation					
Follow-up and monitor implementation of intervention plan					
Rework conceptualization of problem and intervention based on data					
Share problem-solving process with consultee and make joint decisions through the process					
Assessment					
Conduct Curriculum-based Assessment (CBA) in reading					
Conduct CBA in math					
Conduct CBA in writing					
Conduct systematic observations across multiple settings					
Evaluate student progress using data					
Intervention Design					
Use instructional match in intervention design and selection					
Incorporate student's or groups' prior knowledge into intervention plan					
Select materials to build on student's skills					
Professional Interaction Skills					
Work through obstacles and difficult issues with supervisor					
Focus on best interest of consultee and client					
Respect the culture and practices of the school					
Interact effectively with school personnel					
Consider cultural differences in consultation triad					

(Continued)

Consultation Skill Area	*NA*	*AW*	*CU*	*SA*	*AP*
Recognize, respect, and respond appropriately to the effects of personal values and belief systems of self and others in the consultation process					
Exhibit caring, respectful, empathic, congruent and open consultation interactions					
Be willing to admit that you do not know an answer and willing to explore possible solutions with others					
Demonstrate willingness to learn from others throughout consultation experience					
Give and solicit feedback to maintain, revise, or terminate consultation activities					
Relate to peers in professional manner					
Engage in self-evaluation of strengths and weaknesses to modify personal behaviors that may influence consultation process					
Systems Change					
View self as change agent and continue development of the role of change agent					
Conduct system wide needs assessments					
Identify benefits and consequences from proposed change efforts					
Evaluate programs that seek systemic change					

APPENDIX D

University of Maryland

School Psychology Consultation Evaluation

Student Name: Date:
Supervisor: Course:

<u>Competency Scale</u>

1 = Novice: demonstrates partial understanding, high levels of anxiety, difficult to integrate skill areas, very motivated and requires close supervision with a lot of structure

2 = Advanced Beginner: start to master technical aspects, start to see patterns and consider context, more autonomous but requires supervision to set priorities and determine relative importance of information

3 = Early Competent: begin to see relationships better, able to balance skills and empathy, able to plan and think ahead, begin analyzing own skills, supervision used to aid in reflection of skills

4 = Competent: largely self-sufficient, able to apply skills with flexibility in a variety of situations while preserving relationships, able to analyze own skills well, supervision typically used for consultation
5 = Proficient: work successfully with very complex cases, decreased reliance on guidelines, flexible use of skills in many areas of practice, utilize self-analysis often and appropriately, supervision used for consultation as needed

Acceptability Scale
1 = Not Acceptable
2 = Marginally Acceptable
3 = Acceptable/Expected
4 = Exceeds Expectations

Consultation Skill Area	*Competency*	*Acceptability*
Collaboration and Consultative Skills		
Form working relationships with diverse consultees		
Understand consultee's strengths and needs		
Flexibly adhere to problem-solving process		
Successfully address difficulties that arise in consultation		
Use Student Documentation Form (SDF) to facilitate consultation process		
Share problem-solving process with consultee and make joint decisions through the process		
Interpersonal Communication Skills		
Clarify consultee's concerns through use of paraphrasing, summarizing, and asking questions		
Reflect feelings of consultee		
Adapt communication to meet needs of consultee		
Respond to non-verbal cues of consultee		
Reflect on thoughts and ideas of consultee		
Use clarifying questions appropriately		
Acknowledge differences of opinions and resolve conflicts		
Problem-Solving Process		
Address all areas of contracting		
Create a shared understanding of consultee's concerns		
Conceptualize consultee's concerns in observable and measurable terms		

(Continued)

Consultation Skill Area	*Competency*	*Acceptability*
Problem-Solving Process		
Gather data based on curriculum expectations to aid in problem-solving process		
Assess student's instructional match		
Conduct Curriculum Base Assessment (CBA) and/or Instructional Assessment (IA) appropriately in cases		
Conduct systematic observations across multiple settings		
Evaluate student progress using data		
Prioritize concerns of consultee		
Set measurable goals with consultee		
Elicit teacher's ideas for strategies in coordination with goals		
Discuss intervention plans related to EBI		
Use instructional match in intervention design and selection		
Incorporate student's or groups' prior knowledge into intervention plan		
Select materials to build on student's skills		
Anticipate potential barriers to implementation		
Follow-up and monitor implementation of intervention plan		
Rework conceptualization of problem and intervention based on data if needed		
Professional Interaction Skills		
Work through obstacles and difficult issues with supervisor		
Focus on best interest of consultee and client		
Respect the culture and practices of the school		
Interact effectively with school personnel		
Consider cultural differences in consultation triad		
Recognize, respect, and respond appropriately to the effects of personal values and belief systems of self and others in the consultation process		
Exhibit caring, respectful, empathic, congruent and open consultation interactions		
Be willing to admit that you do not know an answer and willing to explore possible solutions with others		
Demonstrate willingness to learn from others throughout consultation experience		
Give and solicit feedback to maintain, revise, or terminate consultation activities		
Relate to peers in professional manner		
Engage in self-evaluation of strengths and weaknesses to modify personal behaviors that may influence consultation process		
Demonstrate investment in becoming a skilled consultant		

Consultation Skill Area	*Competency*	*Acceptability*
Systems Change		
View self as change agent and continue development of the role of change agent		
Conduct system wide needs assessments		
Identify benefits and consequences from proposed change efforts		
Evaluate programs that seek systemic change		

2
Supervision of School-Based Consultation Training: Addressing the Concerns of Novice Consultants

Daniel Newman

Advance Organizer Questions

- **What are the main content and process concerns that arise for consultants-in-training (CITs) during their pre-service level coursework and practicum experiences?**
- **How are CIT concerns addressed through consultation supervision?**
- **What consultation skills are demonstrated for CITs across all three case examples?**
- **What unique consultation concepts are demonstrated by each case example?**

Introduction

Clinical supervision is the primary pedagogical tool used by trainers in mental health fields such as clinical and counseling psychology (Bernard & Goodyear, 2009). Supervision is also expected to be an essential facet of training in school psychology, as is reflected in professional practice standards and ethical guidelines by the National Association of School Psychologists (NASP, 2010). Yet, despite calls from the field for increased implementation of supervision practices, school psychology trainees and practitioners do not receive adequate supervisory support (Crespi & Dube, 2005).

As was confirmed in a study by Anton-LaHart and Rosenfield (2004), school-based consultation training is not immune to the lack of supervision practices in school psychology; the authors found that even though most training programs offer at least one semester of consultation coursework, consultation practicum experiences and consultation supervision are not always provided. The absence of consultation supervision is in conflict with the changing nature of the field of school psychology, including the ever-increasing emphasis placed on the consultation role (Reschly, 2008; Ysseldyke, Burns, & Rosenfield, 2009; Ysseldyke et al., 2006).

There are a handful of available articles in the consultation literature regarding training and supervision (see, e.g., Cramer & Rosenfield, 2003; Rosenfield, Levinsohn-Klyap, & Cramer, 2010), but consultation training and supervision have rarely been the focus of research studies (Alpert & Taufique, 2002). Perhaps the lack of consultation training research is one reason for limitations in consultation training at the pre-service level, as recently described by Hazel, Laviolette, and Lineman (2010). Using several different case examples, this chapter will build upon existing descriptions and studies of consultation training and supervision. Supervision of consultation will be treated as a pedagogical tool, working in concert with consultation coursework and practicum experiences, to help students develop the clinical skills needed to function effectively as school-based consultants. Content and process concerns that most frequently surface for consultants-in-training (CITs) will be identified and described. Supervision strategies that may help address these concerns will be explored using real supervision case examples.

The Role of CIT Concerns during Consultation Training and Supervision

Experiencing heightened levels of anxiety is normal for novice-level trainees. According to developmental process models of supervision (e.g., Bernard & Goodyear, 2009), CIT concerns can be viewed as trigger events that spark reflection, discussion, and CIT skill development (see, e.g., Chapter 10, this volume). The following sections contain a description of how CIT concerns can be triggers for supervision interactions within a supervisee-centered supervision model, and a brief overview of two research studies on the main concerns faced by CITs.

Concerns as Catalysts

Supervision is in many ways a reactive process, both for the supervisor and the supervisee. A developmental process model of supervision described by Bernard and Goodyear (2009) provides an accurate representation of many interactions during consultation training and supervision, and is illustrated with an accompanying case example in Figure 2.1. In this model, CIT reflection commences with a trigger event that brings forth surprise, discomfort, or confusion from the supervisee, who in turn connects the catalyzing event to his or her own skills, personal issues, and/or case conceptualization. The supervisor then helps the supervisee facilitate a "critical reevaluation of the situation" (p. 93) in favor of a new perspective on handling a similar instance in the future. In short, the main concerns faced by CITs during consultation training  are catalysts for a reflective supervision process, which ideally leads to enhanced capacity for CITs to apply skills effectively in future circumstances.

For example, CIT Bonnie experienced feelings of surprise and confusion immediately following her completion of a classroom observation (i.e., the trigger event). As part of supervision requirements, Bonnie listened to an audiotape of the consultation session and reflected in writing about the case, including her use of communication skills and her developing frame of the problem. Bonnie realized her case conceptualization was disparate from the

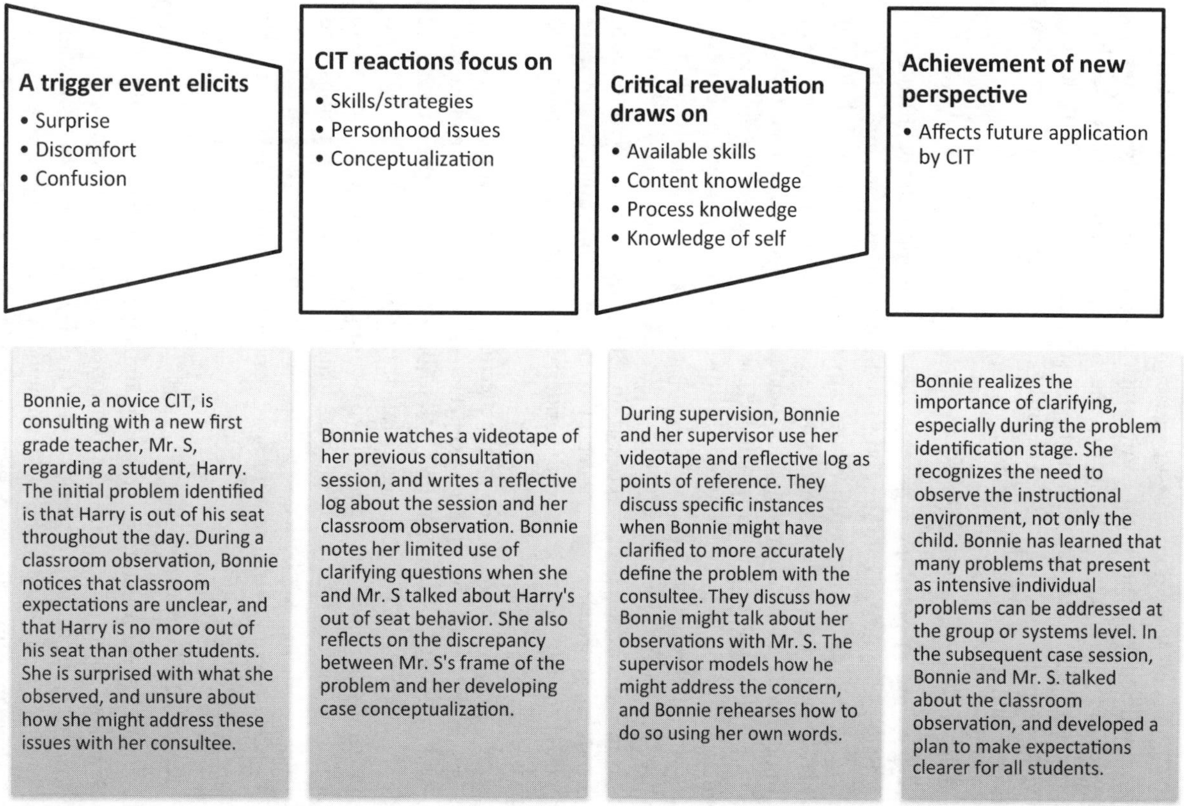

A trigger event elicits

- Surprise
- Discomfort
- Confusion

CIT reactions focus on

- Skills/strategies
- Personhood issues
- Conceptualization

Critical reevaluation draws on

- Available skills
- Content knowledge
- Process knolwedge
- Knowledge of self

Achievement of new perspective

- Affects future application by CIT

Bonnie, a novice CIT, is consulting with a new first grade teacher, Mr. S, regarding a student, Harry. The initial problem identified is that Harry is out of his seat throughout the day. During a classroom observation, Bonnie notices that classroom expectations are unclear, and that Harry is no more out of his seat than other students. She is surprised with what she observed, and unsure about how she might address these issues with her consultee.

Bonnie watches a videotape of her previous consultation session, and writes a reflective log about the session and her classroom observation. Bonnie notes her limited use of clarifying questions when she and Mr. S talked about Harry's out of seat behavior. She also reflects on the discrepancy between Mr. S's frame of the problem and her developing case conceptualization.

During supervision, Bonnie and her supervisor use her videotape and reflective log as points of reference. They discuss specific instances when Bonnie might have clarified to more accurately define the problem with the consultee. They discuss how Bonnie might talk about her observations with Mr. S. The supervisor models how he might address the concern, and Bonnie rehearses how to do so using her own words.

Bonnie realizes the importance of clarifying, especially during the problem identification stage. She recognizes the need to observe the instructional environment, not only the child. Bonnie has learned that many problems that present as intensive individual problems can be addressed at the group or systems level. In the subsequent case session, Bonnie and Mr. S. talked about the classroom observation, and developed a plan to make expectations clearer for all students.

Figure 2.1 The Reflective Process in Supervision of Consultation, adapted from Bernard and Goodyear (2009)

consultee's but was unsure how to address these issues. In a subsequent supervision session, Bonnie's reactions, concerns, and reflections acted as primary points of discussion. The supervisor helped Bonnie reflect on lessons learned, modeled how she might communicate with the consultee to address concerns, and encouraged Bonnie to rehearse how she might discuss her concerns with the consultee. Through the support of supervision, Bonnie achieved new perspectives on the case, and gained consultation skills that she will take with her in her future practice.

Responding to Concerns with Supervisee-Centered Supervision

Supervisor and CIT reactions and interactions can be more deliberate if both parties have awareness of common problem themes that surface for CITs. For example, prior to site entry, a university supervisor–CIT dyad might discuss gaps between applied course expectations (e.g., CITs are expected to engage in ongoing, formal consultation with a teacher) and practicum site realities (e.g., the fast-paced on-site practicum supervisor mostly engages in ephemeral consultation in the hallway). Having this discussion early may prevent CIT confusion and, through supervisor modeling and CIT rehearsal in supervision, empower CITs with words to describe their role as consultant to their site-supervisor, and others at their practicum site. Being deliberatively responsive to CIT needs and prioritizing CIT learning creates a maximally supportive supervision environment; these are the underpinnings of a supervisee-centered supervision process (Conoley, 1981).

CIT concerns are triggers that spur reflection inside and outside of supervision sessions. It can be beneficial for supervisors and CITs to be knowledgeable of typical concerns likely to arise for CITs, while responding to the unique case issues of individual CIT experiences. Moffett (2009) suggested, with regard to psychotherapy supervision, "rather than waiting for problematic events to occur before learning from them, anticipating problematic reactions and preparing for them may better serve" the supervisor, supervisee, and client (p. 78). Next, the topics that tend to be of concern for novice consultants will be more precisely defined.

Research on CIT Concerns

Research studies on consultation training and supervision by Conoley (1981) and Newman (2009) provide insight into some of the most common concerns that arise for CITs at the pre-service level. Conoley (1981) analyzed tapes and notes of small group supervision with 56 novice CITs over the course of three years while implementing and evaluating a framework for consultation training. Nine CIT problem themes were identified; six were categorized as field concerns (entry; lack of knowledge in specialized areas; consultant–consultee incongruity; territoriality; ambivalence of the consultative role; student status of consultants) and three as supervision concerns (giving/

receiving personal and professional feedback; dealing with dual supervisory input; emergent versus structured supervision time).

In a constructivist grounded theory study, Newman (2009) explored the process of supervision within pre-service level consultation training. The main concerns faced by five female second-year doctoral students engaged in the second semester of a two-semester consultation course that included a practicum experience were described and explored with regard to their consideration during a supervision process. Although the study did not include a comprehensive list of CIT concerns, as that was not the study's primary focus, 37 of the most prominent concerns were identified and categorized within the following five topic areas: the problem-solving process as a whole; the individual problem-solving stages; communication processes; use of data; and, relationships.

Many of the concerns that arose in Newman's (2009) study overlapped with the concerns faced by CITs in the study by Conoley (1981). The synthesized results and categories from these two studies are illustrated in Table 2.1. Three topic areas of concerns—consultative role, student status, and processes of supervision—were found by Conoley (1981) but not included in Newman's (2009) study; these three topic areas are described in Table 2.2. The reader should also note that each topic area includes some concerns that are content focused and others that are process oriented. Content concerns often overlap with conceptual knowledge covered during consultation coursework, while process concerns tend to relate to nuanced application of consultation skills in practice.

Table 2.1 Main Concerns Faced by Consultants in Training: Overlaps between Conoley (1981) and Newman (2009)

Topic	*Area*	*Concern*
Problem-solving process, general		• Learning the components of each stage of the process • Problem-solving in order of stages • How to document the case • Working with more than one party/ knowing who is the consultee • Case not progressing/"going in circles" • "Staying true" to the process • Slow moving process • Difficulty scheduling with the consultee
Problem-solving stages	Entry and contracting	• How to establish a consultative contract • How to identify a case • Not feeling a part of the school culture • Communicating expectations to administrators, site supervisor, consultee

(Continued)

Table 2.1 *(Continued)*

Topic	*Area*	*Concern*
	Problem identification and analysis	• Lack of academic knowledge such as principles of effective instruction • Lack of behavioral knowledge such as principles of behavioral support • Clarifying the problem • Prioritizing a concern • Creating a shared problem frame • Conducting a needs assessment (in systems-level cases) • Understanding the relationship between academic and behavioral concerns
	Intervention design, implementation, and evaluation	• Intervention does not match problem • Lack of academic intervention knowledge • Lack of behavioral intervention knowledge • Coordinating interventions and/or resources • Intervention is not clearly described • Intervention is not acceptable to consultee • Intervention lacks treatment integrity
	Closure	• Writing a summary letter • When to end the case • How to transition the case at the end of practicum
Using data		• Conducting an instructional assessment • Measuring baseline data • Setting goals • Collecting data • Interpreting data • Purpose of data
Communication skills		• Using skills covered in coursework such as clarifying, paraphrasing, perception checking, and summarizing • Using collaborative language (e.g., "we" instead of "I") • Using "nuanced" communication skills (e.g., being assertive when necessary; nonverbals; addressing sensitive case issues) • Using communication skills with a purpose

Topic	Area	Concern
Relationships		• Collaboration with the consultee • Working with more than one culture in the consultation triad • Working with a team • Negative relationships (CIT–consultee and consultee–student)

Table 2.2 Main Concerns Faced by Consultants in Training Identified by Conoley (1981) but not Newman (2009)

Topic	Area	Concern
Consultative Role		• Consultative role is not relevant at practicum site • Practicum site emphasizes direct service over indirect service • Unsure about own beliefs of utility of consultation in school psychology practice
Student Status		• Lack of knowledge of school/district • Feeling a lack of credibility among experienced staff people • Balancing multiple requests for time at practicum site • Evaluations from site supervisor and/or university
Supervision	University	• Discomfort with activities such as simulations, role-playing, and rehearsal • Poor relationship with supervisor • Insufficient quality of supervision • Insufficient time for supervision • Confidentiality across supervisors
	Practicum site	• Lack of support on consultation case(s) • Lack of support in pursuing consultation activities • Poor relationship with supervisor • Insufficient quality of supervision • Insufficient time for supervision • Confidentiality across supervisors

Note. The topic areas and concerns identified only by Conoley (1981) were also seen in Newman's (2009) work, but not included in his study because the focus was on processes of supervision rather than CIT concerns.

The Problem-Solving Process

Problem solving, a critical skill utilized daily by school psychologists, is particularly pertinent for functioning in the role of school-based consultant (Ysseldyke et al., 2006). CITs experience concerns in content areas of the problem-solving process such as knowing with automaticity the order of problem-solving stages, the components of each problem-solving stage (considered in more detail in the subsequent section), and how to document the case as it progresses. CIT challenges regarding the problem-solving process are often interrelated. For example, a CIT might inadvertently navigate the stages out of order leading to a slow moving case, or a CIT may feel pressured to move forward in a case hastily due to the consultee's busy schedule, and jump into the intervention stage of problem-solving prior to clearly defining a problem.

The Problem-Solving Stages

In the studies on consultation training and supervision by Conoley (1981) and Newman (2009), CITs engaged in the problem-solving stages of entry and contracting; problem identification and problem analysis; intervention design, implementation, and evaluation; and closure. In each stage there is a particular set of tasks that are to be accomplished. For example, during site entry and contracting, some CITs have difficulty describing their consultant role and the consultation process learned at the university to site supervisors, consultees, or others at the practicum site. This is particularly true for CITs' first cases, since they have never completed the process themselves. CITs are also challenged by their perception, which is sometimes accurate, that they lack the academic or behavioral content knowledge that will allow them to complete the business of each stage.

Deficits in content knowledge—real or perceived—may impact CITs' contributions to accurately identifying and prioritizing a problem, developing an appropriate intervention to target the problem identified, and knowing when and how to close out the case. For example, a CIT–consultee dyad might immediately try to address a salient behavioral problem if neither party is aware that academic deficits are frequently the root causes of behavioral concerns. Related, a novice CIT with gaps in content knowledge, or simply lacking self-confidence, might take a consultee's problem description at face value when in reality the consultee may have a limited or partial understanding of the problem.

Using Data

According to the NASP Standards (2010), school psychologists in training are expected to develop skills in data-based decision-making and accountability throughout coursework, and during practicum and internship experiences. Throughout the school-based consultation practicum experience, as well as within each problem-solving stage, the use of data may present an array of concerns for CITs. Determining what data appropriately measures a concern (i.e., construct validity), what data are necessary and what data are superfluous, how to collect data in the classroom despite schedule complexities and teacher resistance, how to interpret data, and how to set goals and graph data in a manner that demonstrates a student's response to an intervention, are but a few of the matters that arise for CITs (see cases in this volume for multiple examples of data collection issues). School psychologists are often designated the "data experts" of the school building; accordingly, learning how to use data during a consultative problem-solving process is critical, and requires extensive support during supervision.

Communication Skills

Irrespective of consultation model, communication processes during consultation interactions are of vital importance (Rosenfield, 2004; Witt, 1997). Perhaps more than any other consultation models, consultee-centered consultation (CCC) models emphasize "the power of words," "the communication experience," and the overall complexity of CIT–consultee interchanges (Rosenfield, 2004, p. 343). Therefore, CIT concerns in CCC models not only include *what* particular communication skills to use (e.g., clarifying, paraphrasing, perception checking, and summarizing), but also *how* to use them. CITs need supervisory support, including opportunities for modeling and rehearsal, to learn how to apply nuanced communication skills. Examples of communication challenges include clarifying a consultee's high inference language in order to define a concern that is observable and measurable and broaching sensitive but necessary topics with a consultee, such as how to improve ineffective instruction.

Relationships

Concerns about communication are often related to concerns in the area of relationship development. For instance, CITs in CCC models may struggle with using collaborative communication skills in order to promote sufficiently collaborative relationships. Relationship concerns may arise for CITs when consulting one-on-one with a teacher, or when participating as part of a team (e.g., grade level or school wide problem-solving teams). Further, if collaboration is lacking or absent in the school culture, a CIT's relationship with individuals and with teams may be experienced as negative. For example, a teacher in a school where collaboration is not the norm may feel evaluated or defensive about her instructional practices when working with a CIT, especially if the teacher did not seek out the assistance.

In addition to concerns regarding collaboration, relationship challenges may arise for CITs when there is cultural divergence within the consultation constellation. For example, a Caucasian female consultee teaching an English Language Learner of Mexican descent who was a struggling reader discounted the student's success when he read a book about Mexican culture during an instructional assessment. The teacher failed to recognize the importance of prior knowledge in reading, even after it was pointed out by the consultant, replying that "the student cannot always be reading Mexican-themed books." The role of culture in consultation is a critical area that arises as concerning for CITs, and deserves specific attention in consultation supervision.

Consultative Role

Most pre-service level CITs are learning about the role of consultation in their professional practice for the first time, a process that may present some areas of dissonance when moving toward skill application. For one, it can be challenging for CITs to decipher the fit of consultation practice within their burgeoning conceptualization of the school psychologist role. Consultation is unique from many other areas of school psychology practice because it is an indirect service delivery approach (Gutkin & Conoley, 1990). Consequently, consultation might not match well with CITs' preconceived notions or preferred methods of practice that focus more on direct service to students. What is more, many sites remain largely influenced by the traditional school psychologist role of special education gatekeeper (Curtis, Grier, & Hunley, 2004). CITs at such sites have difficulty finding willing consultation "dance partners," and as a result, might perceive consultation as less relevant to school psychology practice. These perceptions are reinforced when a CIT works with a site supervisor who either does not engage in consultation at all, or whose consultation practices are unstructured and/or transient.

Student Status

Being a practicum student presents myriad concerns for CITs. An overarching problem is that, generally speaking, practicum students spend a limited amount of time in schools. Even in an intensive competency-based model, specialist-level practicum students are only expected to be in schools 255 hours per semester (Welsh, Meche, & Broussard, 2010). During this applied time, practicum students are expected to engage in multiple activities informed by both site- and university-based expectations; rarely do CITs have a consultation-specific practicum experience (Anton-LaHart & Rosenfield, 2004). Many CITs express that it is challenging to find the time to engage in structured, ongoing consultation when there are so many requests for their time. Furthermore, practicum students' schedules are often fragmented. As a result, feeling disconnected from the school staff and school culture is common. Spending limited time in the school can combine with CITs' lack of confidence and experience in consultation to result in feeling a lack of credibility among school-based personnel; these dynamics often surface as part of the consultation relationship.

Supervision

Concerns are also commonly present for CITs regarding both university- and site-based supervision processes. At the university level, activities such as simulations, role-plays, modeling, and rehearsal are important contributors to CIT learning, but may result in CIT discomfort. It is critical for supervisors to be aware of CIT apprehensions with the supervision process, and to work with CITs to address such concerns (Cramer & Rosenfield, 2003; Rosenfield et al., 2010). Regarding supervision from site supervisors, CITs may feel a lack of support in pursuing or working through consultation cases. This is not unexpected as most site supervisors have themselves not had adequate consultation training or supervision (Anton- LaHart & Rosenfield, 2004), and perhaps do not know the best way to support consultation skill development. Other CIT concerns related to supervision include poor supervisor–CIT relationships, insufficient quality of supervision, not having enough time for supervision, and worries about the communication dynamics between site and university supervisors.

Supervision Techniques and Strategies

Contemporary perspectives on supervision in school psychology advocate using developmental (e.g., Stoltenberg, 2005) and transtheoretical (e.g., Aten, Strain, & Gillespie, 2008) approaches, because these models highlight the important integration of skill development and self-awareness (Kaufman, 2010). Consistent with such perspectives, there are several supervision techniques hypothesized to augment the development of key consultation skills over time (Cramer & Rosenfield, 2003; Harvey & Struzziero, 2008; Rosenfield et al., 2010). These techniques overlap with clinical supervision interventions outlined by Bernard and Goodyear (2009), including the use of self-report, process and case notes, audiotaping/videotaping of fieldwork, and ongoing opportunities for reflection. For a comprehensive definition and description of these components of supervision of consultation training the reader is referred to Rosenfield et al. (2010) and to Burkhouse (Chapter 1, this volume).

The integrated implementation of techniques as part of a model for supervision of consultation training was described at length by Newman (2009). This study noted that supervision of consultation includes events both inside and outside of supervision sessions. Within supervision sessions, the supervisor and CIT engage in a variety of strategic interactions that can be categorized into (1) those focused on the past, (2) momentary bridges in the present, and (3) those related to future application. Strategies in the second category, moment-to-moment strategies, often act as connectors between CIT reflection about the past and the CIT's application of skills in future consultation sessions. Several strategies used in supervision are defined and exemplified in the Appendix. For a more extensive description of each strategic interaction in supervision, the reader is referred to Newman (2009).

Outside of supervision sessions, CITs are ideally engaged in ongoing coursework to enhance their consultation content knowledge in various domains (e.g., consultation models, the problem-solving, school culture, and school change variables, characteristics of effective instructional practices, instructional assessment, and evidence-based interventions). They also use e-mail communication with the consultee and supervisor, and engage in ongoing reflection.

The Role of Supervision in Addressing CIT Concerns

In the previous sections, the main concerns that CITs face during pre-service level consultation training were highlighted and several supervision strategies that may be useful in working through such concerns were identified. In the sections to follow, three case examples will be presented, each demonstrating concerns faced by CITs and how they were addressed in supervision. As would be expected, concerns are highly interconnected, so more than one category of concern is present in each example. All of the following examples are real, with the author in the role of supervisor. All names are pseudonyms, and none of the cases have been described in other chapters of this book.

Case Example 1: "Staying True to the Problem-Solving Process"

The first case example involves several common CIT concerns with the problem-solving process, and touches upon the need for consultants to work through each stage of the process with integrity. Novice CIT Alice, a second-year school psychology doctoral student taking on her first consultation case, began working with a second-grade teacher, Mrs. B, in late November. Mrs. B was concerned about the writing skills of one of her students. Alice and Mrs. B had difficulty coordinating meeting times because of a hectic school schedule, including pending Thanksgiving and Winter breaks and Alice's practicum schedule, which placed her in the school less than a full day per week. The dyad's third case session did not take place until mid-January, and Alice sensed urgency and frustration from the consultee, who had referred the case to the school-based problem-solving team back in early November. Understandably, Alice felt pressure to move forward in the case and she led their dyad into the intervention stage of problem solving before having clearly defined the problem they would be working on.

Several steps, over multiple supervision sessions, were involved in helping Alice work through these concerns. Alice and I were unable to schedule a supervision session between her third and fourth session with the consultee, the week following the consultation case session described earlier. However, Alice had audiotaped her case session and composed reflective logs, which I listened to and read even though we could not meet in person. In her process log, Alice wrote about the scheduling difficulties she faced with the consultee, but did not demonstrate awareness that she was preemptively moving forward in the problem-solving process. When listening to the tape, I realized the dyad had prematurely moved from the problem identification stage into the intervention stage before clearly defining the problem. My access to the tape and log provided a window for me to see into Alice's ongoing consultation process, and acted as a catalyst for CIT reflection, supervision discussions, and Alice's re-conceptualization of her actions as a consultant.

Since we could not meet in person, I e-mailed Alice immediately with feedback that it sounded to me as if she and her consultee were moving through the problem-solving stages too quickly, offered explicit information about the order of the stages, and inquired as to whether they had clearly defined and prioritized a problem. As Alice expressed in a subsequent process log, the e-mail helped her realize that she had "jumped around" and clarified for her the need to backup and work through the problem-solving stages in order and completely. During our next in-person supervision session, I used the strategy of making CIT to CIT comparisons; Alice and I discussed how some of her classmates also had experienced scheduling concerns in their cases, and what was done to address those concerns (e.g., another student had met with the teacher on the phone when she was not able to do so in person, and a second maintained ongoing e-mail dialogues about the case with her very busy consultee). Our discussion helped to normalize Alice's experiences, and offered pragmatic solutions for her work in this case and others in the future.

Asking reflective questions was another strategy used in our supervision sessions. While listening to her tape, I heard Alice apologize to the consultee for the case taking so long. As a result, I asked her: "What are your thoughts when I say [don't apologize for the problem-solving process] to you?" In response, Alice described worrying that she was "trampling" on the "time," "space," and "energy" of her consultee. Once these feelings emerged in our supervision session, we were able to move toward a discussion about how to recognize consultee concerns by using communication skills such as perception checking, without apologizing for the problem-solving process. In our final supervision session together, I asked Alice to reflect on her case as a whole. She described a newly developed perspective that for effective problem solving to take place, which eventually occurred in her case, it is important to balance "staying true to the problem-solving process" even when feeling pressured to move forward quickly.

Case Example 2: Addressing the Process

The second supervision case example demonstrates a CIT and supervisor working together through consultation case process concerns, the importance of the CIT–consultee relationship, and using communication skills to discuss instruction with the consultee with the purpose of enhancing instructional practices. At the time of this case, Kathy was a second-year school psychology doctoral student working on her second consultation case during her second semester of consultation coursework, including applied practicum experience and ongoing university supervision. Kathy can be described as a highly reflective student, which she demonstrated during coursework, supervision, and in writing her reflective logs. She is self-described as "detail oriented," a cognitive and communication style that had implications for her work with fourth-grade teacher Mr. Y.

For example, Kathy labeled both herself and Mr. Y as "lengthy communicators" who would often meet for very long sessions, some longer than an hour, without making much progress through the problem-solving stages. Despite her awareness of the dyad's lack of progress, Kathy expressed concerns about being too "assertive" or "directive" during case sessions. In supervision she stated, "I don't want to be too directive … and I think … I'm being so concerned that I'm ending up passive." As a supervisory dyad we contemplated whether communication challenges might also relate to gender dynamics; in other words, as a female CIT working with a male consultee, perhaps Kathy was "ending up passive." Kathy wrote in her reflective log:

> I also have a difficult time being assertive … when there isn't a natural pause in his dialogue because I do not want to seem rude or seem like I am minimizing what the teacher is currently talking about. OK yes, so there are likely some male/female dynamics going on!

In general, Kathy was aware that the consultee's communication style, and their communication as a dyad, presented her with many challenges such as not being able to find a "natural … breath spot" to stop dialogue, getting "lost" in Mr. Y's lengthy storytelling, and feeling as though she and the teacher were "spinning our wheels." Further, Kathy and I discussed the possibility that Mr. Y's communication style within their consultation sessions—verbose and sometimes lacking clarity—might parallel his instructional style. As the case progressed, it became clear that the consultation problem, which was originally identified as one student's behavioral issue, was actually, as stated by Kathy, "a wider instructional concern." As a result, Kathy needed to discuss instructional concerns with the consultee, a sensitive topic area that can be anxiety provoking for CITs to address with teachers (see also Chapter 4, this volume).

Kathy's natural tendency to be reflective—verbally within supervision, and with her actions outside of supervision (e.g., writing thoughtful, rich process logs and listening/re-listening to case tapes *and* tapes of our supervision sessions)—was a starting point for us to address consultation case concerns during supervision. For example, to support Kathy in finding a balance between being sufficiently directive while still being collaborative, we first discussed how to address her ineffective communication process with Mr. Y. We revisited specific examples from her audiotapes, and utilized transcript excerpts from her process logs to inform our discussion. I modeled how I might address concerns and Kathy rehearsed what she would say in her own words. The subsequent CIT–consultee conversation resulted in the dyad developing an intervention where Kathy would use a "stop sign" (i.e., raise her hand) to stop the teacher to paraphrase, clarify, or summarize what he was saying. She later expressed in a process log feeling that this was "respectful to him and comfortable for me" and that addressing their communication concerns "helped to improve and advance both the process and the content of the case consultation."

As has been suggested thus far, Kathy and Mr. Y had a difficult time clearly identifying, clarifying, and prioritizing a single problem to work on together, but they had begun to talk about Mr. Y's instructional practices. Kathy and the supervisor discussed the teacher's instruction within supervision sessions and created a shared hypothesis based on all of the available data. Data included several classroom observations by Kathy, which indicated that there might be a mismatch between instruction, the tasks the student was given, and the student's prior knowledge (Rosenfield, 1987). To further support this notion, the teacher expressed that he was differentiating instruction for this student, suggesting an academic concern was present, yet the teacher wanted to focus the problem solving on the student's off-task behavior. In supervision, Kathy and I discussed our lack of clarity on the form and function of Mr. Y's differentiated instruction. Moreover, Kathy stated "I got the sense that he's also sort of struggling with wanting to differentiate instruction for all of the students that need it and not knowing how."

After discussing the nature of the problem in supervision, and having addressed process communication concerns in an earlier supervision session, Kathy was able to communicate with the teacher about instruction in a manner that created a shared CIT–consultee frame of the problem—one that was not located within the student. In the end, instructional practices became the concern Kathy and Mr. Y worked on together. Kathy reported in supervision that she got the sense from Mr. Y that "our working together … helped him to have a different understanding of instruction in general and particularly, even just with this one child … to see that there were things that he could do." Kathy also reflected on how supervision worked to address both content and process concerns in her consultation case: "I've been feeling like [in the consultation case] … the process has been getting in the way of talking about content … It seems like what we've talked about [in supervision] is a way to rein both of them back."

Case Example 3: A "Fictional" Case?

The final case example demonstrates how a CIT can move from a contrived or forced relationship (i.e., a consultee that is "assigned" to work with the CIT) toward a collaborative relationship by using communication skills. Sheena was a specialist-level school psychology trainee working on her first consultation case while concurrently engaged in consultation coursework, a general (not consultation-specific) practicum experience, and ongoing university-based small group supervision. Sheena's site supervisor, a full-time school psychologist practitioner, assigned her to work with a seventh-grade teacher, Ms. Q, regarding an academic concern for a student in the domain of writing. Sheena felt that the consultation case was, to use her words, "fictional"—that Ms. Q had agreed to work with her as a favor to her site supervisor, but not because she actually needed consultative support, or because the student was having significant difficulty.

Whether Sheena's frame of the case was true or false, it shaded her perceived ability to assist the consultee. Despite her initial skepticism, Sheena practiced newly learned skills (e.g., using communication skills and instructional assessment) in her consultation case, and readily discussed concerns and successes in her written logs and during supervision. In her final reflection paper, Sheena wrote:

> I know that the teacher that I have been working with agreed to help me out as a favor to my supervisor and I am not really sure that she was ever truly fully invested in the process. Though she remained positive and always put forth effort and enthusiasm during our sessions, I do not think that the chosen concern felt all that pressing to her and I am not sure that she would have ever even addressed this concern were it not for my supervisor asking if she would mind helping me with this process ... Even with these complications, I feel the overall experience was extremely beneficial for me ... and ... I was able to see how effective this process could be in really helping a teacher learn about his/her own instruction.

Even though Ms. Q was perhaps more a passive volunteer rather than an active partner, over time Sheena realized she could offer something to Ms. Q through the consultation process. The process by which Sheena enhanced her collaborative relationship with Ms. Q, and subsequently worked together with Ms. Q to improve the student's writing skills, was supported through supervision from the beginning of the case.

In fact, prior to her initial consultation session with Ms. Q, Sheena participated in small group supervision with two other students from the consultation course, with me in the role of supervisor. Small group supervision provides several opportunities for CITs to learn from each other's experiences. During this supervision session, the other students described their experiences of contracting, and both expressed that they had a difficult time making contracting a collaborative dialogue with their consultees. We discussed how to make contracting collaborative by asking the consultee about her prior experiences, expectations, and understanding of the process. As illustrated by her first process log, Sheena applied these lessons in her contract session with Ms. Q: "I made a significant effort to make the session dialogue conversational rather than lecture-like" and "to make sure it was known that we were working on equal levels." Sheena also was genuine with the consultee, expressing she was a student learning a new process. On one hand, this may result in the CIT losing expert power in the eyes of the consultee (see, e.g., Erchul, Grissom, & Getty, 2008), but on the other hand lets the consultee know she will need to be an active collaborator in the consultation process.

Following contracting, Sheena continuously worked on sharpening her communication skills while consulting with Ms. Q. I provided written feedback on her process logs and verbal modeling during supervision sessions about how certain issues (e.g., scheduling difficulties) might be addressed during the case. All the while, Sheena improved her purposeful use of communication skills, in particular paraphrasing. For example, after Ms. Q explained that the student had difficulty in responding to literature in writing, Sheena recognized that "[paraphrasing] was enough for [Ms. Q] to have that moment of realization" of what the problem was, and where the dyad needed to intervene. Sheena later reflected: "I feel that we really had a few 'aha' moments and the teacher is beginning to appreciate this process more as a result." As the supervisor in this case, I perceived that such "aha moments" also helped Sheena to appreciate the consultation process and what she had to offer the teacher.

A common strategy in supervision, one that is quite applicable to use in final supervision sessions, is asking reflective questions that begin with stems such as "How do you feel about …?" or "What are your thoughts about …?" In supervision, Sheena and I discussed how she would apply consultation in her role as a school psychology intern next year and a practicing school psychologist in the future. Sheena expressed her increased valuing of consultation as a service delivery tool as the semester went on; this seemed to coincide with the consultee's increasing sense of the value of the process and of the CIT–consultee relationship.

Summary

CITs encounter a multitude of concerns as they begin to bridge newly learned conceptual knowledge with their first applied consultation case experiences. Such challenges act as triggers for CITs to think about their own skills, to consider the content and process issues of their cases, and to reflect in ways that lead to alternative, hopefully improved, methods of practice in the future. However, for novices, reflection without supervisory support may result in a misguided discovery process. In the absence of supervision, Alice and her consultee would have likely prematurely implemented an intervention before clearly defining a problem, while Kathy and her consultee might never have progressed past the problem identification stage of problem solving. Sheena may have dismissed the value of school-based consultation altogether since it was not utilized at her practicum site.

In contrast to misguided discovery, reflection augmented by various training and supervision techniques including audio/videotaping, composition of process logs, and strategic supervisor–CIT interactions inside supervision sessions, promotes CIT skill development. Given the complexity of consultation practice and the numerous concerns that arise for CITs, consultation training may be most effective when a multi-faceted supervision model is included as part of the training process.

Questions for Reflection

1. **What is the role of supervision of consultation at the pre-service level? Internship level? In-service level?**
2. **What supervision models or strategies might be adopted to enhance on-site supervisors' effective contribution to the CIT consultation learning experience?**
3. **How can consultation-training practices be incorporated or strengthened in your training program?**
4. **What concerns have you faced as a CIT? How were they addressed, if at all, through training or supervision?**

Appendix Strategic Interactions in Supervision: Reflections about the Past, Bridges in the Present, and Future Application

Reflections about the Past		
Strategy	*Definition*	*Example*
Use of Logs	Revisiting a CIT's previous consultation case session(s) by referencing a process log written by the CIT	S: One of the things you pointed out in your log was … [the teacher] mentioned grade retention? What was that all about?
Use of Tape	Revisiting a CIT's previous consultation case session(s) by referencing something seen or heard on a tape of that session	S: So the thing to talk about is really the integrity of the intervention … CIT: The teacher will be doing it … drilling him on [sight words] … so that was the part of the tape when I was like, "Just to make sure we all are on the same page …"
Bridges in the Present		
Strategy	*Definition*	*Example*
Challenging	Following up a CIT's statement or action with a question or statement intended to push the CIT to a deeper level of reflection	S: I want you to be comfortable but I also want you to be uncomfortable …
Comparisons	Using comparative reference points to point out similarities or differences including case to case, CIT to CIT, and session to session	S: It did seem like you were more at ease in the latter [consultation case] sessions … in terms of your flow of communication then … if you think back to September or October when you were first starting

Bridges in the Present		
Strategy	*Definition*	*Example*
Deferring	Supervisor accepting information provided by the CIT rather than immediately providing an opinion, answer, or feedback	S: You definitely have more experience working with [the consultee] … so you would know that [better than me]
"Less is More"	Discussing fewer CIT concerns in greater depth rather than briefly touching on multiple concerns	S: I gave you so much stuff now, that I don't want to give you more stuff … I don't want to overwhelm you.
Personal Experiences	Supervisor sharing his or her own experiences with the CIT	CIT: I will ask more specifically about the data … if it's broken down in those ways. S: It's worth considering. I could tell you this from my own experience now in a high school … if you broke down [the data] … there's one teacher who has probably given 30 referrals
Prioritizing	Determining what issues to discuss first during a supervision session	S: Do you have a particular spot where you would like to begin [or] things that you want to talk about to start off?
Supportive Comments	Offering a CIT genuine compliments tied to specific examples to let her know she is doing a good job	S: And so it was … kind of the struggle that was the hard piece, and you were … just talking about it as narrowing it down … I thought you were doing a really nice job with that. That was a really tough spot in the session
Research	Referring to specific course content or other research studies to provide relevant information	S: Have you ever read the NASP position statement on [student] retention?
"Thinking Out Loud"	A mutual discussion by the supervisory dyad when neither party may have a firm answer about an issue at hand	CIT: Clearly this teacher has academic concerns … there are academic issues. But the specifics about what those academic issues are, are never really discussed … S: And I think it could be okay to say it, depending on *how* you say it … I can give you some manner of saying it, but I'm just also thinking out loud with you so we can kind of play with this together …

(Continued)

Appendix *(Continued)*

Bridges in the Present		
Strategy	*Definition*	*Example*
Reflective Questions	Open-ended questions intended to stimulate thoughtful reflection	S: So let me turn it on you, what have you taken from the work that you've done?
Inquiry Questions	Questions intended to encourage CITs to answer their own questions instead of the supervisor providing the answer	S: It's … intervention evaluation. So you're evaluating what's going on, tweaking this. So, what do you think your main question for the teacher will be when you come to these sessions?
Future Application		
Lessons Learned	Discussing potent themes that recurred for the CIT during their consultation training experience	S: Would you have done anything differently if you could? CIT: I don't know. I don't know what I would have done. I mean, meet with her more frequently … but … she didn't want to meet more frequently because she felt overstressed …
Modeling	Supervisor demonstrating with words how the CIT might address an issue in a future consultation case session	S: Or … in the morning when you go in … just say, "I would love to come and … observe class for a little bit and get an idea what the classroom is like and see the student in the classroom environment"
Rehearsal	CIT practicing how to say something in a future consultation case session	S: How would you say it to the teacher? How would you be direct with her? CIT: "I think we will be able to make great progress with [the student] … if we have a consistent time to meet …"
Plan for Upcoming Case Session	Strategizing a plan of action for what the CIT will do in their next case session	S: Well now you have a couple [of ideas] … CIT: Definitely and I think I will set some goals for myself for the next session about stopping the [consultee's] long stories
Writing Notes	A CIT taking written notes during the supervision session	CIT: I want to continue to talk about this idea … so, I'm circling that on a piece of paper so we can go back to that

Note. S: Supervisor; CIT: Consultant in Training

References

Alpert, J.L., & Taufique, S.R. (Eds.). (2002). Consultation training: A field in need of review, revision, and research [Special issue]. *Journal of Educational and Psychological Consultation, 13*(1 & 2).

Anton-LaHart, J., & Rosenfield, S. (2004). A survey of preservice consultation training in school psychology programs. *Journal of Educational and Psychological Consultation, 15*, 41–62.

Aten, J.D., Strain, J.D., & Gillepsie, R.E. (2008). A transtheoretical model of clinical supervision. *Training and Education in Professional Psychology, 2*, 1–9.

Bernard, J.M., & Goodyear, R.K. (2009). *Fundamentals of clinical supervision*(4th ed.). Boston, MA: Pearson.

Conoley, J.C. (1981). Emergent training issues in consultation. In J.C. Conoley (Ed.). *Consultation in schools: Theory, research and procedures*(pp. 223–263). New York: Academic Press.

Cramer, K., & Rosenfield, S. (2003). Clinical supervision of consultation. *The Clinical Supervisor, 22*, 111–124.

Crespi, T.D., & Dube, J.M.B. (2005). Clinical supervision in school psychology: Challenges, considerations, and ethical and legal issues for clinical supervisors. *The Clinical Supervisor, 24*, 115–135.

Curtis, M.J., Grier, J.E., & Hunley, S.A. (2004). The changing face of school psychology: Trends in data and projections for the future. *School Psychology Review, 33*, 49–66.

Erchul, W.P., Grissom, P.F., & Getty, K.C. (2008). Studying interpersonal influence within school consultation: Social power base and relational communication perspectives. In W.P. Erchul and S.M. Sheridan (Eds.). *Handbook of research in school consultation* (pp. 293–322). New York: Routledge.

Gutkin, T.B., & Conoley, J.C. (1990). Reconceptualizing school psychology from a service delivery perspective: Implications for practice, training, and research. *Journal of School Psychology, 28*, 203–223.

Harvey, V.S., & Struzziero, J. (2008). *Professional development and supervision of school psychologists: From intern to expert* (2nd ed.). Bethesda, MD: Corwin Press and National Association of School Psychologists.

Hazel, C.E., Laviolette, G.T., & Lineman, J.M. (2010). Training professional psychologists in school-based consultation: What the syllabi suggest. *Training and Education in Professional Psychology, 4*, 235–243.

Kaufman, J. (2010). Contemporary issues in supervision. In J. Kaufman, T.L. Hughes, & C.A. Riccio (Eds.). *Handbook of education, training, and supervision of school psychologists in school and community* (Vol. II) (pp. 19–36). New York: Routledge.

Moffett, L.A. (2009). Directed self-reflection protocols in supervision. *Training and Education in Professional Psychology, 3*, 78–83.

National Association of School Psychologists. (2010). *Standards for the graduate preparation of school psychologists*. Bethesda, MD: Author.

Newman, D.S. (2009). A grounded theory of supervision in pre-service level consultation training (Doctoral dissertation). University of Maryland, College Park, MD.

Reschly, D.J. (2008). School psychology paradigm shift and beyond. In A. Thomas & J. Grimes (Eds.). *Best practices in school psychology V*(pp. 3–15). Bethesda, MD: National Association of School Psychologists.

Rosenfield, S. (1987). *Instructional consultation*. Hillsdale, NJ: Erlbaum.

Rosenfield, S. (2004). Consultation as a dialogue: The right words at the right time. In N.M. Lambert, I. Hylander, & J.H. Sandoval (Eds.). *Consultee-centered consultation* (pp. 337–346). Mahwah, NJ: Erlbaum.

Rosenfield, S., Levinsohn-Klyap, M., & Cramer, K. (2010). Educating consultants for practice in the schools. In E. Vasquez, T. Crespi, & C. Riccio (Eds.). *Handbook of education, training, and supervision of school psychologists in school and community: Vol. I* (pp. 259–278). New York: Routledge.

Stoltenberg, C.D. (2005). Enhancing professional competence through developmental approaches to supervision. *American Psychologist, 60*, 857–864.

Welsh, J.S., Meche, S., & Broussard, C. (2010). Competency-based school psychology practica: A collaborative training model. In J. Kaufman, T.L. Hughes, & C.A. Riccio (Eds.). *Handbook of education, training, and supervision of school psychologists in school and community: Vol. II* (pp. 37–54). New York: Routledge.

Witt, J.C. (1997). Talk is not cheap. *School Psychology Quarterly, 12*, 281–292.

Ysseldyke, J.E., Burns, M.K., Dawson, M., Kelly, B., Morrison, D., Ortiz, S., Rosenfield, S., & Telzrow, C. (2006). *School psychology: A blueprint for training and practice III*. Bethesda, MD: National Association of School Psychologists.

Ysseldyke, J., Burns, M.K., & Rosenfield, S. (2009). Blueprints on the future of training and practice in school psychology: What do they say about educational and psychological consultation? *Journal of Educational and Psychological Consultation, 19*,177–196.

Part II
Starting at the Beginning

Four kindergarten cases demonstrate the variations in working on even simple concerns such as learning the alphabet letters and sounds. However, when the concern is not complicated in content, novice consultants are able to focus on applying the processes they are learning. In these four chapters, different issues arise to complicate the experience for Emily Gustafson, Kathleen Gifford, Erica Sherry and Cyril Pickering, even when the grade level and concerns are similar. As you read the chapters, focus on the different school cultures, the issues in building working relationships even when the teacher and consultant are alike on many variables, the communication skills being used, and the problem-solving process.

3
The Importance of Collaborative Communication

Emily Gustafson

My first case as an instructional consultant (Rosenfield & Gravois, 1996) was working with Ms. Harris, a kindergarten teacher. The referral problem was academic in nature. Ms. Harris was concerned that a student in her kindergarten class, Marcus, was having difficulty learning letters, letter sounds, and numbers. She noted that Marcus spent two years at the school's preschool program and was worried that he was not further along in these skills.

This consultation case proved to be an excellent learning experience both for myself, the consultant, as well as for Ms. Harris, the consultee. While reading through the case report consider the following

Advance Organizer Questions:

- **How did my actions and styles of communicating affect Ms. Harris' attitude toward the case?**
- **How did Ms. Harris' conception of the problem change from the beginning to the end of the case?**
- **What principles of learning enabled the teacher to create a more effective instructional match?**

Culture of the School

The elementary school where I did this consultation case is a welcoming place, reflecting the warm and kind faculty members. The children in the hallway are orderly and well behaved. There is a behavior plan in place throughout the school, which is used consistently and successfully. This helps to make the school as a whole feel orderly, welcoming, and comfortable. For this reason, starting my first consultation case was relatively unintimidating.

While there is some stress and tension in sections of the building over test scores and resulting administrative pressure to improve them, this feeling was not pervasive, especially not in the kindergarten wing, where my experiences were always pleasant and stress-free. The students were well behaved and the general sense of order that pervades the school was certainly present in the kindergarten suite. I had already been welcomed into several meetings in the kindergarten cluster and so already felt comfortable with the teacher with whom I would be working. The staff worked collaboratively and helped each other plan or work out student concerns regularly. The kindergarten team interactions seemed to stem from a general sense of cooperation and commitment to enhancing teaching and student learning.

This struck me as particularly true in my interactions with Ms. Harris. Her concern for her students seemed to stem from a personal concern with the students' learning instead of pressure from above. She was genuinely concerned with her kindergarteners' academic performance. Ms. Harris was welcoming to me as a consultant and, while always slightly pressed by time constraints, was generally open to working with me. At the end of the case she made sure I knew I was always welcome in her classroom at any time. The friendly atmosphere of the school was certainly present in this classroom.

Relationships

Ms. Harris was demographically similar to myself, a Caucasian female in her mid- to late twenties. I found it easy to establish an amicable relationship with Ms. Harris from the beginning of the consultation process. That being said, I did sense reluctance in Ms. Harris to engage in the process at the very start, and building a working relationship took time. Thus, while our relationship was congenial from the first meeting, Ms. Harris' level of commitment to the process increased over the course of the consultation process. In this section, I will describe my perceptions of how this occurred and the skills that I learned in the process.

Early Stage of the Relationship

The referral process itself likely contributed to Ms. Harris' initial caution about the consultation process. Ms. Harris was new to both the school and to consultation. She was prompted, and I believe somewhat pressured, by the school psychologist, who headed the Instructional Consultation Team (IC Team), to refer Marcus after the student had been brought up in team problem-solving meetings several times. Ms. Harris knew little about the process and did not immediately submit a formal referral to the IC Team even after a verbal agreement to do so with the school psychologist. As a result, I was asked by the school psychologist to fill out the referral form with Ms. Harris, which we did. Thus, starting the process was somewhat externally driven, but she was concerned for her student, wanted to find solutions for him, and was, therefore, willing to try.

Her lack of early commitment was demonstrated in another way. She had to cancel our first meeting, but we were able to reschedule it for later that week. The first two meetings after that she forgot the meeting, but once I located her in the school, we were able to meet anyway. During the second meeting she clearly wanted the meeting to be as short as possible. While she was very nice to me and we seemed to work well together, I was aware that she was not completely committed to the process.

Using Communication Skills Effectively

While she had always been kind and welcoming, the relationship started as more of an expert than a collaborative one, because I made the decision to do much of the initial data collection on my own. While these data could have been presented in a way that invited her to share in the analysis, I did not initially do this, as I was inexperienced in collaborative communication techniques. This resulted in me telling her what *I* had found as well as what *I* thought it meant. Although I felt that my collecting the data was unavoidable due to her schedule and her initial reluctance, I came to understand that had I been more collaborative in at least developing a shared interpretation of the results, we could have moved into a stronger collaborative relationship more quickly. As my use of communication skills improved through supervision, we were able to create a more collaborative relationship and Ms. Harris slowly became more invested in the project. We began to do data collection together and eventually Ms. Harris took on this responsibility by herself and would share the results with me instead of vice versa. By the time we were doing the last data collection before intervention implementation, she was making comments such as "This is fun!"

I think that her being more involved in the process was a turning point for her engagement. Because data collection at the beginning of the process was not collaborative, I ended up shouldering more of the responsibility for the process than was ideal at the start of the case. Making sure she was involved in the data collection and in our further problem identification was very important in making our relationship a more collaborative one. By about the fourth or fifth week, she was engaged and excited about the process and had already started planning on implementing some of the strategies with some of the other struggling students in her class. I have now clearly seen the importance of working "shoulder to shoulder." Even seemingly small things can greatly alter or limit your relationship with a teacher. Seeing the process in action and that we were actually making progress seemed to inspire her as well.

Communication Skills

While I think that my communication skills and collaboration strategies are certainly still in need of improvement, they improved greatly through the course of this first consultation case. With each session I become a little more comfortable with the process. Taping each of my sessions and reflecting on how my communication skills affected my work with Ms. Harris was essential to becoming more aware of my skills, and therefore being able to improve them. From the beginning, I was fairly successful at explaining new concepts such as the IC process or the limits of working memory to Ms. Harris. I found that using summaries, paraphrases, providing information, and asking for her feedback/feelings quickly became more natural to me and proved successful tools in our conversations.

However, I found using communication skills that required me to solicit responses from Ms. Harris in appropriate open-ended ways to be more difficult and required more conscious effort. In the beginning I more often asked close-ended questions or stated what I thought would be an appropriate direction for our conversation, and then asked if she agreed. In retrospect, this is unsurprising since, in my experience, it is often easier to talk and promote your own agenda than to really hear and understand someone else. I found it particularly difficult to open up the conversation since I was trying to shape the direction of the dialogue in order to stay true to the IC process and to maintain the focus on changeable academic concerns.

I think the first step in my development and improvement of communication skills was in being more analytical of my own skills when reviewing session tapes. One cannot improve skills until one knows what to improve. As I listened to myself more closely and discussed my cases with my supervisor, my areas of strength and my areas of needed improvement started to become clearer. I was also beginning to see more clearly how the words you use (e.g., I versus we) and how you present information (e.g., asking a relevant question versus a request for clarification) (Rosenfield, 2004) shapes the kind of relationship you form. Using the appropriate communication style in each of those cases helped me facilitate a collaborative relationship that addressed my consultee's needs and concerns.

One of the skills I worked very consciously on was my response to my consultee when she was taking initiative in a way that reflected the principles of learning we had been using during our case. Initially, I responded to her with simple remarks such as "great!" As my supervisor and I talked about "giving away psychology" and the importance of reinforcing specific skills she was using, I started responding to her more specifically. Here is an example from one of my latter sessions that I feel reflects some of my efforts to improve:

> Consultant: And how many words are you planning on teaching them at a time? These are sight words?
>
> Ms. Harris: There are 10 here. So I'll figure out how many he knows and then do that plus 1.
>
> Consultant: Okay great. So, just to sort of keep the ratio and his working memory limit?

While I am becoming better about using my skills consciously and am certainly improving in some areas, I clearly still have room for improvement. However, as I have found with improvements of other skills, being able to identify the problem areas is half the battle. My skills have progressed to the point where the process is more natural, so I am better able to concentrate on my skills. At the same time, many of the skills are also becoming more natural to me and so do not require as much conscious thought. For example, I now more naturally frame concerns in terms of "we" or "our" instead of "you" or "I."

I believe the overall success of my case speaks to my growth in communication skills. Our relationship went from having an expert feeling in which I was dispensing wisdom to a truly collaborative relationship, in which we both shared in identifying problems and solving them. As the case progressed, Ms. Harris became comfortable with both the process and the principles of learning we discussed each meeting. By the end, she was confidently planning new interventions for her students (more than just our initial student), using the evidence-based principles we had discussed.

Problem-Solving Stages

I will now more systematically explain the progression this case took through the IC process. The IC process involves six stages, the first of which is Contracting in which the process is explained and the consultant and consultee agree to enter a voluntary problem-solving relationship. The next stage is Problem Identification during which the consultant and consultee work together to identify the primary and secondary concerns. During this phase, data are collected on the concerns presented in order to help clarify the concerns as well as to potentially serve as baseline data. Additionally, the consultant and consultee determine if the child is being taught at an appropriate instructional level: one that is challenging enough to facilitate learning, but that is not too difficult for the student's current level of functioning. The child's prior knowledge is considered as central, leaving the task and the instruction as adjustable to help create an appropriate instructional level. Once the problem has been identified and mismatches in instructional level have been evaluated, the consultant and consultee move on to intervention planning and implementation, during which they identify and implement an intervention that both fits the student's needs as well as is feasible in the consultee's classroom. Ongoing data collection to track the outcome of the intervention is of primary importance during this stage. This data collection allows for continual evaluation of the intervention. If the intervention is successful then either the case will be closed or another concern that has not yet been addressed will become the primary concern and the problem-solving process will start over again. The particulars of each stage for this case follow.

Contracting

After the referral is made, the first stage is contracting. While the school has a formal IC referral process that the teachers are expected to initiate on their own, I was asked to reach out to Ms. Harris to initiate the process. Once we had filled out the formal referral paperwork, we set up our first meeting to work together. During our initial session I explained the IC process to Ms. Harris.

Since she knew very little about the process, I delineated each stage for her in detail and explained the concept of an instructional match. She had limited time so we did not have a chance to start problem ID, but we did successfully contract. She seemed comfortable with the process and agreed to work with me without hesitation.

Problem Identification

At the next meeting we started the problem ID process. We started with the student's background. Marcus is an African American student. He attended pre-K at the school the previous year and had started with limited academic skills. Most students in Ms. Harris' class entered kindergarten with a fairly good handle on letters and numbers, having been taught these basic skills at home. Marcus, however, had no such head start at home. While there may have been some exposure to the alphabet or numbers in pre-K, there was no systematic or formal teaching mechanism in place. However, Ms. Harris' initial presentation of Marcus was of a student who could not learn.

Ms. Harris came up with three concerns initially. These concerns were: retention of letters, retention of letter sounds, and retention of numbers. As we talked about each of the concerns and fleshed them out a little more, each one got more specific. By retention of letters, she essentially meant the student could not consistently remember many of the names of letters he had been taught. We broke down letters into upper-case and lower-case letters, since we decided it would be easier to tackle them one at a time, given that many of the upper- and lower-case letters look quite different.

As we talked more about letter sounds, Ms. Harris told me how the students are taught the sounds. Knowing the current instructional design is an important component of the problem identification process with an academic concern. Teachers in this school use the Open Court (SRA/McGraw-Hill, 2002) model, in which letters come with a visual cue. For example, the letter L goes with a lion. When they learn letter sounds they learn them in conjunction with the visual cue as well as a physical cue (in the case of the L, they claw the air like a lion). She said that she thought the most important thing would be for Marcus to know the letter sounds in conjunction with the cue card.

Her final concern was with the student's retention of numbers. Like the letters, she felt that Marcus was inconsistent in remembering the numbers. The teacher felt that being able to count would be sufficient for his current level. She was less concerned with him being able to identify numbers by sight, but wanted him to be able to consistently count from 1 to 10, or higher, as they learned more numbers.

We then prioritized, which meant deciding the concern we wanted to concentrate on first. Knowing the letter sounds was her biggest concern for Marcus, so Ms. Harris wanted to begin there. We decided that the next step would be to do an instructional assessment (IA; Gravois & Gickling, 2008) of

Marcus' letter sound knowledge. Ms. Harris was unable to do a joint evaluation that day, but agreed to do some additional data collection later that week if needed. We decided to use the Open Court cards to do the assessment, since her primary desire was that Marcus know the letter sounds with the aid of the prompt cards. Doing all of the cards with cues would not have been fruitful, since they had not yet been taught what the prompts were and the student could not have picked this up elsewhere. We agreed to focus on the letters that had already been taught by the teacher.

That afternoon I was able to do two trials with Marcus using the Open Court cards. When shown the cards, the child knew all of the letter sounds that the teacher had taught the class. If he were just shown the letter without the cue card, he would only occasionally know the correct letter sound. During the second trial I also asked him what each letter was called. He only knew the letter T and the letter A. For the most part, the student seemed to be associating letter sounds with pictures, and not with the actual letters. He could not associate the letter sound with the letter because he did not know what the letter was. When learning his letter sounds, he always was shown both the letter and the visual cues, which he seemed to have focused on more than the actual letters.

The next week I met Ms. Harris again and told her what I had seen during the assessment. I shared that he already knew all of the letter sounds that he had been taught using the cue cards. I also expressed my concern that he was associating the letter sounds with a picture more often than a letter, as that was the way he had been taught in the class. Ms. Harris picked up on this problem right away. I asked if we might be better served by concentrating first on letter names since this was a clear weakness and Marcus was already on target with the letter sounds. Ms. Harris agreed that this would be a good course of action.

We decided to do an assessment of his letter knowledge. We decided to concentrate on lower-case letters first. Ms. Harris felt they were more important since they are more commonly used. We decided to gather three data points, each containing three assessments, based on Gickling's model of IA (Gravois & Gickling, 2008). Setting letters as "knowns" only after he had identified them three times over the course of a couple of days was particularly important, since one of the main concerns we identified was retention of the material. Ms. Harris had noted that some days the child knew his letters and other days he seemed to have forgotten them.

Ms. Harris readily agreed to do the bulk of the data collection over the next week, since I would not be there to assist. This way we could look at it at our next meeting and she would be more involved in the process. We decided that it would be possible to do the first two assessments of the first data point that afternoon. I would do the initial one since I was available and she had to teach. She thought she would be able to use her classroom assistant for a short time later on that afternoon, however, and that we could collect a data point together. When I came for the second time, however, she was unable to find coverage and could not leave her class. I took the last data point on my own but was able to thoroughly go over the process of data collection with Ms. Harris. I gave her a set of cards to use and asked her to record the date and the knowns after she had completed each data point (after three assessments). This way we would know how many letters he knew and which ones were knowns and unknowns.

We found that Marcus consistently knew the letters x, t, o, w, p, i, and a. Five of these seven letters (t, o, p, i, a) had been taught in class. At the time of assessment, six additional letters had been taught in the class. He therefore knew 27% (seven of 26) of the alphabet and 45% (five of 11) of the letters he had been taught in the class so far that year, indicating that he was able to learn what was being taught. We also determined that he is not at an instructional match, since the classroom curriculum was moving too fast for him. We decided that his lower-case letters would be our primary concern.

We set a goal for Marcus to learn one unknown letter and one emerging letter (sometimes known but not consistently) at a time since this is what his working memory would most likely allow, given his age. Hoping that he would be able to learn one new letter a week, we set a short-term goal of knowing 13 letters in six weeks. With hopes that his rate of learning would accelerate, as sometimes happens with new learners once the correct instructional match is made, we set a goal a long-term goal of learning all of the letters within 20 weeks.

Intervention Planning

I offered two suggestions that work well with both the principles of working memory and repetition, the concepts that we discussed in our session as guiding principles for our intervention design. The suggestions were the "drill sandwich" technique and pocket cards. Drill sandwich is a flashcard technique that folds in both knowns (in order to give the student confidence) and a small number of unknowns that matches the student's working memory capacity. Pocket cards is a simpler technique, in which the teacher carries around a few unknown flashcards in her pocket so she can randomly and commonly present them to the student (Gravois & Gickling, 2008). She agreed and we began talking about what letters to use. We initially decided to use six knowns and two unknowns. We did not hammer out any of the specifics of how the intervention would actually be implemented at this session.

At our next session we got more specific about what our intervention would look like. We decided how often to do both the drill sandwich technique and the pocket cards based on conducting between 35 and 55 repetitions of each letter Marcus was learning per week and what would realistically work for Ms. Harris in the context of her classroom. While I advised Ms. Harris about the structure of the activity and how often is optimal, when to do the interventions was largely directed by Ms. Harris. We decided that she would do the drill sandwich twice a day with five repetitions each. Repetitions are important in supporting the student in retention of new information. We decided to use six knowns (o, w, t, a, x, i), one emerging letter (l), and one unknown (g). We also decided to further reinforce the emerging and unknown letters by using them as pocket cards two or three times daily. Ms. Harris was nervous that she might be committing to too much with this part of the intervention, so we decided she would try it for the first week and see if it seemed feasible. We also decided that we would do one data point (three-trial method) per week (two on Friday and one on Monday morning). This way we could easily track his progress and present new unknowns when appropriate.

Implementation

We started the intervention that afternoon. I volunteered to assist on Monday afternoons. When I entered the classroom, Ms. Harris was in the process of making a second set of note cards. We had discussed implementing the intervention to a couple of her other struggling readers in our previous session after waiting until we saw how it went with our primary client. Ms. Harris, however, had decided that she felt comfortable with the intervention and wanted to start with one other student right away. I agreed to help with this new student and we discussed the importance of doing a three-point data collection to determine her known and unknown letters. I did the first data point with the student. The teacher would continue the assessment the next day and choose which cards to use based on this. She planned on using six knowns, one emerging, and one unknown, if possible.

Evaluation

Marcus was indeed learning even before the intervention began. Although Marcus' learning rate was uneven across the weeks, he averaged about two letters per week. At this rate, he made the long-term goal we set for him during the planning phases of the intervention in 20 weeks. He also made his short-term and intermediate goals along the way. A graph of Marcus' alphabet knowledge over the four months of intervention (Figure 3.1) shows steady progress over time.

Closure

We discussed if there was any need for continued assistance after the child had met his goal on our first objective. However, by the time Marcus had mastered his lower-case letters, the area we decided to focus on initially, he had also managed to learn the vast majority of his upper-case letters at this point and most of his letter sounds. These had both been initial concerns, but were no longer a problem. He was also making sufficient progress in his math skills. Given that these were all of the other areas we had identified as problem areas at the beginning of the case, there was no need to continue with the problem-solving process. Ms. Harris and I hypothesized that this was, in part, due to Ms. Harris incorporating many of the principals of learning we had

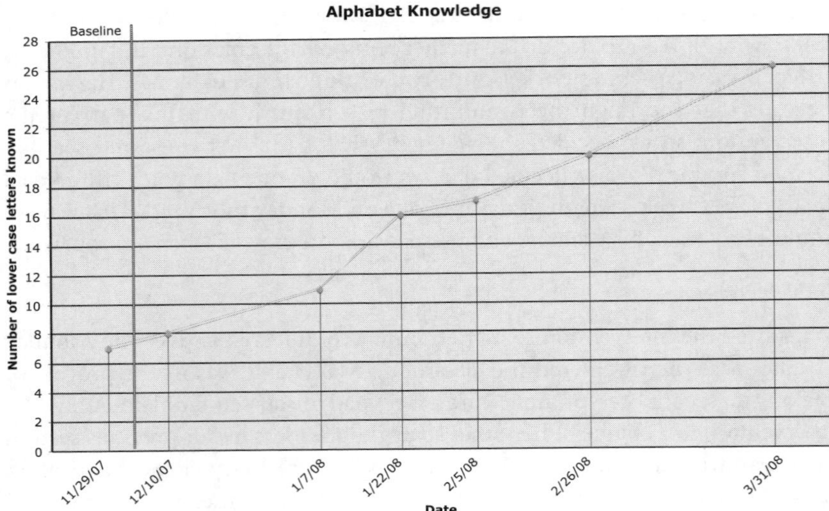

Figure 3.1 Changes in Alphabet Knowledge Over Time.

talked about in the context of learning lower-case letters into the other areas she was teaching.

When we started the case, Ms. Harris viewed Marcus as a student who could not learn. However, with systematic instruction that honored his working memory limits in the areas he was having difficulties, Marcus did, in fact, learn. The consultee's conception of Marcus shifted over the course of the consultation process from viewing him as a child who could not learn to a child who could learn when information was presented in small chunks, and with appropriate levels of repetition.

We closed the case but I left a standing invitation to work with her again if she found she needed assistance in the future. Likewise, Ms. Harris left a standing invitation for me to visit her classroom any time. The case closed on a positive, successful note.

Lessons Learned

My first case provided me with a very large learning curve. Understanding concepts theoretically and having to put them into actual practice are two very different things, particularly when you engage in the process as an active learner. For me, recording my sessions, listening to them afterwards, and reflecting on my skills and the general direction of my sessions proved an invaluable learning tool. I was able to track what skills I was using and where I needed improvement. I was also able to see how my interactions affected the course of the consultation process and the nature of my relationship with Ms. Harris.

A general skill that I developed during my first case is to be able to describe the IC process to another (in particular, a teacher) and be able to successfully guide a consultee through the process in a collaborative manner. Having a clearer understanding of the details that actually go into each step of the IC process has been a major breakthrough in this skill development for me. Reading about a process and actually experiencing it are two very different things and going through the process has brought my understanding to a much deeper level. While each case will present its unique challenges, I felt better equipped to do things such as guide the teacher to be able to describe specific and observable concerns, instead of the vague ill-defined descriptions of concerns, which are often presented in the beginning of a case. I now also have a better understanding of why doing that is very important. If the problem is not clearly defined, then the solution will be nearly impossible to find.

However, even in understanding the process, there are many facets that take a longer time to master—for many of these, I am in the beginning phases. One of these facets is communication skill. While I still have much room for improvement in this area, I have learned a tremendous amount just in the context of one case. I have a better understanding of the different communication skills and their intended use. I have a better understanding of the importance that wording can have in a conversation. While the differences in how you phrase something may be subtle, slight differences, such as using *we* versus *I*, seemed to have a large impact in moving Ms. Harris to a more collaborative relationship.

While I have not had practice yet in many forms of data collection, I am starting to have a better grasp of this part of the process as well. I now understand how to do snapshots of a child's skills using the three-part method to ensure consistency (Gravois & Gickling, 2008). I also understand the basics of an Instructional Assessment (IA). Even though I do not yet know how to collect data on every academic problem I might come across, I now have some general outlines of good practice and the confidence to do it myself.

In the context of just one case I have gained both experience and confidence. I have learned to assess my own communication skills and adjust my use of them as needed. I have learned the importance of working shoulder to shoulder in a truly collaborative relationship. In the process of learning this I have also become a much better listener and observer. Once I made the shift in our relationship from one of me as an expert to one of active collaboration, not only did the case become more successful for Marcus, but Ms. Harris was able to learn and grow as well.

The case closed with a successful student and both a teacher and a consultant with more confidence. By the end, our relationship was warm but professional and very productive. While I certainly have more skills to work on, the ones I have gained so far have served me well. With the confidence of one successful case and the ability to evaluate my own strengths and weakness I have no doubt that I can continue to grow during my next cases. While learning about the IC process and appropriate communication skills in class is useful, only doing a case yourself will help you become fluent in the language of consultation.

Questions for Reflection

1. **How would you use the communication principles described in this case in your own consultation situation?**
2. **Do you agree with the author about what facilitated the turning point in her relationship with the teacher consultee?**
3. **What were the main principals of learning that served as a guide for the overall direction of this case?**
4. **What could be done to potentially mitigate the lack of commitment shown by the teacher early in the process?**

References

Gravois, T., & Gickling, E. (2008). Best practices in Instructional Assessment. In A. Thomas & J. Grimes (Eds.). *Best practices in school psychology V* (pp. 503–518). Bethesda, MD: NASP.

Open Court Reading - Alphabet Sound Wall Cards (2002). Columbus, OH: SRA/McGraw-Hill.

Rosenfield, S. (2004). Consultation as dialogue: the right words at the right time. In N.M. Lambert, I. Highlander, & J.H. Sandoval (Eds.). *Consultee-centered consultation: Improving the quality of professional services in schools and community organizations* (pp. 339–347). Mahwah, NJ: Erlbaum.

Rosenfield, S., & Gravois, T. (1996). *Instructional consultation teams: Collaborating for change*. New York: Guilford.

4

What Do You Do When There Are Multiple Concerns? Using Problem Identification to Clarify and Prioritize a Teacher's Concerns

Kathleen Gifford

Advance Organizer Questions

- **How did problem identification play an important role in this case?**
- **How did the consultant narrow down the concern to observable and measurable terms?**
- **How does working with more than one concern change the process?**
- **How did the school culture influence the problem-solving process and the working relationship between the consultant and consultee?**

The current trend in educational reform calls for increased collaboration in schools as a means to restructure schools (e.g., West & Idol, 2001). Instructional Consultation (IC; Rosenfield, 1987) provides a structure for collaboration among school professionals. I served as the instructional consultant for a kindergarten case. My consultee, Ms. Smith, was a young, female, Caucasian kindergarten teacher referring to the problem-solving team for the first time. We shared relative age, gender, and race. The client for this consultation case was Carla, a six-year-old Hispanic female student in Ms. Smith's kindergarten class. This was my first consultation case as a graduate student CIT.

Working Relationship

In consultee-centered consultation (CCC), the working relationship between the consultant and the consultee is paramount to successful collaboration. According to Rosenfield (1987), the collaborative relationship is a non-hierarchal relationship between two or more professionals working together to resolve a problem. However, establishing the collaborative relationship is not an easy goal to achieve for many CITs. Consultation is a collegial process in which both parties exercise influence. This case gave me a long opportunity to develop a working relationship with Ms. Smith, as we had a total of 21 sessions together. The length of the relationship was a luxury that most CITs would not have, but provided an extended opportunity for our relationship to evolve.

Our working relationship was challenging to establish at the beginning for many reasons. It was the first time Ms. Smith had referred a case to the problem-solving team and I don't think she knew what to expect. According to Rosenfield (1987), many subjects who ask for help believe that the helper will perceive them as generally incompetent. While I don't think that I gave the impression that I thought Ms. Smith was incompetent, she was very defensive of her instruction at the beginning of our work. For example, during one of my classroom observations I noticed that Ms. Smith placed a work sample backwards on the board, text covered, so that the students could not see the example. When I tried to inquire if that might have hindered Carla's work, Ms. Smith deflected the blame back on Carla and said that she probably couldn't see the example because she had failed her vision screening. It took time to gain Ms. Smith's trust and have her believe that I was not trying to criticize her teaching, but instead trying to help her to make an instructional match for Carla.

Rosenfield (1987) also explains that teachers with high investment in their professional competence may be reluctant to view their own classroom behavior as the source of the child's difficulty. This was certainly true in this consultation case because Ms. Smith was highly invested in her competence as a teacher. She was taking graduate-level courses to improve her understanding of the education system, and also looking forward to becoming the kindergarten team leader for the following year. It took some time for us to develop a working relationship in which she felt comfortable letting her guard down and understood that it really was a non-evaluative process. Once she felt comfortable in working with me in this capacity she was much more open to discussing instruction and Carla's learning environment.

Consultants who are learning the problem-solving process feel anxious about what might be required of them both personally and professionally (Rosenfield, 1987). I entered into the relationship anxious about not knowing everything about the kindergarten curriculum and school jargon when I started this consultation case. I wanted Ms. Smith to feel that I was competent enough to work with her, and I also wanted to seem knowledgeable about the problem-solving process.

I believe Ms. Smith came to appreciate the process. She consistently attended our consultation sessions each week over this long time period. She worked hard to make sure that we had time to meet and even gave up planning time to collaborate. In addition, Ms. Smith referred to the problem-solving team a second time before our work was finished. This made me feel that she appreciated our problem solving and valued the work that could be done through consultation. She was much clearer about her concerns at the second referral meeting, and also brought data to demonstrate why she had concerns regarding that particular student. Overall, I believe that our working relationship developed and became much more collaborative by the time we closed the case.

School Culture

Several school culture variables impacted progress in this case, including the focus on the individual child, diversity, and perhaps more pervasively, the quality of collaboration among the staff.

Focus on the Individual Child

Sarason (1996) identifies the tendency to look at the individual child without taking his/her environment into consideration. Historically, training in child development has focused on the individual child and individual differences. I think that this was both a school culture and teacher belief variable for this case. Ms. Smith, the consultee, was in a graduate training program that had a strong focus on developmental education and individual pathology. At times it felt like she was looking for examples of what she was learning in her students. For example, early on in our sessions, Ms. Smith described being highly concerned that Carla sat a particular way because she thought that it was "developmentally appropriate" for a three-year-old and not a six-year-old. This also seemed to be a school culture variable because the special education co-teacher was highly focused on the individual child and viewed her struggles as personal variables, without considering Carla in context.

Sarason (1996) emphasizes an ecological approach to examining school culture for several reasons, noting that it has historically been neglected. First, an ecological perspective takes into account the regularities that are often taken for granted in school settings. School regularities became an important part of this case consultation because the school staff had access to many resources and specialized services. After working with Ms. Smith, it became clearer that the school regularity was to use the problem-solving team to identify a problem, but then a school specialist was often designated to implement the intervention. In this case we spent time narrowing our problem down to handwriting and, once we figured that out, Ms. Smith automatically assumed that she would receive assistance from the occupational therapist, who was the specialist called in for handwriting issues.

Diversity Issues

The next aspect of school culture that I believe could have influenced this case is that the school is very racially homogeneous. Carla was one of the few minority students in a school of primarily Caucasian students, and she was the only Hispanic student in her classroom. I don't think that Ms. Smith purposely discriminated against her because of her background, but she insisted on referring Carla for evaluation for special education although she was not functioning below grade level. I noticed that the majority of the students in this classroom performed above grade level. Carla performed very well on grade level, but appeared behind since she was not above grade level like her other classmates. She could read at the kindergarten level and knew all of her letters upon entering kindergarten, but Ms. Smith still felt that Carla was performing below her expectations for a kindergartener.

Carla was one of the few Hispanic students in the school, spoke English as her primary language, and she came from a typical, if not higher, socioeconomic background compared to the other students in her class. Ms. Smith also knew that one of Carla's sisters had been diagnosed with a disability. Ms. Smith's depth of knowledge about Carla's background often caused her to focus on those issues rather than Carla's classroom performance during our initial problem-solving sessions.

Collaborative Culture Issues

One of the most essential elements in promoting positive working relationships in a school culture is improving staff communication and collaboration. One of the advantages of understanding school culture is that I began to see below the surface. My understanding of the school culture changed as I worked in the school longer. During the first semester I felt that the school had a very collaborative system, with staff appearing to work together in a collegial manner. Collaborative school cultures create interdependence and encourage joint work to improve student academic achievement.

As I worked in the school longer, it felt less like interactive professionalism (Fullan & Hargreaves, 1996), as it became apparent to me that teachers and specialists did not communicate with each other about the work they did with their students. For example, this school had a team in place for collaboration. However, mostly problem identification was conducted through the team and then school specialists, instead of the classroom teacher, conducted interventions. They used a "pull-out" system where the specialists pull the children out for a few hours to work with them and then drop them back off in their classroom. The students not only miss instruction in their classroom, but the teachers are unsure of what the students are working on while they are gone. Essentially, after the students were sent to the specialists, teachers and school specialists rarely came together to problem solve collaboratively, and therefore teachers were often uninformed about interventions being done with students in their class. This became evident when I discussed a "pull-out" handwriting group with Ms. Smith. She knew that the special education teacher and occupational therapist pull the children into a group to work on handwriting, but she had no idea what they did while they were in the group. I came to believe that better communication would have allowed her to understand the intervention and incorporate some of those concepts into her own general education classroom.

Communication

According to Rosenfield (2004), words play a critical role in consultee-centered consultation. Through the words that are spoken the consultant and consultee create a joint conceptualization of the concern. It is critical that the consultant comes to understand his/her communication skills and how communication can be used to solve problems effectively and efficiently.

In school psychology graduate programs, students often receive feedback on their own interpersonal style. I entered the consultation course having received feedback that I can often be perceived as quiet. While I don't think of myself as a quiet person, I am soft-spoken and often have trouble being assertive when I need to be. I have trouble interrupting people when they are speaking and often wait some time to be heard during a conversation. Through my CIT supervision, I was able to discuss my communication skills and role-played having more of a presence and voice in my sessions. This experience gave me the opportunity to work on my communication skills with a supervisor who was able to give me constructive feedback and allowed me to reflect on ways to become active, and at the same time remain true to myself.

In my initial consultation sessions with Ms. Smith, I used a considerable amount of clarification and paraphrasing to understand her concerns. She described concerns using teacher jargon, and it would take me several attempts to clarify what she actually meant. For example, Ms. Smith would describe Carla as "developmentally low" and "distractible" when we first started our problem-solving sessions. Eventually she would expand on her comments and say that Carla sat a particular way on the floor, similar to how she believed a younger child would sit, and would look at others at her table and as a result was not able to complete her assignments.

As we worked together I felt more comfortable clarifying Ms. Smith's jargon and making sure I understood her comments before I moved on in our conversation. Ms. Smith could talk about her concerns at length, and so I had to learn, through supervision and personal reflection, to feel comfortable interrupting her so that I could paraphrase some of her ideas. As we continued to problem solve I became more comfortable paraphrasing and stopping Ms. Smith when she shared several ideas all at once.

Listening to session tapes also allowed me to reflect on how much I was speaking during our sessions. When comparing how long Ms. Smith would speak with my responses, I began to see the importance of taking a more active role in the problem-solving process. Initially I was trying to use active listening to understand Ms. Smith's concerns, but I quickly learned that I needed to become more assertive in order to move the problem-solving process forward. This initial consultation case gave me much more confidence in being an active participant in future consultation cases.

Problem-Solving Stages

The problem-solving process begins with contracting. In this meeting, the consultant clearly describes the process and gains informed consent. Next, the consultant facilitates problem identification and analysis, intervention design, intervention implementation, intervention evaluation, and case closure. Over the course of my work with Ms. Smith, it became clear that she had multiple concerns about Carla. Our work together allowed us to identify and problem solve around three unique concerns.

Contracting

Ms. Smith and I met for contracting in November. Since this was also Ms. Smith's first consultation case as a consultee, she began describing her concerns during this first session. I worked on trying to describe the process before I let us move onto the problem identification stage. I clarified that we would be working together to identify concerns and plan for interventions when Ms. Smith initially expected me to give her feedback about Carla.

Problem Identification

We worked on problem identification for three sessions until the semester break. Ms. Smith initially referred Carla because, in her words, Carla was "showing a variety of behaviors and learning styles that are impacting her ability to move forward in a typically developing way." Ms. Smith often used this type of high inferential language during the beginning of our work together. Over time, I learned that Ms. Smith believed that Carla had difficulty retaining and following instructed activities; difficulty generalizing information; and difficulty following the classroom routine. One of Ms. Smith's main concerns was that Carla became distracted by things in her environment.

During the first semester we conducted an informal observation to understand the antecedents, behaviors, and consequences of when Carla was off-task/distracted during reading. We also planned to conduct an instructional assessment in reading after the holiday break. One purpose of the assessment was to determine if Carla was at instructional match conditions during reading instruction. The instructional assessment demonstrated that Carla was reading at her instructional match, but even in that one-on-one situation, she was distracted by events in her environment (e.g., noises in the hallway).

Since Ms. Smith initially used high inference explanations, such as distractible and developmentally low, I thought it would be helpful to conduct some observations during reading and math to look at the instruction Carla received during both subjects. I also thought the observations would give us some clarity on the antecedents and consequences of her off-task behaviors. Ms. Smith agreed to the observation because she felt that Carla needed a lot of support to move through activities and she wanted to know what was causing her to lose focus.

I conducted five observations over the course of three weeks. The observations took place during three reading lessons and two math lessons. We picked these subjects to observe because Carla was having more trouble during those specific times. I observed for the first 30 seconds of each minute during both subjects. In addition, I recorded the on/off-task behaviors of a "typical" peer every five minutes during the observation. Ms. Smith selected the peer because she felt that he represented a typical student in her class. The observations were representative of Carla during group work and independent activities. She averaged 65% time-on-task, where her peer averaged 92% time-on-task. The observations also demonstrated that Carla looked at her peers frequently during activities, she needed frequent reminders to complete activities, and she finished many assignments late, which caused her to have less time for other assignments.

When Ms. Smith and I began to discuss the observations, it became clearer that she did not have the expectation that Carla remain on-task 100% of the time, but that she complete her work. She expressed that most kindergarteners are not always on-task, but that the rest of the class were still able to complete their assignments, and Carla was struggling to finish her work. Ms. Smith was appreciative of the data that we collected during our observations, because she had not been able to quantify Carla's on- and off-task behaviors up until that point. It gave her more explicit information to discuss with Carla's parents during parent–teacher conferences as well.

Our discussions about the observations allowed us to modify our concern from off-task behaviors to work completion. Ms. Smith was more concerned with Carla completing her work than she was with her looking at peers and noises. In order to assess work completion, Ms. Smith decided that we should look at her weekly letter journal. The letter journal has a page dedicated to each letter of the alphabet. The students are expected to copy the capital letter, copy the lower case letter, copy a sentence that uses the letter several times, and then color a picture. We looked at the letters "J," "W," "V," and "E" because these pages were completed without assistance or intervention. This was important because Ms. Smith used a lot of different interventions with Carla without monitoring their effectiveness. For example, she would have Carla trace letters that she wrote with yellow highlighter and/or use configuration boxes to guide her letter formation, but was never quite sure if the interventions worked, because she would use several of them at the same time with the same task.

Through my CIT supervision, I was able to understand that I needed to conduct a task analysis with Ms. Smith to assess the steps involved in completing a letter journal page. This helped Ms. Smith and me to determine how many steps were needed to complete the work, and made her expectations clearer. We were able to break the task into six parts including copying her capital letters correctly, copying her lower-case letters correctly, leaving finger spaces between each word, copying the sentence, copying the words in the sentence correctly, and coloring the picture using six colors. I think the task analysis helped Ms. Smith to understand that there were more steps involved than she had originally thought when assigning the task. Carla averaged 33% of the steps complete for her baseline performance. Ms. Smith thought that Carla was capable of doing the work, but needed reminders to move on to each new step.

According to Hylander (2004), a turning occurs when the consultee begins to frame the problem she brought to consultation in another way. It was around this point in the problem-solving process that it seemed that Ms. Smith had a turning. The turning usually occurs because the consultee changes her way of understanding the student. I began to notice that Ms. Smith talked more about what Carla could do and less about what she couldn't do. It was nice to hear her put her concerns in perspective and realize that most kindergarteners are off-task some of the time, but that she really wanted Carla to be able to complete her work. If Carla mastered the skills to be able to complete her work, Ms. Smith would not mind if she occasionally looked at other students during the day.

Intervention Planning

With this in mind, I thought that Carla might benefit from having some prompts to move on to each new step of a task, given that she required many reminders to complete the letter journal. It seemed that this would give Carla more confidence to complete her work independently, and would allow Ms. Smith to work with other students without being interrupted. Ms. Smith and I discussed the idea of using prompts, and she shared that picture prompts would likely help Carla to work more independently. Ms. Smith had general picture prompts that she kept on the blackboard at the front of the classroom.

However, we found out that Carla was near-sighted and could not see objects that were far away. We tried to keep this information in mind when problem solving because Carla's parents did not purchase glasses for her even though it was difficult for her to see distance. The school nurse conducts a routine hearing and vision screening at the beginning of the school year, and recommends additional screening outside of school if students do not perform as expected. When this was recommended to Carla's parents, they did not follow the recommendation even with ongoing encouragement from the school nurse. Therefore, Ms. Smith and I attempted to make sure that all of Carla's materials were presented to her at a distance close enough that she could read them.

Ms. Smith really owned the picture prompt intervention, and volunteered to create individual picture prompts to help Carla move through the steps of the activity. She created a folder for Carla to take with her to her different independent activities. The folder included many picture prompts with Velcro strips that Carla could use to create a list of prompts to help her to move through an activity.

Intervention Implementation

Ms. Smith began using this intervention immediately and noticed that Carla could complete all of her work independently using these prompts. The teacher also shared that Carla enjoyed the intervention and became excited to bring her folder with her to the different activities. After one week of using the folder, Carla was able to choose her own prompts and follow them to complete an activity.

Problem Identification for Second and Third Concerns

Ms. Smith and I were excited that Carla was able to complete her work, but I began to hear that Ms. Smith was now focused on the quality of Carla's work and not just work completion. As a result, I decided that it was important to discuss Carla's work quality in more detail, a second concern. I asked Ms. Smith to bring samples of other students' letter journals that met her expectations to our meeting so that we could discuss how they were different from Carla's work. It became very clear that Ms. Smith's expectations were that the students would use the lined paper as a guide to write their letters, so that the letters touched the top and bottom lines. Carla's letters were legible but she did not use the lines as a guide when writing. For example, she would write the letter 'A' so that it sat on the middle dotted line of the page, but the letter was much smaller in size than what was expected. Ms. Smith and I decided together that I would collect writing samples of Carla's alphabet so that we could measure her baseline performance for correct letter formation.

During the same meeting that we discussed letter formation and expectations, Ms. Smith shared a third concern, that Carla had been struggling to understand the word "different" on a benchmark assessment. Ms. Smith had tried to describe the word "different" several ways but Carla did not seem to understand the meaning of that particular word. I took this conversation as an opportunity to suggest that we might want to give Carla the *Boehm Test of Basic Concepts* (Boehm, 2000) to assess her understanding of academic vocabulary. It would be difficult for Carla to complete her work accurately if she did not have a solid understanding of academic vocabulary that is used when giving directions. Ms. Smith agreed that it would be helpful to understand which basic words Carla did and did not know. We planned for me to assess Carla's handwriting and give her the Boehm the following week.

Carla knew 60% of the Boehm vocabulary, which placed her in the 38th percentile for kindergarten students. The Boehm describes the student's performance range on a scale from 1 to 3, with 1 being the highest level of understanding and 3 being the lowest level of understanding. Carla performed within level 2, which means that she knew most of her basic concepts to perform at grade level, but that she lacked understanding of some key concepts. Carla only made it into this level by one word, which meant that she was closer to the lowest level of understanding and she probably needed some teacher/

parent help in learning these critical concepts. Ms. Smith and I went through the results of the Boehm one word at a time because I wanted her to have a clear understanding of how the assessment works, and how each word is conceptualized on the assessment. I thought that this allowed us to have a very collaborative session. As I explained Carla's answers, Ms. Smith marked down the words that the student knew and those she struggled with. Ms. Smith also completed the parent handout of the Boehm so that Carla's parents could know which words she needed more practice with and could help her at home. The form also gives the parents suggestions on how to fold in the new words into their daily activities.

Ms. Smith decided that she wanted to share the information about Carla's academic vocabulary with the special education co-teacher before we decided whether we would be planning an intervention. We also looked at Carla's handwriting sample, and Ms. Smith decided that Carla did not meet expectations for forming any of her letters on that sample. We planned to collect a second handwriting sample the following week and review it for our second baseline point for handwriting.

Intervention Planning for Additional Concerns

When Ms. Smith and I met the following week she shared that the occupational therapist (OT) would be pulling Carla into a morning handwriting group. Ms. Smith felt that the group would be really helpful in working with Carla and her handwriting struggles. I tried to get more information about what the OT would be doing as an intervention in the handwriting group, but I got the sense that Ms. Smith only had a vague idea that they would work on the mechanics of handwriting. If I were staying in the school longer, I would have liked to include the OT and special education teacher in one of our sessions, so that Ms. Smith could hear more about the handwriting group, and potentially incorporate the same instruction into her classroom. This would help to minimize the difference between morning group and class instruction on handwriting. This is important to do so that students get repetition of the same instructional concepts throughout their academic day.

Since Ms. Smith felt that the morning handwriting group was a sufficient intervention, I suggested that we create an intervention to work on Carla's academic vocabulary. I felt that it was really important to create an intervention with Ms. Smith that we could track to measure student progress. I wanted to make sure that we followed this step in the problem-solving process so that Ms. Smith did not think that we only did problem identification, and then assigned the intervention to a school specialist. I also wanted her to be able to see the data that showed that the intervention was successful.

Ms. Smith and I used the Boehm to see which words Carla struggled with and created a list of six words she wanted Carla to know by the end of the year. The six unknown words were: last, before, different, third, second, and starting.

We decided that Carla would concentrate on learning three unknown words at a time in order to not overload her working memory. Ms. Smith chose seven known words from the Boehm to fold into the unknowns. The known words were: top, above, first, most, between, below, and under. Our initial plan was to give Carla exposure to the new words by creating cards with pictures and the word, and using classroom materials to teach the concepts.

When we met again the following week Ms. Smith had decided to change the method of teaching Carla her unknown words, indicating that she had taken ownership of the intervention. Ms. Smith drew a picture that allowed her to teach and assess Carla's knowledge of the unknown vocabulary words. For example, she would draw a line of people and assess the word "last" by pointing to the person standing last in the line. Our baseline was that Carla knew none of six unknown words. Ms. Smith used the picture to show Carla the concepts and then asked Carla to demonstrate her understanding.

Intervention Implementation

The first week Carla knew three new words, and the second week she had learned four new words (only two words were the same words as the week before). During our last session I had to clarify that we should only introduce three of the six new words at a time so that we didn't overload Carla's working memory. I worked with Ms. Smith to understand that Carla would need to consistently understand the word at least three times before we considered the word known. Ms. Smith seemed receptive to this, and said that she would only work on three new words at a time until Carla knew those same three new words three times in a row. Ms. Smith planned on continuing to teach Carla the new words for the remainder of the school year with the hope that she mastered all six unknowns. She also planned to give the parents information about how to work with Carla on her unknown words over the summer.

Our last few sessions made me realize that I should have checked in with Ms. Smith more during the week to see how the intervention was going, an important element of the intervention implementation stage. It seemed that she wanted to work on the intervention, but had a lot of end-of-year activities that were taking up her time (e.g., individual benchmark assessments, school play, etc.). As a result, she was not providing the repetitions that we had planned together. I reflected on this before our last session, and I asked Ms. Smith if there might be another adult who could also work on the unknown words during the day. She thought that Carla's morning group leader might be able to go over the concepts with her as well. I didn't want her to feel that I was taking the intervention away from her because she enjoyed working with Carla. However, I wanted to try to find a way to provide Carla with more repetition of the unknown words during the school day.

The school psychologist, who was my site supervisor, and Ms. Smith, both had a copy of the Student Documentation Form (SDF; Rosenfield & Gravois,

1996) to continue monitoring progress. The school psychologist offered to check in with Ms. Smith for the remainder of the school year to see if she needed any additional supports. Ms. Smith planned to continue to collect data and monitor the vocabulary intervention for the rest of the school year.

Carla was referred to the IEP team toward the end of our problem solving because Ms. Smith still felt that she might qualify for services and she also seemed to feel some pressure from her co-teacher to refer the student. Although Carla had been referred, Ms. Smith made it very clear that she valued our problem solving and wanted to continue working together for the remainder of my time in the school. Carla was never formally assessed for special education, and the family moved the following year.

Lessons Learned

Reflection involves a deeper level of thinking that leads to new insights and improvements in practice (Fullan & Hargreaves, 1996). This case allowed me to reflect on my ability to introduce instructional consultation to a teacher who had never participated in it before. This proved to be challenging for my first case because I was still learning the process as well. I had the opportunity to work on being more assertive with a teacher who liked to talk and do things a certain way. It took me time to feel comfortable pointing out instructional mismatches, but it proved to be helpful in narrowing our concerns. Ms. Smith viewed problems as child centered, and this process allowed me to expose her to a more ecological approach to problem solving with some success. She did implement two interventions in her classroom, for example, and her language about Carla began to change. Ms. Smith did eventually refer Carla for special education services, reflecting her level of continued concern, in spite of Carla's progress on the implemented interventions.

Looking back I wish I had felt more confident in designing an intervention and monitoring it earlier in the process. We did not have a real opportunity to track and monitor the picture prompts because Ms. Smith began using them quickly and she felt that the concern was resolved. I think we could have still tracked that intervention as we moved on to the next concern. However, since the process is consultee-centered I was glad to see that Ms. Smith owned the intervention and was excited to put it into place.

This case gave me the opportunity to see why problem identification is so critical to the problem-solving process. We spent the majority of our time trying to narrow down the concerns into observable and measurable behaviors. Once we were able to target the specific area of concern, we could design an intervention that was effective. It appeared as though Ms. Smith also began to observe Carla in a more positive light as we moved through the process. At the beginning of the process, it seemed that Ms. Smith was biased by Carla's ethnic background and family history. Once we were able to focus on Carla's progress in school we were able to make more objective decisions.

This case helped me to reflect on my own communication skills. Listening to session tapes and discussing them in supervision allowed me to understand that I needed to become more active and involved in my sessions, which I worked at for the remainder of the year. This also allowed me to begin new cases with more of a presence and place, beginning with contracting. I realized that I would have to work on my own communication skills as well as be more active in the session with this teacher in particular, because she had some strong assumptions about the student from the beginning. I used paraphrasing and clarification to make sure that I understood Ms. Smith, and this encouraged her to slow down during our sessions and reflect on her communication. As a result, she started to realize that she wasn't always very clear when describing her concerns.

This case taught me a lot about consultation and the importance of following the process. I think my work with this teacher helped me to improve my skills and be more assertive in my other consultation cases. I hope to incorporate consultation into my work as a practicing school psychologist and to continue to develop my skills in working with teachers. Since most of my experience has been working with young children, I'm still learning how to navigate working more with the adults in the school. This experience has made me feel much more comfortable working in the schools and using a collaborative framework.

Questions for Reflection

1. **What are the issues for you as a consultee-centered consultant in a school that has a culture of assigning interventions to school specialists?**
2. **What are some ways to improve your own personal communication strategies?**
3. **How does attention to the problem-solving process enable you to address multiple concerns of the teacher?**
4. **How might you address teachers' perceptions that frame the problem as solely within the child versus the interaction between the child and their environment?**

References

Boehm, A. (2000). *Boehm Test of Basic Concepts*, Third Edition. Upper Saddle River, NJ: Pearson.

Fullan, M.G., & Hargreaves, A. (1996). Interactive professionalism and guidelines for action. *What's worth fighting for in your school?* (pp. 37–62). Andover, MA: Regional Laboratory for Educational Improvement.

Hylander, I. (2004). Analysis of conceptual change in consultee-centered consultation. In N.M. Lambert, I. Hylander, & J.H. Sandoval (Eds.). *Consultee-centered consultation* (pp. 45–61). Mahwah, NJ: Lawrence Erlbaum Associates.

Rosenfield, S.A. (1987). *Instructional consultation.* Hillsdale, NJ: Lawrence Erlbaum Associates.

Rosenfield, S.A. (2004). Consultation as dialogue: The right words at the right time. In N.M. Lambert, I. Hylander, & J.H. Sandoval (Eds). *Consultee-centered consultation: Improving the quality of professional services in schools and community organizations* (pp. 339–347). Mahwah, NJ: Lawrence Erlbaum Associates.

Rosenfield, S., & Gravois, T.A. (1996). *Instructional consultation teams: Collaborating for change*. New York: Guilford Press.

Sarason, S. (1996). *Revisiting "The culture of the school and the problem of change."* New York: Teachers College Press.

West, J.F., & Idol, L. (2001). The counselor as consultant in the collaborative school. *Journal of Counseling and Development, 71*, 678–683.

5

Making the Case for Consultee-Centered Consultation: A Novice Consultant's Perception of Culture and Relationships

Erica Sherry

Advance Organizer Questions

- **What are the essential concerns that this case presents to the novice consultant?**
- **What skills will the consultant need to bring or develop to consult in this school culture?**
- **What activities may need to precede consultation to help build awareness for the value of individual teacher consultation over group problem solving?**
  - **With the administrator?**
  - **With the faculty?**

School Culture

There are two issues in this school's culture that impacted the consultation process: the role of the principal in establishing a collaborative culture and the school's architecture.

Role of the Principal

Typically, principals are the most influential people within school buildings. Students and staff answer to the principal and look to the principal for approval. Observing the behavior of the individual in this role can offer one insight into the school culture and environment. The principal's preferred style of collaboration makes a difference in the collaborative nature of the school (Fullan & Hargreaves, 1996).

The principal at my practicum site stated that she encourages collaboration among her staff, but has one main format that she prefers for such collaboration. She strongly endorses a model of grade-level assistance teams that teachers utilize when a student (or multiple students) does not make sufficient progress, academically or behaviorally. The principal made grade-level meetings mandatory for all teachers in the school. Many teachers in the school stated that they find grade-level teams to be an integral support to their individual student concerns.

However, from personal observations of a kindergarten grade-level team, I witnessed a number of problematic issues. One issue I saw was a lot of storytelling at the meetings. Instead of talking about intervention-related issues and data on student progress, there was talk about students' family homes and behaviors unrelated to the concern on the agenda. Also, there were six students listed on the agenda of a 15-minute meeting, which is hardly enough time to effectively problem-solve concerns for all of the students.

Along with these issues, two types of ineffective collaboration existed in the meetings: balkanization and contrived collegiality (Fullan & Hargreaves, 1996). Balkanization occurs in schools when teachers and administrators form cliques based on personal interests and possible competition with others not in that group. Contrived collegiality occurs when school staff are required to meet in groups for planning and consulting, as opposed to being given the opportunity, skills, and structures to participate, which is more likely to recruit devoted staff members. I witnessed both forms in the same kindergarten grade-level team meeting, both with teachers forming cliques and others who were clearly not interested in being present at the meeting.

School Architecture

The architecture of a school building can provide further information about the school's culture. Most classrooms are connected in some way to other classrooms. The teachers engage in conversation with each other regularly and with students in other classes, which seems to facilitate a friendly, comfortable environment in the building. Two aspects of the kindergarten classroom setting are noteworthy. Unlike other grades, they were closed off from each other. This may have interfered with the collaborative relationship among kindergarten teachers. Second, kindergarten classrooms are set in their own hallway in the building. Sarason (1996) hypothesized that the isolation of kindergarten classrooms from the rest of school limits the interactions between kindergarten students and older students, which might prevent the younger students from maturing at a more rapid rate. Although I believe the reason for this is to have the kindergarteners near the entrance to the door so there is as little hallway time for them as possible in the mornings and afternoons, the consequence is to separate the teachers and students from the other grades.

Relationships

When I started this process, I did not understand the concept of a working relationship as it would be used in a consultation context. I had a difficult time differentiating it from a personal relationship. Before starting the case, I had observed this teacher's classroom and interacted with her a few times. After our first consultation session, I thought we had developed a good personal relationship, but I didn't feel comfortable describing it as a working relationship. By the end of the second session, I had a stronger grasp on the difference between the two concepts. The teacher, Ms. Simon, was able to disclose to me a personal worry of hers and I addressed it in a way that told her I understood her emotions involved in the situation. Once we discussed this, she seemed relieved and was ready to discuss her concerns for the student, Samantha. I realized at this point that we were able to discuss personal issues and still return to the business of the case in a professional manner.

From the beginning of the contracting stage, I purposefully used more "we" language than "you" and "I" language. I did so to express the collaborative nature of the process. I noticed by the end of the second session, she was beginning to use the word "we" more often, as well. I think this was a sign that our working relationship was continuing to build because she was viewing it as a collaborative process as well. This shared language continued throughout the remainder of the consultation process, showing both of us perceived our work as shared collaboration.

Communication Skills

One of my main goals over the last four sessions of the case was to sustain awareness of appropriate use of communication skills while also remaining engaged in an active conversation with the teacher about the concerns. This was more difficult than I imagined it would be in a number of ways.

One skill that I wanted to focus on was paraphrasing. By restating what the teacher had said in my own words, I was checking to see if we had the same understanding of the meaning behind her words, as well as reflecting her comments back to her so she could think further about what she had said. Paraphrasing allows for clarifying instances in which I may have understood something she had said in a different way than she intended.

However, I found myself struggling with this skill because Ms. Simon had a lot to say about Samantha and did not pause much in her narrative flow. I was not confident enough to interrupt her so that I could paraphrase or summarize what was just said. This posed a few problems. First, when the teacher talked for extended periods of time, she tended to jump around between concerns. This made paraphrasing more difficult because, instead of having to paraphrase her words on one topic, I had a few running through my head. It is helpful to learn how to make the conversation more of a dialogue, instead of a monologue by the teacher. Even though it sometimes feels awkward to interrupt someone, through supervision I worked on doing so in a way that conveyed that I wanted to hear everything she has to say, but I also want to stop periodically to make sure I understand her correctly.

Also, I found that when I did not interrupt the flow of conversation, she worked her way up the ladder of inference (Argyris, 1993) to a more abstract and more pathological possible reason for the concern, locating the problem within the student. For example, she mentioned a few times that she thought Samantha had a "visual-spatial" problem. During our third session, she said:

> So there's this whole visual spatial concern, visual discrimination that I really continue to have concerns about. Even when she's holding a book, she'll hold it upside down or backwards, same thing putting numbers on a calendar, she'll place them upside down.

When the conversation got to that point, I started to feel so far off track. In addition, as she expressed her concerns in these terms, she became increasingly sure of their validity, a process described by Higgins (1999) as developing a shared reality.

A good tactic that I learned to use when she used these labels is the bond and move communication skill (see Introduction), where I would use a perception check, which focuses on acknowledging the consultee's feelings without conveying approval or disapproval (e.g., conveying to her that it must be upsetting to think that Samantha has an issue that might be out of her hands), and then bringing the conversation back to the specific point we had reached in narrowing down her concerns through clarification. After clarifying with the teacher, I realized her concern was whether Samantha knew how to form letters and how to recognize them.

> Consultant: So you're saying that Samatha is having a lot of difficulty visually recognizing her letters?
> Teacher: Yes!
> Consultant: That sounds like its very frustrating for you when you're trying to work on them with her. And probably frustrating for her, too. Well, let's look back at where we're at with narrowing our concerns and finding out what Samantha does know in regard to letter identification now.

By doing this, I showed her that I understood what she was saying, but since it was not something we could observe or intervene with, I moved on to continue discussing the concern about letter identification in observable terms.

Problem-Solving Stages

Contracting

My first session with the teacher consisted of contracting. During this session, I started by introducing myself as the case manager and also as a graduate student. I knew the teacher was already aware of this, but I mentioned it to introduce a conversation about how I was learning the consultation process and how we'd be navigating our way through it together. The teacher was very receptive to this, so we continued by talking about her expectations for the process. She wasn't sure what to expect, but she talked about how she had worked with the grade-level team and was looking for another way to go about helping one of her students. That naturally led into a discussion about the purpose of consultation and how we'd be sharing ownership of each step of the process. During this session, I also talked about the non-evaluative nature of the process and the possibility of coming up with intervention ideas that could be applied to other students in the class or future classes.

Our first meeting was only 15 minutes long, and because of this, I felt rushed. I discussed all of the components of the consultee-centered consultation process with the teacher, but because of the short amount of time, I didn't think I had spent enough time ensuring that the teacher knew enough about the process to truly feel comfortable with it and agree to go forward. Because of this, we spent the first few minutes of our next session reviewing some of the things we had discussed about the consultation process, such as the different steps and how it would remain collaborative throughout, and addressing questions and concerns she had with the process, before beginning a conversation about the student.

Problem Identification

Our second meeting together was focused around problem identification. The teacher came into the meeting with four concerns about Samantha's progress at that point in the school year with literacy skills. These concerns were clearly defined and in order of her priority:

1. identification of lower-case letters;
2. left to right progression when the student was writing her name;
3. identification of upper-case letters; and
4. isolating sounds of letters.

I was surprised and pleased to start with such well defined concerns, none of which the teacher implied were due to Samantha's behavior or internal deficits. We did not need to make our way too far down the "ladder of inference" because the teacher was very clear about the academic nature of her concerns. However, as previously noted, she did go back to issues higher on the ladder of inference during a later session.

However, it was during this meeting that the teacher brought a strong concern to the table. She had been discussing this particular student at the bi-weekly kindergarten grade-level meetings in her school and had been informed by another kindergarten teacher who facilitated the meetings that if she were to continue the consultation model with me, Samantha would be taken off the grade-level agenda. This was a concern because she felt the grade-level team offered her a level of support that she had come to value and she did not want to forgo that in order to participate in the consultation process. She expressed this concern as a dilemma, but not as a reason she did not want to continue our process together. Therefore, I paraphrased what she had told me and assured her that I would do what I could to make sure she kept any support she needed in the school. I wanted to assure her that I understood her concern and we would work through it together to assure that she received any supports she needed. This was also a good time to utilize perception checks to convey to the teacher that I understood the emotional experience she was going through.

> Consultant: Ok, and that's understandable. I can talk to the school psychologist about what she thinks the best route would be for that. If the team ever gets to a point where they want to drop her from the grade-level team's agenda because we're working on it together, and you're not comfortable with that, then talk with me about that and we'll see how we can compromise with the team to get as much support for Samantha as necessary and for you. I don't want you to lose any supports because I'm here, so however we can best go about that, we will.

Our third meeting continued our problem identification stage. I started the meeting by summarizing what we had accomplished in the preceding meeting, which led into a discussion about the importance of knowing what the student knew in regard to the areas of concern. I told the teacher that by examining Samantha's prior knowledge, we could fold the new information into the known information at the appropriate level of challenge, to not overload her working memory and to enable her to feel success (Rosenfield, 1987). At her age, Samantha was only expected to be able to hold two new pieces of information in her working memory at a time (Gravois, Gickling, & Rosenfield, 2007). In order to keep her at an appropriate instructional level where she can successfully learn and maintain new information, we also needed to keep the known information at a high level, somewhere between 70 and 85% of information presented. Therefore, it was crucial for us to know what letters Samantha knew at baseline.

The teacher agreed and volunteered to do the first instructional assessment (IA), using the three-trial method (Gravois et al., 2007) to collect data on lower-case letter identification, the concern we had prioritized. This strategy allows the student to show consistent knowledge of a newly acquired piece of information across multiple trials, and in this case, multiple days, before the teacher assumes it to be mastered at the rate of automaticity. When using the three-trial method with letter identification, the teacher has the student identify each one individually. A pile is made of the letters the student knows (with quick identification; hesitation is treated as an unknown). Later in the day or the next day, the known letters are given to the student again individually for identification and a pile is made of the letters the student knows. Sometimes, the student will know all of the letters at the second trial and sometimes will only know some of them. This process is repeated again later in the day or week with the known letters from trial two and a third pile of known letters is compiled. After the third trial, the known letters are assumed to be the student's baseline of letter knowledge.

During this meeting, the teacher started to use more "we" language, conveying to me that she was beginning to understand the partnership nature of the process. She also demonstrated more ownership of the case by volunteering to conduct the first assessment for baseline data. During previous meetings, the teacher had asked if I would be working with the student and had alluded to her being pulled from the classroom for intervention. Now she was volunteering to assess her current knowledge and also mentioned that she should remain in the classroom for intervention because the hallway can be a distraction. The fact that the way this teacher was thinking about the case had changed by the third session confirmed my belief that we were engaging in a consultee-centered consultation. It was also during this session that the teacher talked about the visual spatial problem and I was able to use communication skills to move us back to the more observable and measurable problem with the letters.

During our fourth meeting, we continued with the problem identification stage by discussing the data that the teacher had collected on Samantha's lower-case letter identification. The teacher found that Samantha had four letters that she identified automatically at the first assessment. However, the teacher continued to assess her knowledge three times each following school day. We looked over these data together and realized that there was only one lower-case letter that the student identified automatically each day, the letter "c."

Once we had determined what the student knew, we were able to set goals for the letter identification concern. Per the teacher's expectations of her rate of progress, at four weeks, we had planned for Samantha to learn 10 lower-case letters. At eight weeks, we had planned for her to have learned 18 lower-case letters. Finally, by the end of the school year, in approximately 12 weeks, we had planned for Samantha to learn all 26 lower-case letters. It was important for us to discuss these goals and arrive at these numbers together. Setting goals together kept the process collaborative in nature and continued to build on our working relationship.

Intervention Design

The teacher expressed during this meeting that she was interested, from her prior experience, in using the drill sandwich to teach the unknown letters (Gravois et al., 2007), a process that uses a ratio of 70–85% known and 15–30% unknown. This ratio obviously would not be possible with only one known letter. However, during supervision on this case, I realized that we could have 10 cards with letters on them and have seven of those cards be the letter that the student knows to automaticity. In addition to drill sandwich, we decided to create pocket cards for the student's known letters and target letters. We wrote the student's known letters, along with the letters currently being targeted, on small cards for her to keep with her at all times. This way, she could practice identification throughout the school day with multiple people, as well as at home with her family.

With our intervention of choice in mind, the teacher and I spent the next session discussing initial implementation. We ironed out the major details, such as how the intervention would be implemented (keeping a 80% known: 20% unknown split), who would be responsible for implementing it, how many times a day it would be implemented, and where it would be implemented. We had decided to do the drill sandwich three times a day (as soon as she arrived in the morning, halfway through the day, and at the end of the day) in the classroom. The teacher and classroom assistants would be responsible for implementing it. When she was able to identify a target letter immediately across all drills, three days in a row, we would consider that letter mastered and add in a new one.

Intervention Implementation and Evaluation

Over the next three sessions, we monitored treatment integrity, as we discussed current implementation and how we could continue its effectiveness. Samantha was beginning to acquire more letters to automaticity, so we knew, overall, the drill sandwich strategy was a good fit for her. However, the teacher expressed concern with data collection. Although the staff were practicing her letters with her multiple times a day, the frequency of data collection was variable. We decided at this session that data collection would only occur once per day. They would run through Samantha's letters with her at the beginning of the day before she had a chance to practice and take data then. By doing this, we knew for sure which letters she was truly maintaining and, also, the data collection process became less cumbersome for the staff. Figure 5.1 details the case progression, using the Student Documentation Form (SDF).

Closure

At our final meeting, after eight weeks of intervention, the teacher stated that because of state testing and the end of the school year approaching, the intervention had become too much for her to do on a daily basis. I asked her if she wanted to work on making it easier to implement, but she was ready to stop. I could tell this teacher was under a lot of stress and I did not want to continue an intervention that would not be implemented with integrity. So at this meeting, we closed the case. Samantha had acquired 16 letters in eight weeks. Although we had set our intermediate and long-term goals for more, we were both happy that she had met the short-term goal and was close to meeting the intermediate term goal.

My initial reaction was to feel disappointed that we were closing early, although I understood that she was finding the time commitment too difficult. However in supervision, we discussed how else I might have addressed the issue with the teacher, recognizing that I had not considered some other possibilities (e.g. less frequent meetings/a different time for meetings, others who could implement the intervention with Samantha, etc.) prior to closing.

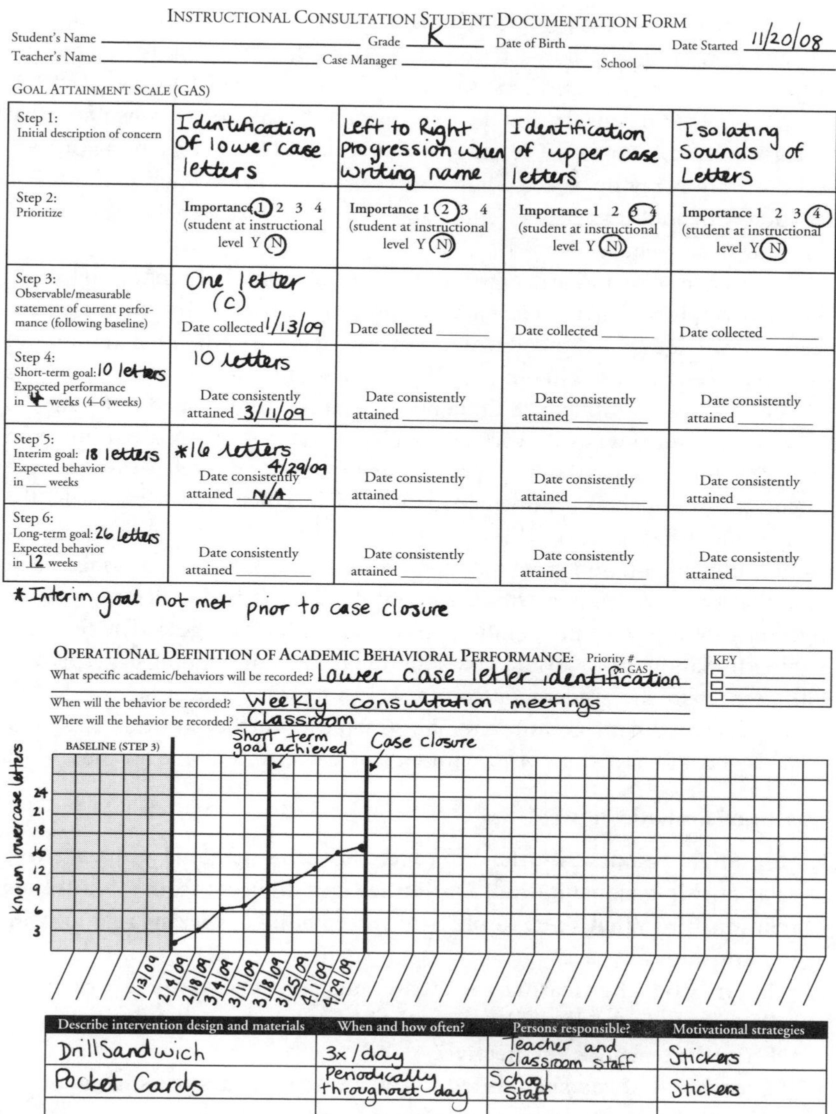

INSTRUCTIONAL CONSULTATION STUDENT DOCUMENTATION FORM

Student's Name ______ Grade K Date of Birth ______ Date Started 11/20/08

Teacher's Name ______ Case Manager ______ School ______

GOAL ATTAINMENT SCALE (GAS)

Step 1: Initial description of concern	Identification Of lower case letters	Left to Right progression when writing name	Identification of upper case letters	Isolating Sounds of Letters
Step 2: Prioritize	Importance (1) 2 3 4 (student at instructional level Y (N))	Importance 1 (2) 3 4 (student at instructional level Y (N))	Importance 1 2 (3) 4 (student at instructional level Y (N))	Importance 1 2 3 (4) (student at instructional level Y (N))
Step 3: Observable/measurable statement of current performance (following baseline)	One letter (c) Date collected 1/13/09	Date collected ______	Date collected ______	Date collected ______
Step 4: Short-term goal: 10 letters Expected performance in 4 weeks (4–6 weeks)	10 letters Date consistently attained 3/11/09	Date consistently attained ______	Date consistently attained ______	Date consistently attained ______
Step 5: Interim goal: 18 letters Expected behavior in ___ weeks	*16 letters 4/29/09 Date consistently attained N/A	Date consistently attained ______	Date consistently attained ______	Date consistently attained ______
Step 6: Long-term goal: 26 letters Expected behavior in 12 weeks	Date consistently attained ______	Date consistently attained ______	Date consistently attained ______	Date consistently attained ______

*Interim goal not met prior to case closure

OPERATIONAL DEFINITION OF ACADEMIC BEHAVIORAL PERFORMANCE: Priority # ______ on GAS

What specific academic/behaviors will be recorded? lower case letter identification

When will the behavior be recorded? Weekly consultation meetings

Where will the behavior be recorded? Classroom

KEY

Describe intervention design and materials	When and how often?	Persons responsible?	Motivational strategies
Drill Sandwich	3x/day	Teacher and Classroom staff	Stickers
Pocket Cards	Periodically throughout day	School Staff	Stickers

Figure 5.1 Student Documentation Form.

Lessons Learned

This consultee was a good one to start with as my first experience with consultee-centered consultation, even though she backed out early in the intervention implementation stage. The teacher was eager to participate and collaborative by nature. She was open to the process, understood the time commitment involved with our meetings, began implementing an intervention, and seemed to look forward to meeting with me each week. Because of this, I was able to practice the process and enjoy it at the same time, reinforcing my belief in the power of consultee-centered consultation. I would suggest that all novice consultants try to start with a "warm fuzzy" teacher consultee. It is a time-consuming process and there are many unexpected glitches that can arise, but when you're collaborating with another person, it motivates you to troubleshoot the glitches and enjoy the time spent.

However, in spite of that, a new (or experienced) consultant may find him or herself disappointed if the consultation process ends early before goals have been reached. It can be difficult to end a case prematurely when much time and effort has been put into building it. When the consultee in my case told me she wanted to stop, my immediate thought was that the student had not achieved the goals and there was still work to do. However, after talking about my own concerns during supervision, I realized that there had been some positive outcomes. Although the student had not reached her long-term goals, the teacher and I had developed a collaborative relationship through the intervention implementation stage and had begun to think about her concerns in ways that did not imply a within student deficit. We had collected baseline together, developed an intervention, and attained the first goal. The teacher's early termination, prior to full goal attainment, was disappointing, especially with respect to the student outcomes. Understanding why teachers do not continue successful interventions remains a topic for further study, and learning what else I could have done was an important learning outcome for me as well.

Questions for Reflection

1. **How might you describe the difference between a personal and a working relationship in consultation? Do you see it as different from a counseling relationship? What skills would help you to build a working relationship in a consultation case?**
2. **What may be other reasons the teacher may have ended the case early?**
   - **From a student-centered perspective?**
   - **From the teacher's perspective?**
3. **If a teacher told you she wanted to end a case early despite success of the student, what might be some strategies to handle it?**
4. **What are the ideal criteria for closure in a consultee-centered consultation relationship? Student long-term goal attainment as success? Teacher change as success? A combination? What information might this consultant use to rate the success of this case?**

References

Argyris, C. (1993). *Knowledge for action: A guide to overcoming barriers to organizational change*. San Francisco: Jossey-Bass.

Fullan, M.G., & Hargreaves, A. (1996). *What's worth fighting for in your school?* Andover, MA: Regional Laboratory for Educational Improvement.

Gravois, T.A., Gickling, E.E., & Rosenfield, S. (2007). *Training in instructional consultation, assessment, and teaming.* Catonsville, MD: ICAT Publishing.

Higgins, E.T. (1999). Saying is believing: effects: When sharing reality about something biases knowledge and evaluations. In L.L. Thompson, J.M. Levine, & D.M. Messick (Eds.). *Shared cognition in organizations: The management of knowledge* (pp. 33–48). Mahwah, NJ: Lawrence Erlbaum Associates.

Rosenfield, S.A. (1987). *Instructional consultation.* Hillsdale, NJ: Lawrence Erlbaum Associates.

Sarason, S. (1996). *Revisiting "The culture of the school and the problem of change."* New York: Teachers College Press.

6
Relationship Building and Objectivity Loss: The Importance of the Process in Consultation

Cyril Pickering

Advanced Organizer Questions

- **How do you balance being a child advocate and working collaboratively with the teacher during the consultation process?**
- **What are you willing to sacrifice or change to maintain a working, collaborative relationship with a teacher? When should you risk fracturing that collaborative relationship, if ever?**
- **Why is it important to honor the process, even when the solution to the concern seems straightforward?**
- **Who determines the success of a case?**

Introduction

In consultation cases, the seeming simplicity of the concern can mask how intensive the case will be. This was true for my first consultation case. Having completed an academic assessment course the semester prior to the consultation course, I believed that the case would have a straightforward intervention. I forgot, however, that the crucial difference between my belief and the reality of a consultation case is that the latter requires a collaborative, working relationship with the teacher. Focusing on the intervention rather than the consultative process led to many difficulties in this case and to some important lessons.

School Culture

As a practicum student in Westwood Elementary, my first task was to understand the school culture, which in the context of this case, was particularly important. The culture of the school created expectations for the nature of the consultation relationship, which would have an effect on the implementation of the intervention. My supervising school psychologist spoke with me at length about the characteristics and regularities of the school. Two aspects of the school culture had a particularly large impact on this consultation case:

1. the short time the consultation-based problem-solving team had existed; and
2. the availability of school specialists.

The New Team

This school was relatively new to consultation teams and the collaborative consultation process that I had been learning. The team, in its current form, had only existed for one year, beginning with the arrival of the present school psychologist. The school psychologist became the leader and was in the process of teaching the consultation process to the members of the team. The psychologist told me that the teachers in the school had received the new process with mixed reactions, and consultation was not universally accepted as a support system.

During my time in the school, I got the opportunity to attend some of the meetings to observe how the team operated. I noticed there were a lot of cases that were extreme problem behaviors, which were unresolved through typical interventions. There was a sense that the team was the last stop before special education referral. The consultation team was likely viewed as a barrier to special education rather than a means to improve student learning. It was clear that, across the school, there was a lack of understanding of the nature and purpose of the consultation process. This aspect of the school was also affected by the second major aspect of school culture, the large number of specialists who worked in the school.

The Role of Specialists

This Title 1 school had a wide variety of staff members available to work with students. The school had a highly mobile population and many students experiencing academic problems. Because of the high need, the school was well staffed with specialists, including para-educators (classroom aides) and special educators. There were often several adults in a class at one time. I observed many team-taught classes or classrooms that had a teacher and a para-educator. While the availability of other staff members is certainly a useful resource in any school, the presence of specialists created a regularity where students who were having academic concerns were pulled out of the class to work individually with the interventionist and the classroom teachers were rarely required to implement interventions. Since the goal of consultee-centered consultation is to improve the skills of the classroom teacher, this school-wide mindset was frequently a barrier to ideal implementation of a system of consultation.

The role of specialists impacted this case significantly when it came to establishing a classroom intervention for the student. The practice of having another staff member pull the student to do an intervention runs counter to the goal of enabling the teacher to handle similar problems more effectively in the future. The psychologist reported that many teachers felt the consultation was a more useful process for schools that did not have enough resources to go around. They felt that Westwood had enough people who were willing to come in to do interventions, so that consultation did not fit in anywhere. Teachers were not perceived to have a role with struggling students.

The Specialist-Filled Team

These two aspects of school culture combined to impact the formation of the consultation team. The team was almost entirely populated by specialists, without a single classroom teacher. In fact, the principal in charge when the team was formed did not allow any teachers to be on the team. This was still the case when I was placed in the school, even though the principal and assistant principal had changed. The psychologist noted that the new administration was very supportive of the consultation team and she was working on getting teachers to join the team, although by the end of that school year, there were still no teachers trained in the process.

The lack of teachers contributed to the continued misunderstanding of the team's purpose. First, there were no teacher members who could report to their peers about the process. Second, specialists usually took on referrals that appeared to be about concerns related to their specialty, blurring the lines between consultation and direct intervention. For example, the math specialist on the team tended to take the math cases. Thus, teachers might be unable to view the team members as taking a role that is different from their job title. When a specialist comes into the classroom, it usually means that a student is getting taken out for direct intervention services. It was natural for the teachers to assume that a specialist coming in as a consultant would take a similar role. This perception would become obvious during the course of my case, as I came to see that the teacher viewed me as another person who would pull the student out to do an intervention in spite of my assertions of another framework. Another problem, in combination with the team composition, is that the name of the team included the word *intervention*, suggesting a team of people who do interventions. The team name, in concert with the reality that all of the team members are in the school to do interventions, can significantly affect the perception of a teacher new to the consultation process.

Working Relationship

Participants

Between the consultee, the student, and myself, there were a variety of demographic characteristics that affected the case. I am an African-American male graduate student. At the time of the case, I made it clear to the teacher that I was still learning the process and was working with her on my first case. The consultee, Ms. Williamson, was an Asian female kindergarten teacher. She had several years of experience teaching. The difference in experience and status of the teacher and me also played a role in the relationship. The teacher could draw on her experiences in the past to inform the progression of the intervention. Though I could reference the instructional principles that I had been learning in class, I did not have comparable experiences, which made things difficult when the teacher made suggestions that would violate some of the instructional principles that I believed were essential to the student's academic progress.

The student, Walter, was a five-year-old Caucasian male. The shared attribute of gender between the student and me was a factor in how the teacher viewed my role in the case. The teacher was eager to have me work with the student because of the fact that we are both male. The teacher made constant reference to the age of the student and his maturity level. When the student entered kindergarten, he was five years old, which did not seem unusual to me, as that was the age that I was when I entered kindergarten. However, I discovered that at Westwood, it is typical for students to enter kindergarten at the age of six. Additionally, the student did not have any previous schooling and he came to kindergarten not knowing any letters. The teacher would continually refer to these facts, often stating that he had some maturing that he still needed to do. This was a big issue for me, since I was a student who came into kindergarten at five years old with no prior learning experience and no letter knowledge. I can remember that I first learned letters in kindergarten, whereas there seemed to be an expectation that students in this school would come to school with significant letter knowledge. There were a couple of times, while evaluating the student's progress, when Ms. Williamson said that hopefully he would have enough letter knowledge by the end of the year to be ready for kindergarten next year. In this case, I found myself having a strong connection with the student, not only because of our gender, but also because of the similarity of our educational history.

Issues in the Working Relationship

My working relationship with the teacher was extremely complicated. Even after almost two dozen sessions and several months working with her, it is still difficult for me describe how we worked together. On the surface, we accomplished a lot and had very little overt tension in our sessions. Anybody listening to our sessions would probably be unable to detect a problem in our interaction with each other. The difficulty in describing our working relationship stems from my internal concerns. We had very different perspectives on the problem, which resulted in some strong feelings of tension on my part. Though I was able to contain my feelings, the relationship was not comfortable for me, since there was a lot on my mind that I left unsaid because I believed it would negatively affect our working relationship. The way that I was presenting myself in the sessions was not necessarily how I actually felt, which is inauthentic; but I believed that it was necessary to continue working together. There were several issues in our working relationship that complicated and prolonged the case. These include the following.

The Impact of the Specialist Driven Culture

Because I was committed to a consultee-centered process, it was important to me that the teacher take full ownership of the intervention. When we discussed intervention, there were several people that the teacher listed as being responsible for the intervention. I wanted the teacher to be the primary person responsible for working with the student and collecting progress data. The teacher eventually took responsibility for coordinating the intervention implementers. I think this was evidence of progress, since it was a step away from the typical school process.

The Retention Issue

The retention issue was a big factor in the way that I felt about working with the teacher. She brought up retention early, which I heard but interpreted as a passing reference to something that was unlikely to happen. Later, she e-mailed the school psychologist and asked her to sit in on our session to make sure that the consultation process was going right. This bothered me a lot since the teacher did not discuss her concerns with me first and instead felt the need to speak with the team leader. Although I felt this way, I did not express it to anybody at the school. Since she had not brought up the topic of retention in our meetings again since the first time that she mentioned it, the reference to it in the e-mail was unexpected. I later concluded that retention was in the back of her mind the entire time. At the point in the case where she raised it again, there was a lot of frustration over the intervention and what letters would be included, how many he would learn at once, and the progress that he would make. I did not feel it was right to discuss retention since I did not think that it was appropriate in this case, and it upset me when the retention process was set into motion. I still felt that the student would be able to make more progress and that retention would not be the best option.

Eventually the retention meeting happened and I was asked to attend. For that meeting, I decided to leave my personal and professional opinions out of the discussion to prevent any discord and simply reported the data from the intervention. In the end the child was retained, which did not sit well with me. When reflecting back on the case, I wonder if retention would have been necessary if Walter had been working in an environment that was a match to his instructional level and if the teacher and I were more efficient with the process.

An Unshared Perspective

Ultimately, these issues hurt the working relationship. The teacher may have felt that I was not listening to her, which was not far from the reality, as I was intentionally ignoring some of her statements. I felt as if I needed to be the advocate for the student and I let that feeling interfere with my work with the teacher. My feelings influenced my communication with the teacher and prevented me from developing a shared understanding of the problem with her. We were never looking at the problem from the same perspective. I saw the child's instructional match as the problem, meaning that the instructional environment should be changed; the student should be given a manageable workload and brought up to the level of the rest of his classmates. The teacher seemed to think that the problem was a developmental/child-centered problem and that his workload should not change, despite his lack of success, since he would need another year of kindergarten. She expressed that keeping him in the current curriculum was the best way to handle his class work. I thought that we should have the freedom to make modifications to the student's work, but the teacher did not share my perspective.

Even when looking at the data from the intervention, we interpreted it differently. Where I saw progress, the teacher saw *slow* progress. We both saw the same plateau, but she would mention the plateau as a feature of the student's learning, whereas I interpreted the plateau as the result of a change that she insisted we make in the intervention. The entire time, the teacher and I were looking at the same student, the same concern and the same data, but developing two separate explanations and interpretations, resulting in two different solutions. I realized through this case that not all data are going to have one interpretation, depending on your perspective.

Loss of Objectivity

I had been interpreting the situation as the problem being entirely with the teacher, but came to realize that I had a loss of objectivity because of the differences in basic assumptions about the problem and my unwillingness to bring them to the forefront. I began to misinterpret what the teacher was saying, perceiving her statements as more negative than they actually were. One instance, where she made a comment about not needing an IEP, made me think of the first time she brought up retention; as a result, I began to worry that she was thinking about special education. In another session, she wanted to see if the student would do well with three unknown letters. I felt that she was ignoring what I said about working memory, but I was conflicted in what I wanted the outcome of the modification to the intervention to be. If the student succeeded, then the teacher would have been reinforced in her belief that working memory is not that important. However, the alternative was that the student would be unsuccessful, but the teacher would learn about the effects of violating working memory. I wanted the teacher to understand that working memory is important and that, for a five-year-old, it is limited, but I did not want the student to suffer. It became difficult for me to see things from her perspective because I believed that our differences were so obvious and that neither of us would budge. This became what Hylander (2004) referred to as "The Hidden Fight." The teacher was communicating how she felt about the student's progress. I had a different view of the case, but I was apprehensive about expressing it since that may result in more tension.

Fortunately, I received support, through supervision, on the way that I had been working with Ms. Williamson. Through supervision, I began to change my communication style so that I could clearly understand the teacher's perspective. I changed the way that I communicated to better match the consultee's feelings so that we could avoid a break in the relationship and still make progress.

Communication Skills

Better use of communication skill, particularly early on, could have helped facilitate the relationship. This was my first case and I thought that it had a very simple solution, so I entered the sessions with a particular goal in mind and was very expert/directive. Several communication issues were discussed in supervision that helped me to move toward a more collaborative stance. In our later sessions, my communication skills would become more collaborative, but the majority of our sessions were characterized by my directive, expert communication style.

Information Giving

I tended to offer information, as would be typical for somebody who would be developing the intervention alone. From that perspective, there was some information that needed to be given and reiterated. However, when I found myself repeating principles related to the intervention development multiple times, I recognized there was a problem. In addition, it was clear that, even if the teacher understood the principles, she was comfortable violating them in her practice. For example, the limits of working memory were violated in the intervention because the teacher felt that the student could learn more letters than was recommended for a child his age. I expressed my disagreement, but we tried it anyway, resulting in a period of one month where the student did not learn any letters from his intervention. Through supervision, I came to realize that the teacher's perspective and beliefs are important and that through collaboration, we can come to a faster consensus about the effectiveness of the intervention and interpretation of the data. Rather than forcing my opinion on the teacher, collaboration will produce results that reflect the desires of both members of the consultation relationship.

There were other times where I offered information at the wrong point in time. For example during the intervention planning session, I was very brief in my attempt to find out what the teacher had in mind. Instead, I took her first response, and interpreted that to mean that she did not have any intervention ideas. I used that assumption as a platform to offer information about the drill sandwich, an intervention that I thought was appropriate. This was an example of my taking control of the session, rather than working collaboratively with the teacher to develop the intervention.

Repetition of Concerns

There were issues that I brought up multiple times, which might have ultimately affected the working relationship. The teacher's concern was the student's letter recognition, so I wanted to work on the lower-case letters first, before working on capital letters. The teacher expressed that she would prefer to keep the capital and lower-case letters together, since that was how the class was learning the letters. I was fine with that reasoning at the time, but I brought the issue back up two more times. I also brought up the instructional match in the classroom, as he was still exposed to a large number of unknown letters in the work that he did daily. The student was never in an instructional match in the classroom, since the teacher viewed the intervention as being enough of a match. I occasionally would bring up the possibility of modifying the classroom material, but the teacher felt that the student needed to do the same work as the rest of the class, even though he did not know most of the letters. My general response to a denial in one of these areas was to bring the topic back up again later to see if the teacher changed her mind, but the teacher always responded the same way. This could have been damaging to the working relationship. Through supervision I realized that this might be perceived as ignoring the teacher's previous preferences.

As the sessions progressed, my communication style developed and I intentionally became more collaborative. My supervisor pointed out my lack of paraphrasing in my sessions. I learned that paraphrasing serves the dual purpose of ensuring that I am clear about what the teacher is saying and letting the teacher know that she had been heard. I realized that it would be difficult to change my communication style, so for a few weeks I used a prompt to remind myself to use paraphrasing as a skill. Prior to each session, I wrote the word "paraphrase" on my hand as a reminder, until I began to incorporate the skill more consistently. As I began to paraphrase the teacher's statements, the sessions began to become more collaborative and I think we began to work more effectively together.

Problem-Solving Stages

Contracting

It is important to begin a consultation process with a solid contracting session, and that is even more critical in a school whose culture is not structured for the process, as in this case. Unfortunately, we rushed through contracting. The meeting had to be brief because of time constraints. Because I recognized, through listening to my tapes, that all of the steps of contracting had not been completed, I did some piecemeal revisiting in our later sessions. However, we never had a discussion about the process and some of the problems that developed were due to the teacher's lack of a clear understanding of the process.

Problem Identification

The problem identification stage went smoothly, as the teacher knew exactly what concerns she wanted to address. Letter identification was our primary focus, which we worked on for our entire case. We prioritized the concerns and began to plan for the baseline collection. I thought that we would be assessing the student on all 26 letters (small and caps), but the teacher believed that we would just test the student on the six letters in his name, which she identified as her short-term goal for him. I discussed with her that it would probably be a good idea to get as much information as possible for the baseline. At that point, she asked when I would be able to come in to collect the baseline, reflecting the school norm that outside personnel come into the class to work with students, rather than the teacher developing skills to deal with problems. I offered to have us collect the baseline together, using the three-trial method: taking a full assessment of letter knowledge and repeating the assessment with the previously known letters, to find out which letters are known consistently across the three trials. However, the teacher came in the next week with baseline collected. It was a little surprising that she collected the baseline on her own, since I thought that we were going to collect the baseline together. I thought it was a good sign that she had taken the initiative to collect it. We found a stable baseline point, revealing that the student knew six out of his 52 total letters.

Intervention Planning

At the point that we had baseline, the teacher asked me when I would be able to come in and do an intervention, showing that she was still under the impression that the process was intended to develop an intervention for someone else to do. I also learned how much intervention this student was actually getting with a variety of people to work on his letter knowledge. It seemed that the student was receiving at least two separate interventions on letters already, with the potential for another intervention to be added after winter break. That fact raised concerns for me about overloading the student's working memory. I wanted to make sure that once we started an intervention, everybody doing an intervention was working on the same letters. I asked the teacher to contact those staff members to ensure that everyone working with the student knew which letters were being targeted.

After we had the baseline, however, it took us longer than I had expected to begin the intervention. Most of the teacher's concern was about the progress that the student would make if he only worked with two unknown letters at one time. She was concerned that he would take the entire year to learn the rest of his letters. We worked through some of these issues, but I still felt we could have implemented an intervention earlier. Rather than the intervention itself, we would have likely come to a faster consensus if I had focused more on the consultee's perspective.

We finally got all of the components of the intervention settled and set the short-term goal for the student of learning all the letters in his name. We also agreed that the student would have no more than two unknown letters in his intervention so that his working memory would not be overloaded. We discussed progress-monitoring procedures and developed a way to keep track of when a letter becomes known and how to record his progress for our chart. Soon after, we wrote a script to ensure that everybody who was doing the intervention was working with the student in the same way.

Intervention Implementation

Despite the difficulties discussed above, the teacher and I developed a solid intervention for the student. There were numerous modifications that we needed to make, but the intervention proved to be effective. The intervention went smoothly, until we realized together, from looking at the data, that the student was not benefiting from having capital and lower-case letters on the same card. We decided to present the letters to the student individually, on separate cards.

After that, my concern was that the student was not getting the intervention often enough. We set a minimum of two times per day for the intervention, which I thought would not give him enough repetition to make significant progress. I reasoned that our intervention, which took a few minutes to go through, could be performed multiple times throughout the day, particularly during transitions in the morning or between classes. This was an issue that was not resolved the way that I believed would be most effective, but the teacher felt that there was not enough time in the day to do the intervention multiple times. While this difference of opinion did not harm the working relationship, it is a topic that I brought up multiple times, trying to find ways to increase the student's repetitions.

The student began to make steady progress for a few weeks. The teacher then decided to increase the number of unknown letters to three, as she wanted to introduce a capital and lower-case at the same time, though there was still one unlearned letter in the drill. I disagreed with this approach, but we came to the conclusion that we would make the modification, evaluate his progress and make a decision based on results. When it became clear that the student's progress had stopped entirely, the teacher still did not want to reduce the unknowns, since she did not feel comfortable pulling a letter out once it was in the drill. After four weeks passed and the student still had not learned any new letters, we placed the student back into his working memory range. The result of the student's return to his match was that the student made even more progress than he had previously. He began to learn his letters more quickly than before and also consistently recognized some letters that we had not yet included in his drill. When we honored working memory, the student made progress and when working memory was overloaded, progress stopped, resulting in an ABA intervention design. When I discussed this with Ms. Williamson, we agreed to put phase lines on the graph of the student's progress, to indicate what was happening in the separate phases of the intervention.

Evaluation

At the end of the process, the student was a single letter away from knowing all of the letters in his name and, including the letters he learned incidentally, knew 23 out of 52 letters, compared to his baseline measurement of six letters. In the first two months of the intervention, he learned eight new letters. During the period that the third letter was added, he only learned one additional letter, though that letter was not in his drill. In the month after returning to his working memory range, he learned eight new letters.

Closure

During the closure stage, I discussed these three phases with the teacher and we agreed to put phase lines into the graph, to make sure that somebody else looking at the graph would be able to interpret his progress in the context of his working memory load. To ease the interpretation, we labeled the middle phase as a period of three unknowns. Additionally, the teacher reported that spring break was during that time and the student had some absences, so that was also written on the graph.

During closure, we completed the articulation form required by the school for all consultation cases, which the teacher began to work on prior to our session. We talked about some of the information that would be included, but the teacher did most of the writing. We also discussed the teacher's comfort level with the process and how she would work with similar students in the future. After this discussion, we officially closed the case.

In our final session, I asked the teacher for her impressions of the process. The teacher said that she was pleased with the process overall. She said that, in particular, the structure provided by the process was helpful. She reflected that the charting of the student's progress really helps make decisions about intervention progress and tells the story of the student's skills in a way that is easy to understand. She did say that it takes a little bit of extra effort to actually do the charting, but it was something that she would try to do in the future. It was particularly helpful in this case when the student stopped making progress and we were able to see a visual representation of the plateau and do something about it.

She said that she would be willing to use the consultation team in the future, because of the structure that it provided, with the case manager helping to manage student interventions. She remarked that in the future, starting on an intervention earlier would probably be the better course of action, so she would not wait until the middle of the year to approach the team. When I asked her how comfortable she would feel using the same problem-solving process on her own in the future, she was a little bit hesitant. She said that she would be able to do it and would feel comfortable playing the role of the manager of the interventionists working with a particular student, facilitating communication and making decisions. However, she seemed to prefer the presence of a case manager working with her to facilitate everything. I believe that she learned a lot of information that would affect her instruction, like the ratio concept regarding known and unknown information, although during the session, she did not specifically reflect on any instructional practices that she would change.

Lessons Learned

Reflecting on this case, I learned a lot about myself that will be helpful for the future and that might be helpful for other new consultants as well. I know that in general I am a very solutions-focused individual, but I was unaware of how this would affect my case. It is important to have an understanding of your own personality and to consider how your personality will affect your work with teachers.

My communication with the teacher for the first half of our sessions was not very collaborative, since I was more concerned with getting an intervention started and having the student make progress. I lost sight of an important goal in consultee-centered consultation, which is to work together with the teacher to ensure that her comfort with the problem-solving method will lead to implementation of an intervention and change future practices. I was focused on the tangible, measurable goal of student progress and frustrated that the teacher was getting in the way of the intervention that I had in my head. Knowing this gives me a starting point to learn how to adapt my personal style to the collaborative process. During this case, I used a prompt to encourage myself to paraphrase more (literally writing the word "paraphrase" on my hand), which resulted in more collaborative sessions. As I learned more about myself, the sessions across this and other cases became more interactive and less expert on my part. Consultants should know what they are bringing to the table when they enter into a consultation relationship with a teacher. Reflection on one's practice is critical to building a collaborative working relationship.

My loss of objectivity with the teacher was also a humbling experience. In class, I learned that lack of objectivity is one of the main barriers that can prevent a teacher from effectively managing a classroom problem (Caplan, 1995). That became even clearer to me when I realized that consultants can experience the same thing, which was damaging my ability to interpret the conversations with my teacher and prevented me from being an effective consultant. Analyzing why I lost objectivity was helpful in identifying future triggers that may cause a strong reaction in the future. It is easy to criticize a teacher for blaming the student for a problem and accuse the teacher of lacking objectivity, but my own loss of objectivity taught me an important lesson. Consultants are also subject to internal biases and perspectives. Through this case, I was able to identify sensitive issues that trigger my negative attitudes.

Another important lesson to draw from this case is the importance of the process. Some of the problems that I faced can be traced directly back to the lack of completing the steps of contracting in the beginning of the case. Spending

10 minutes giving talking points about the process does not mean that the business of the contracting stage has been accomplished. Contracting, like any other part of the process, should be a collaborative dialogue, enabling the consultee to understand the process, consider how intensive the work is going to be, and make an informed decision about whether or not to proceed. It is important to hear the consultee's perspective of the process going in and to discuss the steps of the process that you will go through together. I failed to do that in my first session and did not return to ensure understanding in the following session. As a result, I was seen as yet another specialist coming to do an intervention.

The purpose of consultee-centered consultation is not just to solve the teacher's problem. Even when the case seems simple and a solution immediately comes to mind, the vital outcome of the case is not a quick resolution. The apparent simplicity of the case should not interfere with the reliance on the problem-solving model. Learning to be a consultee-centered consultant requires reflection and skill over and above the content of the referral problem.

Questions for Reflection

1. **Reflect on your educational history. How do you think some of your most salient experiences can influence the consultation process?**
2. **In what way can your personal feelings interfere with developing a collaborative relationship with the consultee? What are some ways to avoid these barriers?**
3. **Is there any part of the consultation process that you have found to be particularly important to the success of the case?**
4. **How did the author distinguish personal and professional opinions? Was there a time when the two overlapped? Is there ever a time that the consultant should share his/her personal beliefs and opinions with the consultee? Explain why or why not.**
5. **How might differences of race and gender impact the consultation process? What could the author have done to address the cultural context of this consultation process in a way that could have improved the process?**
6. **The teacher's solution of retention could be considered her attempt at being an advocate for the student. How could her idea of advocacy conflict with the consultant's view of advocacy and how did this affect the case? With this in mind, what solutions are there to conflicting perceptions of advocacy?**
7. **What are your beliefs about how teachers should serve children who are at risk in their classroom? How can you prepare yourself to address potential conflicts about how teachers should serve children during consultation?**

References

Caplan, G. (1995). Types of mental health consultation. *Journal of Educational & Psychological Consultation*, 6, 7–21.

Hylander, I. (2004). Analysis of conceptual change in consultee-centered consultation. In N.M. Lambert, I. Hylander, & J. Sandoval (Eds.). *Consultee-centered consultation: Improving the quality of professional services in schools and community organizations* (pp. 45–61). Hillsdale, NJ: Lawrence Erlbaum Associates.

Part III

Consulting in the Elementary Grades

A central element of Instructional Consultation is assessing and creating the instructional match, that is, ensuring that the student enters the learning environment with the skills to be successful. Part of the problem for many students is that there is a gap between what they know and are able to do and what the learning environment demands. In the two chapters in this part, the authors confront this issue. Courtenay Barrett helps a second grade teacher construct and monitor instructional match in reading for his classroom. Laura Schussler supports a teacher in understanding how vocabulary is not only a problem in being successful in the social studies curriculum for her English Language Learners, but for her other students as well.

7
Making the Instructional Match Salient for the Teacher

Courtenay Barrett

Advanced Organizer Questions

- **How does this case study fit into a consultee-centered consultation framework?**
- **How did the consultant make instructional match salient for the teacher?**

Instructional level is "the critical point at which the child has the prerequisite skills to enter … the classroom curriculum and can benefit maximally from instruction" (Rosenfield, 1987, p. 101). It provides the student with the ideal balance between challenge and success in order to optimize learning. The concept applies to the suitability of the material a specific individual is working from, rather than the benchmark level of an entire class or reading group. In reading, this match occurs when the student knows between approximately 93% and 97% of the words in the material; frustration level occurs when the student knows fewer words and independent level occurs when the student knows more.

Research has indicated that instructional level can affect task completion, on-task behavior, and task comprehension (Gickling & Armstrong, 1978; Gravois & Gickling, 2008). Students who are at frustration level, knowing less than the optimal 93% of the words in the text to automaticity, show lower rates of task completion, on-task behavior, and task comprehension than students working at an instructional level. Unfortunately, some students may be at frustration level during the majority of the school day (Gravois & Gickling, 2008). As a result, teachers see off-task behavior, distractedness, and dissatisfaction in school. Students are learning at a slower rate than their peers who are working at instructional level and fall further and further behind as the year progresses.

School Culture

One such case is the focus of this chapter. This case took place in an upper-middle class suburban elementary school as part of my consultation practicum experience. The school was significantly diverse with over half the school population consisting of racial minority students (Asian-American, Black, or Hispanic). This case was not formally referred through the problem-solving team that the school had in place. Instead, my site supervisor, the school psychologist, asked the teacher if he would participate in the process as a learning experience for both of us, as he was a new teacher to the school.

The school utilized a pre-referral process, in which teachers would informally discuss student concerns at grade-level meetings and receive feedback from each other. If the teacher's concerns were not subsequently resolved, the teacher would then refer the student to the school level problem-solving team. The school culture focused on the use of specialists within the school. Therefore, typically, when a student was referred to the problem-solving team, the team arranged for a specialist to work with the student, rather than engaging the teacher in the problem-solving process. Lastly, if the concerns were still not improving, the school psychologist would formally begin the assessment and testing process for special education placement.

Relationships

I am an Asian-American female school psychology doctoral student; Mr. Sabins, the consultee, a Caucasian male, was the student's general education teacher. The client, John, was a second grade Caucasian male. I was being trained in an instructional consultation (IC) model (Rosenfield, 2008), but had limited practical experience in the schools. Mr. Sabins had only two to three years of teaching experience and had never before referred a student to the problem-solving team.

As a result of our inexperience, the consultation process was lengthy and challenging. Contracting occurred in December, the intervention was implemented in late March, and the case moved to closure in May. Winter vacation and school holidays further impacted case progress. At each session, though, we moved the case ahead, albeit slowly. As the school curriculum progresses over the year, it is important that problem-solving processes and interventions move quickly so that students do not continue to fall behind as coursework becomes more challenging. Furthermore, it may be difficult for teachers to persist with a time-consuming or slow process without a strong working relationship. This suggests how important it is that all consultants receive sufficient training and supervision so that cases can move ahead more quickly with experience and learn how to develop quality relationships.

After persistent use of my communication skills, our working relationship progressed. Specifically, the strength of our relationship can be illustrated though the teacher's initiative by the end of the process. He would come to our sessions prepared, conducting running records and calculating the percentage of known words, even when there had been no formal agreement to do so beforehand. He was always on time and never forgot that a meeting had been scheduled.

Communication Skills

In order to develop the working relationship, I used several communication skills. Specifically, I focused on the use of perception checking, paraphrasing, and clarification statements, all of which are key communication skills in IC (Rosenfield, 2008). It was important to acknowledge and understand the emotional state of the teacher during the first stages of the process. Often, by the time that a student is referred, the teacher is frustrated and discouraged, as was the case here. In order to move forward, I had to ensure that the teacher felt that I was respectful of his emotions and efforts; that I was trying to work with him rather than against him. Perception checking, which reflects back an individual's feelings, is extremely useful in this regard.

In addition, during the initial problem identification stage, the teacher's concerns were vague and focused on behavioral rather than academic concerns. For example, the teacher was concerned that John was easily distractible and overly interested in his classmates' behavior. In order to help clarify the teacher's opinions, observations, and concerns, it was extremely important to use paraphrasing and clarification statements or questions. Paraphrasing also helped me ensure that we had a shared understanding of the problem. For instance, after Mr. Sabins commented on John's distractibility in the classroom versus the lunchroom, I paraphrased by saying, "It sounds like he's not as distracted in the classroom, like when he's in lunch", followed by a clarification question, "[And], last time, you told me he was more distracted after break. Can you tell me more about that?"

These communication skills were also helpful during the intervention design and implementation stage. For example, as we discussed how he chose vocabulary words from the classroom text, I paraphrased, "So, it seems like the first time you do [the word search], he'll get certain words wrong and those words will become the pocket cards." He then realized that he could be more specific, "I picked words he missed that were [also] on a lot of the pages." Before moving forward, it was important to make sure that we were on the same page. Often, by paraphrasing what the teacher said, he would realize that his statements were unclear and would himself clarify his responses.

Initially, as I was just learning the skills, it was difficult to use communication skills in a comfortable and fluent manner. Therefore, in order to improve the use of my communication skills, I transcribed my sessions. I would highlight all the times during the session where I used a specific communication skill in the color blue and highlight the times where I could potentially have used a communication skill in green. During the "green" parts of the transcription, I would include specific paraphrases, reflections, or clarifications that I could have said. This intentional self-reflection helped me to learn how to use communication skills more effortlessly.

Consultation Process

The consultation process, based on the IC model (Rosenfield, 1987, 2008), involves a series of problem-solving stages, embedded in a collaborative relationship, and is guided by an ecological view of problem-solving. IC is a consultee-centered consultation (CCC) model. CCC focuses on the consultee's presentation of the client's issues rather than the client's assessment and diagnosis. Most types of CCC are non-hierarchical, with both the consultant and consultee having expertise on the problem (Lambert, 2004).

The stages of the problem-solving process are Contracting, Problem Identification, Intervention Design and Implementation, Intervention Evaluation, and Closure (Rosenfield, 2008). The Student Documentation Form (SDF), a document used in the IC process (see Rosenfield & Gravois, 1996, for a full description), helped us adhere to the problem-solving process, collect data, graph progress, and set goals. The SDF is also used to measure process integrity of the consultation process. In this case, the following steps were completed within the model and are described below.

Contracting

The primary purpose of the contracting stage is to discuss expectations and procedures of the consultation process, inform the consultee about the values and perspectives of the consultation process, and then obtain an agreement to move forward with the relationship.

Our contracting phase occurred in December. I ensured that the purpose and function of the consultation model and the various stages of the process were discussed. I received an agreement to move forward with the process from Mr. Sabins. Then, we made a commitment to the process that included shared ownership, confidentiality, and regularly scheduled meetings, the essential elements of the IC contracting stage.

Problem Identification

The problem identification stage focuses on narrowing down the consultee's concerns about the student into observable and measurable behaviors, and then prioritizing which concerns to address first. Instructional Assessments (IAs) are one of the tools with which the IC process helps the team collect data about the concerns and determine if the student is at instructional level (Gravois & Gickling, 2008). These concerns are recorded on the SDF, in addition to data collection methods, baseline data points, and goals.

After contracting, the initial concerns that were discussed were broad and high on the ladder of inference (Rosenfield, 2004). Mr. Sabins' concerns were behavioral, including John's distractedness and off-task behavior, and that he was working below grade level in both reading and math. The problem identification stage, which is a major portion of any IC case, was lengthy and difficult. Often, when a student has been working at frustration level for a period of time, it is extremely challenging to identify what the observable and measurable concerns are, and then prioritize them. It is also often the behavioral concerns about the student, which can be a result of the frustration that the student feels, that are first brought to the attention of the consultant.

As a first step in the process, I gathered background information about the student. According to a record review, John was below grade level in reading and math in both kindergarten and first grade, even "with assistance and reasonable effort." In first grade, he attended supplemental reading with the reading specialist for 30 minutes every day. At the end of first grade, he was assessed as having 29 out of 50 sight words and reading entry-level first grade (E-level) books independently. He had satisfactory attendance since he began attending school.

At the time of referral, John was in the lowest reading group, all of whom attended supplemental reading for 30 minutes every day. During the first half of the year, the group read mid-level first grade (F-level) books in their general education classroom. At that time, they were expected to read out of the more challenging, end of the year, first grade (G- and H-level) books in their classroom reading groups.

I conducted an observation of the reading specialist's classroom, and it appeared the material covered in the general education classroom and the material in the reading specialist's classroom were different, suggesting that the students were challenged by two separate reading curricula. In the reading specialist's classroom, the students were being introduced to different vocabulary words than in the general education classroom. Primarily, they worked on increasing the recognition and automaticity of vocabulary words out-of-context, while reading fluency and comprehension were more of the focus in the general education classroom. Since the vocabulary words differed across classrooms, students in that reading group were being introduced to more new pieces of information than other students in the class. This may have resulted in an overload of the students' working memory. Research on working memory, as applied to learning to read, implies the importance of providing "new information in limited sets so as not to overload working memory" (Gravois & Gickling, 2008, p. 506). Students in the first grade have the capacity to learn approximately three to four new pieces of material, or words, at a time (Gravois, Gickling, & Rosenfield, 2007). If this is violated, as it was in this case, the student's progress will be inhibited and they will be prevented from successfully retaining and using the new material.

Next, we conducted an Instructional Assessment (IA; Gravois & Gickling, 2008) in order to see if John was on instructional level, a standard procedure in every IC case. A specific type of reading IA is the "snapshot," which uses the student's classroom material to move through a series of activities in order to help identify concerns. The steps of a snapshot include:

1. reading aloud to the student and assessing oral comprehension of the material;
2. conducting a word search;
3. having the student read aloud while calculating reading fluency; and
4. assessing reading comprehension.

Implementing a trial intervention if the student is not at instructional level is also part of the IA process.

A word search is used to determine the percentage of words that the student knows in the given text to automaticity. During a word search, the teacher points to a word in the text and the student says the word aloud. The teacher points to the words out of order to ensure that the student is not using context clues to identify the word. The process is "quick and snappy," preventing the student from sounding out the words. Word meaning may be simultaneously assessed, if appropriate. After every word has been pointed to, the teacher calculates the percentage of words that the student knew. If it is found that the student is not at instructional level (93–97% known), the teacher implements an intervention in order to create the match. Common interventions are shortening the passage, teaching a few words or concepts (while not overloading working memory), substituting known for unknown words, and rewriting the story so that a higher percentage of words are known.

We used passages from the F-level book in which John's regular classroom reading group was working for the IA. During the word search, we found that there was not an instructional match between the student and task, since John only knew about 70%, opposed to a desired 93–97%, of the words. With only 70% of the words known, it would be improbable that he could comprehend the passage. After a series of additional snapshots, it became clear that altering the classroom and reading group material to be an instructional match for the student would be an intervention in itself. Therefore, the priority was finding out how to ensure that John was on instructional level during classroom reading instruction.

Intervention Design

After concerns had been identified and prioritized, we moved into the intervention design stage, to design an intervention that would work for Mr. Sabins in the classroom. After the decision was jointly made to work on ensuring instructional match, Mr. Sabins and I designed the plan. In the beginning of this stage, Mr. Sabins decided he would generalize the intervention to the entire below-grade level reading group. Specifically, he agreed to conduct a word search with each student at the beginning of the week, using a part of the story book in which the reading group would be working. Next, he would record what percentage of words the student knew using a colored pencil. Then, the teacher would alter the material as needed, either shortening the passages or replacing unknown words with known words.

Pocket words (Gravois et al., 2007), that is, vocabulary words that are written on index cards that can be carried around in the child's pocket, were selected as the intervention to facilitate instructional match. Each student in John's reading group would have pocket words for four of the unknown words in the weekly reading assignment, in accordance with research on working memory capacity. The pocket words were practiced two or three times each day, in addition to the times they were used during reading group, according to the following procedure:

1. Students lay pocket words out on the table.
2. The teacher asks, "Which word says __________?" The students identify the word. The teacher repeats with the remaining words.
3. Students read the pocket words aloud to the teacher.
4. The teacher says, "Show me the word __________ in the book." The students have to find and point to the word in the book.

Intervention Implementation

Intervention implementation began in late March, as shown in Figure 7.1. In order to aid in treatment integrity, I met with Mr. Sabins for six sessions after the intervention began so that I could make sure the intervention was understood and easy to implement. In order to see if he was implementing the intervention as intended, I observed the intervention during the seventh week of the intervention. At that time, treatment integrity was high; however, I failed to observe the intervention additional times and there are no data to illustrate that there was treatment integrity during the other weeks.

Intervention Evaluation

The intervention evaluation stage is used to measure student outcomes and modify the intervention if progress is not on track to meet goals. Because IC is consultee-centered, it is also important to discuss the consultee's outcomes. They are each described in separate sections below.

ASSESSMENT AND CLIENT OUTCOMES

At the end of the week, Mr. Sabins would conduct another word search and record, in a different colored pencil, what percentage of the words the student knew. A solid line separates the baseline data collection and the beginning of the pocket word intervention. The data points labeled "Pre Intervention" were collected on Mondays, prior to the pocket word intervention for the week. The data points labeled "Post Intervention" were collected on Fridays after that week's pocket words had been used. By late May, the student was on

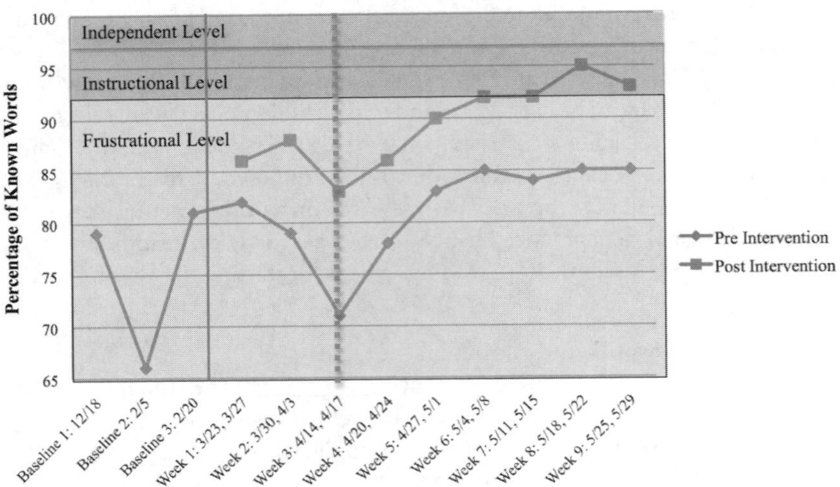

Figure 7.1 Instructional Match Weekly Assessment.

instructional level by the end of the week as documented in Figure 7.1 and had progressed to reading early- to mid-level second-grade books (K-level).

Around mid-April, the teacher recognized that the student was having difficulty generalizing between the pocket words and the identical word when it was used in the classroom material. The intervention was modified by making a direct connection between the pocket words and the words in the story. These changes are illustrated through the dashed phase line in Figure 7.1.

It was unnecessary to provide an extrinsic motivator to the student; he was intrinsically motivated by the process, as were the other students. When I observed the intervention in May, the students were extremely enthusiastic about their pocket words, wanting me to quiz them before Mr. Sabins formally began the reading lesson.

This study exemplifies the effect of instructional consultation on improving academic performance in the classroom. John increased the percentage of known words in the classroom text, advanced to grade level reading material, and became more invested in his academic achievement. Mr. Sabins described him as taking more initiative in his learning and "making the connection that these (pocket) words are in the story." He said, "I think before he thought we were learning words just to learn words." The teacher perceived that the progress the student made over the course of the intervention was high, and if progress continued at the same rate over the next year, he hypothesized that the student could stay on grade level in reading with little additional support.

CONSULTEE OUTCOMES

Because IC is a consultee-centered consultation model, there is an expectation that the teacher, as consultee, will be impacted by the process. This design made instructional match salient for the teacher. Mr. Sabins had no prior knowledge of working memory or instructional match. In addition, he had never used pocket words before. He found them easy to make and use, and successful in engaging the students in his lowest reading group. He stated that he "felt like he had another tool to teach" all his students. Therefore, one of the results was that the teacher's skill level increased as a result of this case.

Furthermore, Mr. Sabins' perception of the source of the problem changed. Initially, the teacher saw the problem as a deficit existing within the student (i.e., his inability to stay focused or on-task), rather than as a result of a mismatch between the classroom material, student's entry-level skills, and instruction. As the case progressed, the teacher no longer discussed his initial behavior concerns and, instead, focused on creating the match. After moving through the process, the teacher noted that he "thought the intervention was helping [John] read" and "he was picking up more words." Mr. Sabins is now more aware that an instructional mismatch may influence behavior, rather than assuming that off-task behavior is the cause for low academic performance.

Mr. Sabins also expressed increased confidence teaching the student. Initially, he claimed that he "felt like there was nothing he could do to help him." Now, he may be more likely to refer a student that presents similar concerns as John to the problem-solving team or to use a pocket word intervention to create an instructional match. Thus, the teacher's future students may benefit from the consultative process in this case. One of the greatest benefits Mr. Sabins found was that he had a new tool to help the student in the classroom.

Closure

The purpose of the final stage, closure, is to formally conclude the collaborative relationship after goals have been met and the teacher feels comfortable continuing to use the intervention strategies when appropriate or fade the intervention so that the student can succeed in the classroom with little or no additional support (Gravois et al., 2007). After reviewing the goals of the process, the case was closed in May. At that time, Mr. Sabins intended to continue using the intervention with the entire reading group and planned on passing his experience onto John's third grade teacher.

Lessons Learned

Limitations

While the teacher generalized the intervention to the rest of the student's reading group, no baseline or outcome data were collected from the other children. This case study would be strengthened if data showed that the intervention increased the percentage of words known for more than one student. Future studies may wish to ensure that data are collected for every student receiving the intervention.

In addition, the data collected only illustrate that the number of words the student knew to automaticity increased within and across weeks. No data on the student's reading skills, including reading fluency or comprehension, were collected. However, the student did progress several book levels over the course of the collaborative relationship (from F- to K-level books), and continued to be on instructional level.

Although I observed the intervention one time, it would have been helpful if Mr. Sabins and I created a formal checklist of activities that needed to occur in order to define treatment integrity. This would have been especially useful when Mr. Sabins passed the intervention on to John's third grade teacher.

Lastly, the intervention did not include the reading specialist. By collaborating with both the reading specialist and the classroom teacher, the pocket word intervention could have been used in both environments, increasing repetition and preventing working memory from being overloaded. Future case studies might focus on the process of developing a collaborative relationship between the specialist and classroom teacher, as well as with the consultant.

Implications for Novice Consultants

This case study provides several lessons for future consultants and school psychologists, including the importance of choosing relevant outcome measures and utilizing supervision and self-reflection to improve communication skills. First, I remember feeling overwhelmed as we approached the intervention design and implementation, and intervention evaluation stages. It seemed as if there were an infinite number of interventions to choose from and an even greater number of methods to measure the effects of those interventions! When creating our data collection and outcome measurement plan, I felt that it was really important to guide our choice toward a data collection method that was simple yet engaging for Mr. Sabins. I knew that I would have to think outside the box in order to capture the importance of instructional match for Mr. Sabins and that a simple post-test measurement would not suffice. I encourage you to think about what your consultee, not only your client, needs in regards to data collection and intervention evaluation.

Furthermore, supervision was initially a confusing hour for me! I was unsure of what to expect each session, what to talk about, and what questions to ask. As the relationship with my supervisor progressed, though, it became clearer to me. I also began to take more ownership over my learning and the process by spending time transcribing my sessions, labeling the communication skills that I used, and thinking about where and how additional communication skills could have been helpful. This not only saved us time to talk about more conceptual or complex issues rather than repeating what I already reflected upon, but it also allowed my supervisor to get to know me better and to better understand where in the learning process I was. I sent my supervisor my notes and transcriptions several days before our scheduled supervision, so that she could also be prepared for the session. In the end, we found a way to make our supervision sessions as efficient, productive, and worthwhile as they could be, which is extremely important in the busy schedule of a graduate student or early-career psychologist!

Lastly, for future consultants and school psychologists, this case is promising in that it can increase confidence in collaborative efforts. Consultants can feel more assured that placing effort and time into consultation activities is successful and worthwhile for teacher and students. Hopefully, as more research is conducted on consultation, more psychologists will shift their focus to classroom-based interventions rather than referring students to specialists, especially if there is a lack of coordination between them and the classroom teachers, thus causing students to lose instructional time and violate their working memory.

Questions for Reflection

1. **Do you think the consultee may have felt overwhelmed by collecting data on all the students receiving the intervention? If so, what might the consultant have done?**
2. **Assuring that the outcome measure is related to the concern being addressed has been found to be a problem for many consultants. With what issues of measurement of outcomes have you struggled in your consultation experiences?**

References

Gickling, E.E., & Armstrong, D.L. (1978). Levels of instructional difficulty as related to on-task behavior, task completion, and comprehension. *Journal of Learning Disabilities, 11*, 559–566.

Gravois, T.A., & Gickling, E.E. (2008). Best practices in instructional assessment. In A. Thomas & J. Grimes (Eds.). *Best practices in school psychology V* (pp. 503–518). Washington, DC: National Association of School Psychologists.

Gravois, T.A., Gickling, E.E., & Rosenfield, S. (2007). *IC teams: Training in instructional consultation, assessment, and teaming*. Books 1 & 2. Catonsville, MD: ICAT Publishing.

Lambert, N.M. (2004). Consultee-centered consultation: An international perspective on goals, process, and theory. In N.M Lambert, I. Hylander, & J.H. Sandoval (Eds.). *Consultee-centered consultation: Improving the quality of professional services in schools and community organizations* (pp. 3–20). Mahwah, NJ: Lawrence Erlbaum Associates.

Rosenfield, S.A. (1987). *Instructional consultation*. Hillsdale, NJ: Lawrence Erlbaum Associates.

Rosenfield, S. (2004). Consultation as dialogue: The right words at the right time. In N. Lambert, I. Hylander, & J. Sandoval (Eds.). *Consultee-Centered Consultation:*

Improving the quality of professional services in schools and community organizations (pp. 337–347). Hillsdale, NJ: Lawrence Erlbaum Associates.

Rosenfield, S. (2008). Instructional consultation and instructional consultation teams. In A. Thomas & J. Grimes (Eds.). *Best practices in school psychology V* (pp. 1645–1660). Washington, DC: National Association of School Psychologists.

Rosenfield, S., & Gravois, T.A. (1996). *Instructional consultation teams: Collaborating for change*. New York: Guilford Press.

8
Improving an English Language Learner Client's Comprehension through Consultee-Centered Consultation

Laura Schussler

Advance Organizer Questions

- **Consider how the consultation process is affected when the client is an English Language Learner and the related challenges that might arise as a new consultant.**
- **In the framework of the problem-solving process, think about the advantages and challenges associated with having two consultees for one client's case.**

School Culture

While completing my consultation practicum, I worked in an elementary school in a suburban area. As I became better acquainted with the school, I discovered that several aspects of the school culture were relevant to and affected the consultation process as I worked with teachers.

Collaboration

Collaboration and the Instructional Consultation (IC) process became engrained into the school's culture over four years of implementation of IC. The school's mission, which was posted boldly in the front lobby, stated, "Teachers, administrators, and parents work collaboratively to ensure student success." I found it significant that the school explicitly included collaboration in their mission statement, and I viewed it as an early indicator that it was an integral part of the school's culture. It is important to have shared norms and values in a school among school faculty and parents (Vescio, Ross, & Adams, 2008). If there are shared values and norms regarding the importance of collaboration, one would expect that the school found forms of formal collaboration, such as the IC team, to be an effective use of their time.

IC Team and the IC Team Facilitator

Using a team model to collaborate and discuss student improvement ideas obtains positive effects for schools (Goddard, Goddard, & Tschannen-Moran,

2007). The team model of IC had expanded in this school over the course of just a few years and the team's size had increased as more teachers became interested in the process and eventually joined the team.

The team facilitator was a key reason for the success of the IC team in the school. She made sure that new team members were well trained, and served as a strong source of support for them as they took their first cases or learned new concepts. For instance, she provided coaching for new case managers as they worked through their first cases as novice consultants. The team facilitator set the bar high for her team and took care to ensure that team members received ongoing professional development throughout the year to keep their skills honed. She offered pragmatic assistance whenever she could, including offering to cover classes for case managers and referring teachers who needed to meet. This was highly valued as time is a critical resource in all schools.

Also, the facilitator helped make IC engaging and interesting to her team and other teachers in the school, as she often brought food to IC meetings or offered small tokens in her office to attract school staff to her room. In her room and hallway, there were several large and colorful displays that described the IC process. Anyone who walked by or entered her room was immediately exposed to the message of collaboration or a colorful flow-chart outlining the problem-solving process. Moreover, the facilitator was genuinely appreciative of the team members' hard work, and often let them know that they were valued each week by explicitly saying it through e-mails or during meetings.

Nature of Collaboration in the School

All of the aforementioned aspects of school culture impacted my experience as a case manager, while other school culture factors impacted the consultees with whom I worked. School culture often takes on variations of two forms: collaborative or individualistic (Fullan & Hargreaves, 1996). Individualistic, or balkanized, school cultures foster teacher isolation and educational conservatism, while collaborative school culture creates interdependence and encourages joint work to improve student academic achievement (Fullan & Hargreaves, 1996). Collaboration falls on a continuum, moving away from balkanization as it moves toward an interactive professionalism that encourages risk-taking, reflection, continuous growth and professional development, and collaboration to improve student achievement (Fullan & Hargreaves, 1996).

Through several observations in different classrooms throughout my practicum placement, I discovered that the school fell on the interactive professionalism end of the spectrum and such collaboration was clearly encouraged by the administration. Teachers met often to schedule activities or plan field trips, yet they also discussed lesson plans and provided feedback to each other about what works well and what does not when teaching the state standards required for the state assessments. Teachers tended to meet most often with other grade-level teachers. They occasionally met with special education or English as a Second or Other Language (ESOL) teachers who taught their students, but it was not common or regularly scheduled.

According to Vescio et al. (2008), there are positive effects of having a professional learning community (PLC) present in schools. In a PLC, interactive professionalism is evident as teachers collectively generate new ideas for practice, especially when problems arise. Also, teachers in collaborative schools with PLCs more often engage in personal reflective dialogue about instruction and then share their reflections with colleagues (Vescio et al., 2008). Lipman (1997) observed that the collaborative process in schools helped teachers gain a better understanding of a student's problems, often leading to the teachers taking extra measures to prevent student failure. Such collaboration seemed to be present in this school, as approximately 60% of the teachers in the school referred cases to the IC team during the 2008–2009 school year. The majority of the school's teachers chose to become part of a PLC through the IC team, which provides continuous professional development and places value on teacher learning and reflection.

Diversity

Another factor that strongly impacted the school's culture was the diversity of its students: 27% of the students were enrolled in the ESOL program, and 34% were considered economically disadvantaged by the county's public school system office of accountability standards for that academic year; 59% of students identified their race as non-White, and Hispanics made up the majority with 28% of students. While the student body was quite diverse, 81% of teachers at the school identified as non-Hispanic White, and 96% of the teachers were female.

Such homogeneity in the teachers when compared to the diversity of the students had a number of effects on the school culture. Many teachers discussed their efforts to take certification or continuing education credits in teaching English Language Learners (ELLs), while some made comments about the difficulty of having "too many" ESOL students in their classroom. One teacher expressed that her school year was especially busy and difficult because of the high number of ESOL students in her class and she viewed it as a heavy burden.

English Language Learners

The ESOL program at this school was generally structured so that students were pulled from their general education classrooms to receive ESOL instruction once a day for about an hour. ESOL teachers had their own separate state standards that students are expected to reach, which did not overlap with the general education state standards. Some ESOL students were exempt entirely from the general education state standards (usually in reading) and were only expected to meet the ESOL standards. This occurred on a case-by-case basis.

During an ESOL classroom observation, it became clear that the class time was not always used as productively as anticipated, given the wide range of students' English proficiency. For instance, one student moved to the United States from a Middle Eastern country in September and knew very little English. This student was placed in the same ESOL reading group as Bao, the client in this case, who was born in the United States and has lived here his entire life. This demonstrates the breadth of language development that made up each ESOL class, as students tend to be categorized in ESOL classes only by grade. Such a wide range in English proficiency within one class created a daunting task for the teacher who must try to effectively teach all students in the class.

Additionally, there was an apparent disconnect between the general education teachers and ESOL teachers, especially in the fifth grade. Teachers appeared to have limited insight into how the ESOL classrooms functioned and what objectives were being met. Classroom teachers also had the impression that the ESOL teachers were too busy helping their students reach the ESOL state standards to be able to help students reach the general education state standards. Therefore, classroom teachers felt that collaborating with the ESOL teachers would be difficult due to time constraints and differences in goals.

Identifying the Consultant and Consultee

Consultant

As a consultant, it is important to recognize how one influences the IC process and collaborative working relationship. As a White Caucasian female born and raised in the United States, I was part of the racial and ethnic majority of teachers at the school. During this case, I was a second-year school psychology doctoral student with some related experience in behavior modification, single-subject research design, and academic assessment. This case was part of my training in school-based consultation with a focus on instructional consultation in a two-semester course that included practicum experience. This was my second case as a consultant. My first case closed during the problem identification stage, meaning that my prior experience was limited. Also, I received weekly supervision from a professor who is an expert in school-based consultation and has much experience supervising consultation practicum students.

Consultee

The consultee in this case, Ms. Parker, was a White Caucasian female. Ms. Parker was an experienced fifth-grade teacher who taught at the school for a few years (the exact number is unknown). She referred students to the IC team at least twice, though she had never served as a member of the team. As a result, Ms. Parker seemed somewhat familiar and comfortable with the IC process.

Client

The client in this case, Bao, was a Chinese male fifth grader who was born and raised in the United States. His family spoke mostly Chinese at home and his parents had a very limited understanding of English. A Chinese interpreter was used during recent meetings between the school and the parents. Bao switched schools from another local elementary school the previous year, during the fourth grade. He had been in the ESOL program for a few years and spoke English clearly in the classroom and with his peers. His social class was not made clear by the teacher.

The Consultation Relationship

Establishing the collaborative relationship affects the process from the problem-solving stages of contracting through closure (Rosenfield, 1987). The working relationship should have a mutual power of influence, rather than being unidirectional, and have an egalitarian and trusting nature (Rosenfield, 1987). Also, empathy, respect, and genuineness should be present from both the consultant and consultee, and open, honest communication is vital to facilitate an effective intervention that satisfies the consultee (Rosenfield, 1987). Reflecting back on the case, there were many struggles between the consultee and myself. It seems that the bulk of my work in this case went toward keeping our working relationship strong, and it was always a point of extra concern for me during supervision and while reflecting on my case logs.

Rosenfield (1987) stated that one problem for instructional consultants is that teachers may not refer their concerns for assistance until they are already in crisis and the concern is difficult to manage, therefore making it more unlikely for the teacher to believe that the concern can be resolved in her own classroom. This was especially true for Ms. Parker who was ready to refer Bao to the special education referral team, known as the "Child Study team," because she saw his problems as too serious for her to handle in her classroom. She requested assistance from the IC team because the Child Study team required prerequisite data that she did not have in order to make a special education referral, and Ms. Parker felt that such data could be obtained from the IC process. She told me this early in the process, which immediately affected our working relationship. I often felt that she was only engaging in the process in order to obtain such data and not because she voluntarily wished to engage in problem solving. This was consistently on my mind as we worked together and sometimes made it difficult for me to remain genuine and trusting of her reasons for the IC referral.

Rosenfield (1987) asserted that it is important to focus on being explicit about one's own belief systems as a consultant, as well as understanding and respecting those of the consultee throughout the process. This posed another challenge to our working relationship because Ms. Parker saw Bao as a student who could not understand anything he read or heard, and she attributed it to an internal child deficit, such as a processing or memory problem. On the other hand, I saw Bao as an ELL who had trouble comprehending what he read because of language differences. The teacher's belief systems are clear in this excerpt:

> *Ms. Parker*: I'm hoping to further identify that it's more than language … I filled out the Child Study form and it sounds like it's language, but it's more than that. I think it's a processing issue. So I am hoping that going through this process, that will give me further evidence that it's not an ESOL issue, that it's something more, so that will help me progress with the Child Study [process].

Ms. Parker also believed in a family-model causation and that Bao's family "babied" him too much. She told me that she saw Bao and his family at a school open house and his mother and sisters "were helping him with everything," and "treated him like a baby." She felt that they helped him too much with his homework and that it was better than the work he did in class. As the consultant, it was important for me to remind Ms. Parker that while those factors are important to consider, they were out of our control. It was important to remain focused on the factors that we had control over—those related to instruction in the classroom (Rosenfield, 1987). As a novice consultant, being directive in this way was especially difficult for me and even more so with a veteran teacher. Also, I pointed out some general cultural differences to the teacher, which I thought about based on previous coursework and discussed during supervision. In this instance, I provided information to Ms. Parker that Eastern cultures, such as the Chinese culture, tend to be collective and reliant on the group or family, as compared to Western cultures that tend to value independence and self-reliance.

The importance of teacher–student relationships and how they affect performance in the classroom when the relationship is strained also came through in this case (Hamre & Pianta, 2006). Ms. Parker was obviously frustrated with Bao's achievement in the classroom and began to feel there was no hope for him to improve. She saw him daydreaming and staring at the clock and viewed working with him separately as a waste of time because he never improved. Similarly, Bao seemed to dislike and be afraid of Ms. Parker, which I observed when I worked with both of them together during the reading Instructional Assessments (IA; Gravois & Gickling, 2008). Bao seemed more timid and quiet in her presence, and lacked self-confidence when working with Ms. Parker compared to working with me. She would often say discouraging comments with an annoyed tone, such as, "Bao we've gone over that word a million times."

As the consultant, it was difficult for me to understand the consultee's perspective and understand her frustration in seeing him fail daily. It helped our progress and working relationship for me to come into the classroom and see Bao with a fresh perspective. When I worked with Bao during the IAs, I was less quick to become frustrated and had more patience compared to Ms. Parker, allowing us to better problem-solve. I helped Ms. Parker to see Bao through a different lens.

Communication Skills

The communication skill of clarifying was vital to our working relationship, as Ms. Parker tended to use high-inference and pejorative terms to describe the student's behavior. This is demonstrated in the following dialogue during the problem identification stage:

> *Ms. Parker*: It's like he has the information but it gets all jumbled up, and so he just pulls what he thinks belongs to that but it's actually from something else he's learned, but it's like it's all jumbled.
>
> *Consultant*: Tell me more about what you mean by "jumbled."

When encountering differences in belief systems, it was important to use the communication skill of bond and move. Bond and move incorporates finding a way to acknowledge the teacher's comment ("bonding") before challenging the teacher's thinking ("moving"), which helps keep the working relationship strong as shown in this dialogue:

> *Ms. Parker*: I don't think it's a language issue because he was born in the U.S., his family speaks Chinese at home and his first language is Chinese, but he speaks English all the time except at home ... It's all women and he's the only boy. They baby him. They help him with his homework.
>
> *Consultant*: How great that his family cares about him so much, but you're finding he doesn't use the strategies himself in the classroom.
>
> *Ms. Parker*: What's interesting to me is that I've been saying all along. I don't think it's language, I don't think it's language. Now, hearing him more, I think his Chinese background *is* affecting his progress in some way. I think he's learned how to read English words and how to speak English, but he hasn't gotten any further than that.
>
> *Consultant*: Yeah, so what you're saying is before you weren't sure if Chinese as his first language was affecting his reading, but after seeing that he's not really getting the meaning of words, you think it could be.
>
> *Ms. Parker*: He knows how to say words ... but I may have absolutely no idea what it means just because I'm saying the words. And I have to say, I'm thinking about him differently suddenly. There are days when he does really well. And now I'm not sure if it's because he has a strategy for it or it's clear in his mind.

As a consultant, I showed Ms. Parker that I understood what she was saying, but then moved forward in a respectful manner to help her see that language, working memory, and repetition were contributing to the problem more than she acknowledged.

Due to Ms. Parker's many frustrations with the lack of ESOL support and the stress of the state testing, perception checking was often vital to our working relationship. The following dialogue provides an example of this:

Ms. Parker: It's been a bad year for ESOL.

Consultant: Tell me more about what you mean.

Ms. Parker: I just think there hasn't been enough support in the classroom, and the [ESOL state standard requirements] have been difficult to do. It hasn't come together very well.

Consultant: I can tell you're frustrated by that because there's little connection between them and your classroom.

Ms. Parker: Yes, there's no connection at all. The reading groups, and he misses our daily review in the afternoon ... I told [Mrs. Johnston, the ESOL teacher] next year they should not be called out twice a day and once during review ... It's time out of the classroom when we're doing something important.

It's clear that the stress from pressure to reach state standards often came through in our case. Again, this dialogue reflects the disconnect between the ESOL specialist and classroom teacher, and how much the child missed by being out of the classroom in a setting that did not provide him the instruction that he needed to reach the general education state standards.

Problem-Solving Stages

Contracting

The IC team received the voluntary request for assistance in January and the case was assigned to me as case manager. The teacher's request read: "Bao: student does not comprehend much of what is taught orally or what is read. Bao is an ESOL student but Mrs. Johnston [the ESOL teacher] and myself feel that it is not because of his language that he does not comprehend."

I contacted the teacher and met with her to begin the IC process with contracting. As a novice, I felt most nervous and unsure of myself during this stage of the process because I was unfamiliar with the teacher and I felt like I was telling her what she already knew. Because this was only my second time contracting with a consultee, I felt nervous going into the session.

I was told that Mrs. Johnston would also be joining us and that she would be late to the session, so I began contracting with Ms. Parker. I started by informing her of the purpose of IC and the stages of the problem-solving process. Because she had already referred a case, I felt as if I was boring her and rushed through it quickly. I discussed the collaborative, confidential, non-evaluative nature of the process and that we would be collecting data together. We also discussed the concept of instructional match and the fact that some interventions may be applicable to other students in her classroom. She nodded her head often and seemed like she already knew everything I was saying to her. I did ask about her expectations for the process and she told me her specific concerns with Bao. I later realized that I could have better worded the question to avoid moving into the problem identification stage by saying something like, "Tell me about your previous experiences with the IC team and how you hope this goes for you," or, "How do you expect this process to go?" Ms. Parker had previously referred to the IC team, so contracting would have been more effectively done if I had asked her about her understanding of the process, her previous experiences with the team, what she liked and disliked about the process, and what she found especially helpful.

At this point, Mrs. Johnston entered the room and joined the meeting. This was difficult because I was unsure whether to restart contracting again or to move forward in the interest of Ms. Parker's time. I decided to rush through what we had discussed with little explanation of each stage of the process and then moved forward after gaining agreement from both of them. I found that working with two consultees posed a challenge because I had to take extra care to keep both consultees on the "same page" and equally informed about the process. I experienced this in a difficult and awkward manner during contracting.

Problem Identification

After contracting, I found that both consultees were eager to vent about the student due to their shared frustration, but not necessarily ready to problem-solve. Simply verbalizing the problem seemed to be cathartic for both of them and a release of pent-up frustration. Both consultees fed off each other and it became overwhelming for me. They seemed to think that because the other teacher agreed about their concerns, it must be true. Together they created a shared reality because their subjective experiences were validated by each other, so they were perceived then as objective and true (Higgins, 1999).

I thought that it was important to them to vent, though I soon realized that it ran the risk of the consultees believing the high-inference concerns even more than they already did. My communication skills were especially important here as much high-inference language was used in describing the problem, such as, "He has things jumbled in his head," "What I say to him might as well be 'gobbledegook,"' "I teach other ESOL students and he doesn't process things like they do," and, "He gets it today but not tomorrow." It was important to slow the consultees down while venting their frustrations because they were becoming emotional, and to help them to clarify their concerns into observable terms. For instance, using clarifications, such as "Tell me more about how he seems to understand something one day but not the next," helped bring to light the importance of working memory and repetition for this student. Also, as a new consultant who felt overwhelmed by the two veteran teachers venting, I often found myself head-nodding or saying "mmm-hmm" as the consultees spoke, which created another inadvertent shared reality. This was brought to my attention during supervision and as I listened to my tapes of the session.

Through the process of clarifying the concerns, the consultees continuously mentioned Bao's difficulties during reading, social studies, and science. Together, we realized that the student had trouble specifically while reading text in each of the three classes. We specified that Bao had trouble "pulling from the text" and could not comprehend much of what he read in ESOL reading, social studies, and science. Later, Ms. Parker also mentioned that Bao had trouble in math class with "problems that are not straight-forward." She mentioned that he especially had trouble with fractions and word problems. We agreed to conduct a reading IA together during our next session.

During the first IA, we used a non-fiction, unfamiliar, peer-expected text, which was a biography of Daniel Boone from Bao's social studies book. Bao easily read every word in the passage, yet it was apparent that he did not understand their meaning and he was unable to answer most comprehension questions. After the IA, Mrs. Johnston and Ms. Parker seemed frustrated that he performed so poorly and said, "See, he just doesn't get it." It was important at this point to conduct another IA and make an instructional match that would allow the consultees to see what Bao *can* do instead of perpetuating their negative view of him. Therefore, we conducted two more IAs using non-fiction, unfamiliar, peer-expected social studies and science texts. These IAs became challenging because it was difficult to find an instructional match when Bao could read almost every word in the passage, yet it was obvious that he did not comprehend it.

The consultees and I began to make the connection that Bao did not understand many of the content words in the text, such as *tropical*, *disaster*, *peninsula*, *settlement*, and *Jamestown*, and that they were directly related to how well he responded to and comprehended the text. We began to minimize the amount of text that Bao read and defined the words for him in order to achieve the instructional match. During one IA, we used only two sentences and, in turn, saw an improvement in Bao's responding when the meanings of the words were clarified.

Next, I conducted an observation of Bao's ESOL class because Ms. Parker and I realized together that she had a limited understanding of how the reading classes were conducted for ESOL students. Looking back, perhaps observing along with Ms. Parker would have been more beneficial, though as a new consultant I was nervous to ask Ms. Parker to do more than she was already. Ms. Parker strongly believed that an intervention should be implemented in the ESOL classroom rather than her own.

I observed in the ESOL classroom that Bao seemed more advanced compared to his peers during a group-read of a narrative fiction text and he seemed extremely bored. The class took turns reading sentences of a passage aloud and then the class period ended. Little comprehension and word meaning work was done in the ESOL classroom, which was important to note, as they were the consultees' main concerns. I brought this information back to Ms. Parker and pointed out that what Bao was learning in his ESOL reading class was very different from her social studies and science classes that she taught. We discussed the fact that the results from an intervention in the ESOL classroom would unlikely generalize to her classroom for science and social studies. She agreed and stated that she would be willing to focus more on the social studies and science concerns in her classroom.

At this point, Mrs. Johnston rarely attended our sessions, and if she did, she stayed for only a short time. I brought up this concern with Ms. Parker and she replied that Mrs. Johnston expressed that she no longer wished to remain a primary consultee on the case because she was working on another IC case as a consultee and felt overwhelmed. Here, it was important to discuss with Ms. Parker how she wished to proceed by revisiting the contracting stage. Ms. Parker decided that she wished to continue with the process and she agreed to keep Mrs. Johnston informed periodically of our progress in the case. In hindsight, this presented an interesting dilemma because the ESOL class was not helpful to the student, but with Mrs. Johnston gone, there was less chance to address this. Also, thinking back on the case, it would have been ideal to officially close with Mrs. Johnston.

We decided to prioritize our concerns and focus on word meaning and comprehension in social studies. We hypothesized that increasing the student's understanding of word meaning would in turn improve his responding and comprehension. We continued to move forward in the process and did a trial-teaching session together with an unfamiliar, non-fiction, peer-expected text from Bao's social studies unit.

We chose to test a word search strategy followed by word maps. The word search is a similar strategy to the one used during the IA process and asks the student to point to words that he does not know how to read or does not understand the meaning. Before starting, it is important to explain and distinguish the difference between known and unknown words with the student. To clarify this, we decided to categorize the known and unknown words into three categories: "See, But Can't Say," "Say, But Don't Know What It Means," and "Proud Words! Know How to Say *and* What it Means" (see Appendix A).

After identifying the list of words during the word search, we used the words in the "Say, But Don't Know What It Means" column to make word maps for each one (see Appendix B). A word map is a common intervention used to improve student's vocabulary and works especially well with content words such as those in social studies and science (Schwartz & Raphael, 1985). The maps provide a clear visual breakdown of the definition of a word for students often making it easier to understand complex meanings.

In the trial-teaching passage, we used only one sentence because it contained many advanced content words. The sentence read: "The economy in the northern part of the United States was industrialized, while in the southern part it was agricultural and relied on slave labor." Bao read each word and I asked him to conduct his own word search using the table. He pointed to the words *agricultural*, *economy*, and *industrialized* as those he could say but did not know the meanings. We used these three words for the word map portion of trial teaching. Together, the student and I discussed the questions, "What is it?" "What is it like?" and "What are some examples?" as outlined on the word map worksheet. We went through each of the three words in great detail, following this format as the student wrote the information on the word maps. After reviewing the meaning a few more times for the purpose of repetition, we re-read the original sentence from the passage once more and discussed the meaning of the sentence as a whole. Bao clearly had a strong grasp of the meaning of the complex sentence and it was exciting to see that the intervention used for trial teaching had, in fact, worked.

At the end of our trial-teaching session, the consultee did not hear Bao read the whole sentence again and discuss his new understanding of its meaning because she left to pick up her class from another classroom. When she returned, she told me, "See, he just doesn't get it." She said, "That was just scary, and I put him up for Child Study again because he's just not getting it." She expressed her disbelief that Bao still did not know the meaning of the words *agriculture* and *industrialized* because they had reviewed them multiple times as a class since the beginning of the school year. The importance of having the teacher observe the entire IA process, recommended by Gickling and Gravois (2008), became even clearer to me.

With her class back in the room, we had run out of time to discuss this more, so we agreed to discuss her thoughts during our next session. I was disheartened and disappointed because I felt that I saw improvement and success, while Ms. Parker still saw failure and was compelled to refer him to the Child Study team again. I felt that I had failed at some point. I knew the consultee had at least been considering the special education referral because of her previous referral that was rejected by the Child Study team due to lack of data, but I expected her to give the IC process more of a chance. It was again clear that she hoped the IC process would provide her with such data that showed Bao failing.

When I came to Ms. Parker's classroom for our next session, I was shocked when she greeted me right away with, "I've actually seen a change in him." Initially, I came to our session quite nervous because I felt that based on her last comments she would want to close the case. I was also apprehensive because I feared she would still be frustrated, causing a strain on our relationship as I was beginning to see Bao as successful. Here, the teacher experienced a clear turning (Hylander, 2004) by expressing that she had seen a change in him in her classroom. She found that since our trial teaching, Bao seemed to pay more attention in class and remembered the meanings of the three words that we dissected on the word map while doing a class exercise. She saw him in a different light and wished to go forward using the same intervention in her classroom.

Before we planned the intervention, we decided to plot baseline data using Bao's past social studies unit test scores. He received scores of 65% in January, 53% in February, and 20% in March, which showed a clear downward trend. Ms. Parker and I set goals with a score of 70% as our short-term goal (three weeks), 75% as our interim goal (six weeks), and 80% as our long-term goal (10 weeks).

Intervention Planning

The teacher and I designed the intervention based on the trial-teaching results. Together we drafted a script of the intervention and the details of how it would be implemented in her classroom (see Appendix C). We decided that each Monday, Ms. Parker would conduct a word search of words that Bao would likely need help with during the social studies lessons that week. We decided to limit it to three to four content words, due to working memory limits. Ms. Parker would take about 20 minutes to review and outline each word using the word map. She decided to do this with Bao and one other student who was an ELL whom she thought could also benefit. On Tuesday or Wednesday (depending when "Core Extension" was scheduled, which was a time used for catching-up on weekly assignments), Bao would transfer the words from the word map onto small index cards on a binder ring. He would follow a basic pocket words intervention procedure and write the word on the front of the card, and the meaning, examples, and a small visual on the back of the card. Transferring the word map to pocket words during Core Extension time was Ms. Parker's idea, since she had previously used the pocket words intervention with another IC case. I liked this idea as well, especially because it provided even more repetition for Bao.

Throughout the rest of the week, Bao would review his pocket cards multiple times a day on his own and Ms. Parker could prompt him as needed. I reiterated the importance of repetition in assisting Bao learn such complex meanings of words. On Friday, Bao would review his pocket cards again with a partner, who was either a more advanced student or the other student who was also participating in the intervention with Bao. Ms. Parker made it clear that Bao could come to her at any time with a word that he did not understand and they would fill out a word map together.

On Monday, they would use the word search to find three to four new words and repeat the same procedure. I made a copy of the script so that we both had one to reference, and I left copies of the word map worksheet in her mailbox so she could start at the beginning of the next week. She confirmed that she felt comfortable with our design and seemed ready to begin.

Intervention Implementation

The intervention was implemented for about a week before we met again, and Ms. Parker seemed delighted that the intervention went smoothly and appeared helpful for Bao. She followed the script very closely and kept it on her desk to refer to often. She told me that in the past week she made a "word wall" for the entire classroom that displayed all of the words the class had a question about and reviewed them together as a group. She found that Bao was not the only student in her class having difficulty with such complex words, and most of her students (both native English speakers and ELLs) could benefit from more time and focus spent on word meanings in the classroom.

During this meeting, we decided to re-design a few minor parts of our intervention design. She found that the original word map which asked the two questions, "What is it like?" and "What are some examples?" were too similar and difficult for her to describe differently. She decided that it would be easier and more beneficial to combine these two questions and also make room for a visual representation of the word to be drawn. Additionally, she found that the boxes on the word map worksheet were too small for the students to write in, so we decided that I would make a new version of the word map (see Appendix B) for her to use beginning the next week.

Evaluation

Over the next three sessions, the consultee and I met to check-in with each other, and examine and plot data after each social studies unit test was completed. On April 17, Bao received a score of 56%, an improvement from his most recent score of 20%.

At the beginning of our next session on April 30, Ms. Parker was frustrated because Bao did not do well on his last unit test with a score of 53%. She felt concerned because she "really pushed him" and felt that he received a high amount of repetition. She also allowed him to go back and re-take the unit test because she could see that he did not do well the first time. She also told me that it seems unlikely Bao would receive services through the Child Study team, and she seemed to realize that IC was her best option for helping him now.

I recognized her frustration and asked if she wanted to change the intervention in some way. She said she felt that the intervention had been helpful, but she wished she could have started it earlier in the year. She continued to tell me that she felt a lot of pressure right now due to the fast-approaching state testing. Ms. Parker was clearly overwhelmed and stressed during this meeting.

Ms. Parker expressed that she hoped Bao could use this intervention next year, starting right away, and that both his regular classroom teacher and ESOL teacher would use the intervention with him. She told me that she felt ESOL was not supportive to Bao or her in the classroom this past year and hoped that he would be pulled out of the classroom less next year. Ms. Parker continually emphasized that she still felt this was a good intervention and that it had helped

Bao, but it was apparent that she was still frustrated. She said, "It's just disappointing," and that the other student receiving the intervention seemed to be improving faster than Bao, though the student began with higher unit test grades than Bao. Here, it was important as the consultant to remain optimistic and use the communication skill of "bond and move." I had to recognize her frustrations yet make it clear that the intervention had only been implemented for a few weeks and Bao may still show improvement. Also, Ms. Parker expressed a number of times that she hoped to use this intervention next year with her new class, especially her ESOL students, because she found it so helpful for her other students.

Closure

The next week, Ms. Parker requested to cancel our meeting because she felt so overwhelmed with the upcoming state testing. I sensed that she was ready to close the case because of the stress she showed during our previous meeting. I asked her if she was ready to close and she agreed. We quickly reviewed the case because I could tell she was stressed out and in a rush. We spent a few minutes reviewing the Student Documentation Form (SDF) on which we plotted our data and tracked our sessions together. The form helped me to efficiently summarize what we had done in each stage of the process.

Then, I asked Ms. Parker for personal feedback and feedback regarding how the process went for her. She was honest and told me that she found the strategies and IAs helpful, but she wished that she had started it earlier in the school year, had more support from the ESOL teacher, and that she still saw the difficulties Bao was having. The IAs allowed her to see the problems that she saw in her classroom in observable and measurable terms. She knew Bao was not "getting it" but she did not know why or in what way. She hoped that the ESOL teacher would be more willing to collaborate for strategies in the future.

She also planned to tell Bao's next teacher that this strategy worked for him and she hoped that his teacher would use it with him from the start of the year. I thanked her for her patience and for working with me as a new consultant and we closed the case. Over the course of the process, Ms. Parker and I met in her classroom for 14 sessions once a week that usually lasted between 15 and 30 minutes each.

Lessons Learned

Hylander (2004) states that a successful consultation process ends with a different representation of the problem compared to how the consultee first viewed it. This conceptual shift in representation, known as a "turning," was apparent in Ms. Parker by the end of our work together (Hylander, 2004). We started in what Hylander calls a "tug of war" in which both the consultant and consultee have different mental representations and verbal presentations of the concern. Ms. Parker saw the problem as unrelated to language and attributed it to memory and processing, whereas I saw the problem related to language, working memory, and repetition. The consultee was quite pessimistic about Bao's chances of improvement and was waiting to send Bao to the Child Study team.

Again, using bond and move was vital to our relationship in this respect, and I feel that it was one of the main contributors to the teacher's eventual turning. It would have been easy to lose the consultee in the process if I never acknowledged that I heard her thoughts and frustrations, yet guided her to see some other issues underlying the problem. The turning came after the trial-teaching took place, when Ms. Parker told me that she saw a difference in Bao and wanted to try the intervention we used during trial-teaching in her classroom. She was forthright about her disappointments with Bao throughout the process and the turning came as quite a surprise to me. I entered that session expecting to close the case because she wanted to go forward with the Child Study referral. However, this unexpected turning allowed us to make some progress with Bao and allowed her to change some of her practices in the classroom, such as encouraging more repetition and not overloading working memory. Further evidence of a clear turning is implied because Ms. Parker explicitly wrote that the concern was not related to language on the IC request for assistance form. Yet, by the end of the process she recognized that her concerns with Bao were related to his language and ESOL instruction.

Though the client did not experience measurable change on his unit tests, the measure we had selected for evaluation, he did experience some improvement and clearly exhibited an enhanced sense of self-confidence compared to when I first worked with him during the IAs. Most importantly, the teacher saw him as a student struggling as an ELL, rather than a student who needed special education due to processing and memory problems.

As a consultant, I also experienced positive outcomes. My communication skills improved as I furthered my paraphrasing, summarizing, perception checking, and clarifying skills. Toward the middle and end of the process, I had more difficulty using paraphrasing skills. However, this was pointed out in supervision and I worked to improve this skill. The meetings with the consultee became shorter in duration during the intervention implementation and evaluation stages making it especially important that I used communication skills as effectively as possible.

Also, I learned the new communication skill of bond and move during supervision, which was difficult for me to use during sessions. I practiced this skill repeatedly in supervision because I found that I often moved forward in the process without bonding and recognizing the teacher's thoughts and feelings first. I feared that if I recognized what the consultee said, I would give the impression that I agreed and it would further solidify her thoughts. However, I learned that I could still recognize the consultee's thoughts, though I sometimes reframed them more positively. This kept our working relationship strong, yet also moved us forward to help the teacher see the concerns in a different way and keep the focus on instructional practices in the classroom.

Second, I learned a great deal about quality instruction for ELLs. I had little prior experience in this regard, so I value what I learned through readings on effective interventions for ELLs, ESOL instruction, and literacy development for second language learners (August & Shanahan, 2006; Gersten et al., 2007). I learned how important repetition, working memory, and content vocabulary instruction is for ELLs. After reviewing the literature on vocabulary and comprehension interventions for ELLs, I gained new knowledge and information that I could impart to the consultee. For instance, I shared with Ms. Parker that word meaning and vocabulary interventions are commonly quite helpful for ELLs because they can often read most of the words in a passage, yet they may not know what they mean (Gersten et al., 2007). The word search allows students to separate words that they can read and know the meaning, from words that they can read and do not know the meaning, from words they can neither read nor know the meaning. The word map is also an effective strategy for ELLs because they tend to have difficulty with larger and more complex vocabulary words such as those in science and social studies (Gersten et al., 2007). It is important to distinguish between core and fringe vocabulary for ELLs. Core vocabulary makes up about 85% of our daily language, includes words that are frequently used and in a variety of situations (e.g., the, and, want), and is often developed first by ELLs (Baker, Hill, & Devylder, 2000). Fringe vocabulary, on the other hand, includes words that tend to be content or topic specific (e.g., slavery, museum, evaporate) and take more time for ELLs to develop (Baker et al., 2000). Fringe vocabulary words are those that need the most practice by ELLs.

We found this to be true for Bao, and the word map allowed him to break fringe vocabulary words down in a visual way. I also learned that pocket words are an effective strategy to couple with the word map because it allows the student to experience the repetition of the words that were mapped out. Simply mapping out the words with no repetition will have less positive outcomes than using it in conjunction with some method of repetition. Overall, sharing the knowledge learned through one's own literature review advances the case and helps the consultee to expand their understanding as well.

Moreover, I learned more about the school's ESOL program and the importance of collaboration between the general classroom and ESOL teachers. This is important in order to encourage congruence across settings and make transitions from the general education classroom to the ESOL classroom as effective as possible. I also gained a new (though limited) understanding of Chinese culture and the need to be aware of cultural differences when instructing and forming belief systems.

Finally, as a consultant I improved my skills in working with more than one consultee and especially the importance of contracting. Establishing guidelines for who will meet regularly and how to keep both consultees informed must be clearly detailed during contracting. When one consultee becomes less invested than the other, it is necessary to discuss how to proceed. In this case, we found that one consultee seemed more invested than the other, and it was important to emphasize that an intervention in one consultee's classroom may not generalize to the other's classroom. I found that working with two consultees is undoubtedly more difficult than working with one; however, keeping a strong working relationship with at least one of the consultees assists in making it more manageable.

It is clear that this case involved hard work and patience, both during and outside of sessions over many weeks. As a consultant, I highly valued this case because I learned such a breadth of skills ranging from the process itself to working with linguistically diverse clients. Despite some disappointment in not reaching our outlined goals for the student, there is still satisfaction to be had—most notably, the changes in the consultee and myself as the consultant.

Questions for Reflection

1. **Based on this case, what would you now consider in any teacher referral of an English Language Learner?**
2. **How might this school and teachers/staff benefit from professional development on issues related to English Language Learners? Should a school psychologist provide such opportunities?**
3. **What would you do as a new consultant when challenges arise in the working relationship with more than one consultee?**

References

August, D., & Shanahan, T. (Eds.). (2006). Developing literacy in second-language learners: Report of the national literacy panel on language-minority children and youth. Mahwah, NJ: Erlbaum. Executive Summary retrieved August 12, 2010 from www.cal.org/projects/archive/nlpreports/Executive_Summary.pdf.

Baker, B., Hill, K., & Devylder, R. (2000). Core vocabulary is the same across environments. Paper presented at a meeting of the Technology and Persons with Disabilities Conference at California State University, Northridge.

Fullan, M.G., & Hargreaves, A. (1996). Interactive professional guidelines for action. *What's worth fighting for in your school?* (pp. 37–107). Andover, MA: Regional Laboratory for Educational Improvement.

Gersten, R., Baker, S.K., Shanahan, T., Linan-Thompson, S.L., Collins, P., & Scarcella, R. (2007). *Effective literacy and English language instruction for English learners in the elementary grades: A practice guide* (NCEE 2007 4011). Washington, DC: National Center for Educational Evaluation and Regional Assistance. Institute of Education Sciences. U.S. Department of Education. Retrieved from http://ies.ed.gov/ncee.

Goddard, Y.L., Goddard, R.D., & Tschannen-Moran, M. (2007). A theoretical and empirical investigation of teacher collaboration for school improvement and student achievement in public elementary schools. *Teachers College Record, 109*, 877–896.

Gravois, T., & Gickling, E. (2008). Best practices in instructional assessment. In A. Thomas & J. Grimes (Eds.). *Best Practices in School Psychology V* (pp. 505–508). Bethesda, MD: National Association of School Psychologists.

Hamre, B.K., & Pianta, R.C. (2006). Student-teacher relationships. *Children's needs III: Development, prevention, and intervention* (pp. 59–71). Washington, DC: National Association of School Psychologists.

Higgins, E.T. (1999). "Saying is believing" effects: When sharing reality about something biases knowledge and evaluations. In L.L. Thompson, J.M. Levine, & D.M. Messick (Eds.). *Shared cognition in organizations: The management of knowledge* (pp. 33–48). Mahwah, NJ: Lawrence Erlbaum Associates.

Hylander, I. (2004). Analysis of conceptual change in consultee-centered consultation. In N.M. Lambert, I. Hylander, & J.H. Sandoval (Eds.). *Consultee-centered consultation* (pp. 45–61). Mahwah, NJ: Lawrence Erlbaum Associates.

Lipman, P. (1997). Restructuring in context: A case study of teacher participation and the dynamics of ideology, race and power. *American Educational Research Journal, 34*, 3–37.

Rosenfield, S. (1987). Establishing the collaborative relationship. *Instructional consultation* (pp. 21–33). Mahwah, NJ: Lawrence Erlbaum Associates.

Schwartz, R., & Raphael, T. (1985). Concept of definition: A key to improving students' vocabulary. *Reading Teacher, 39*, 198–205.

Vescio, V., Ross, D., & Adams, A. (2008). A review of research on the impact of professional learning communities on teaching practice and student learning. *Teaching and Teacher Education, 24*, 80–91.

APPENDIX A

Word Search Table

See, But Can't SAY	**Say, But Don't Know What it MEANS**	**PROUD Words! Know How to SAY *and* What it MEANS**

APPENDIX B

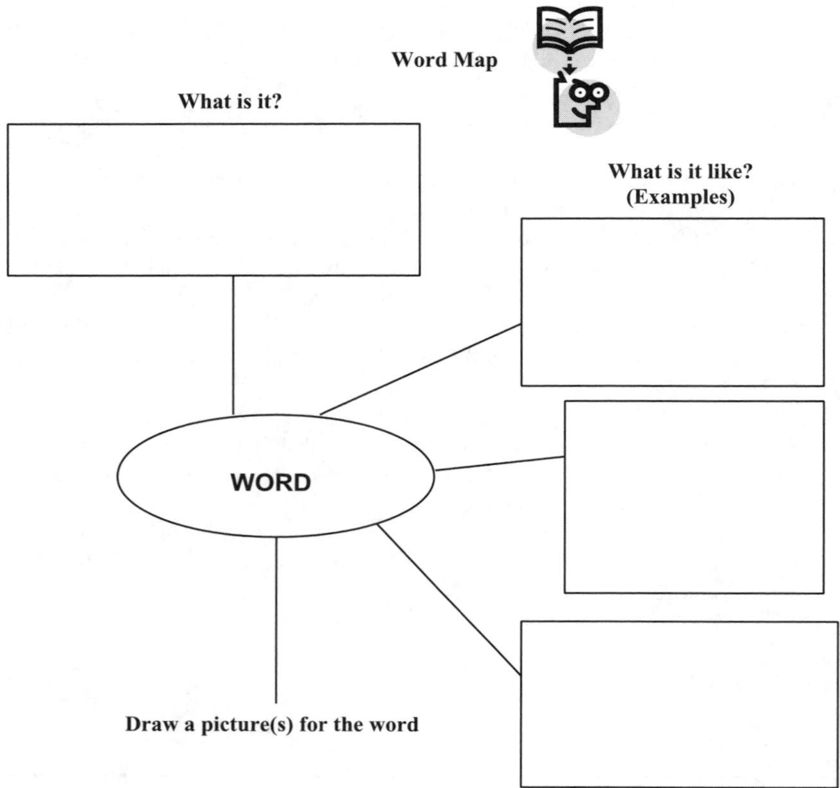

(Schwartz & Raphael, 1985)

APPENDIX C

Script for Ms. Parker

Monday

- Use word map with 3–4 words that you have picked from your own word search
- Remember working memory!

Tuesday or Wednesday

- Bao will transfer information from the word map onto index cards on a ring ("pocket cards") during his free time or Core Extension (may need prompting from you)

Remainder of Week

- Bao will review the cards on his own throughout the day, or you can prompt as needed
- Remember repetition!

Friday

- Bao will review pocket cards with you or a buddy again

Monday

- Repeat with new words
  - Bao can also word search his own words, and come to you to fill out a new word map together

Part IV
Consulting on a Class-wide Concern

Although teachers will sometimes enter the consultation process with a concern about a single student, the consultee-centered consultant is always open to the possibility of working at the class or school level, a more systemic approach to problem solving. In these two cases, there was the opportunity to work with the teacher on a classroom concern. Jill Berger worked through a teacher's concern around homework completion, helping the teacher to change her perspective and her actions. Megan Vaganek entered the consultation with concern about a single student being bullied and found a classroom bullying problem; an interesting aspect here is also the challenge of implementing an evidence-based practice in the classroom. Notice how loss of objectivity plays a role in both these cases as well.

9
Who Owns the Classroom Homework Problem?

Jill Berger

Advance Organizer Questions

- **How do you help consultees recognize their contribution to the "student problem" while still maintaining a supportive, working relationship?**
- **How do you effectively work with a teacher who has strong belief systems about students and classroom management practices that are contradictory to your own?**
- **As a consultee-centered consultant, how do you learn to prioritize helping the teacher develop new skills and competency, when this emphasis may put a direct intervention for struggling students on the backburner?**
- **How can you build opportunities for student engagement into your interventions?**

Culture of the School

My first experience with consultation practicum took place at a suburban elementary school serving approximately 500 students in pre-kindergarten through grade five. Since nearly 30% of the students were identified as disadvantaged, the school received Title I funding. As a result, there were many extra specialists and teaching aides in the school, making the student-to-teacher ratio less than 11 to 1. Pull-out services for students struggling academically were common, and teachers frequently relied on extra staff to assist with academic concerns in the classroom. A school-wide program for students with behavioral concerns was being implemented to provide daily check-ins and positive reinforcement for work completion and good behavior throughout the school day. A few students from each grade level were selected by teachers to receive extra support through this program.

The school had recently begun to implement a team consultation model designed to limit the number of special education referrals by providing assistance to teachers in the beginning stages of a student concern. Volunteer teachers and other school staff were trained to serve as case managers (i.e., consultants) to work with other teachers in the school who requested assistance.

In theory, the consultation team would meet regularly to build team member consultation skills and discuss cases as a team. However, in reality, the team met more for logistical purposes such as assigning case managers to new referrals and providing case updates.

Student behavior was a primary concern for teachers in the fourth grade. School administrators were frequently involved in handling student behavior problems in these classrooms; however, teachers generally felt unsupported by their administrators when behavioral issues arose. There was obvious tension between teachers and administrators around behavior problems, and I was told from the beginning by the on-site school psychologist that I should not address these larger issues as part of my consultation case.

Although the team tended to take individual consultation cases, the school psychologist asked the fourth-grade teachers if they had any interest in being part of a classroom-level case to help me out with my practicum requirements. There were four fourth-grade teachers, and one of them, Mrs. Matthews, was interested in talking to me about some issues in her classroom. Mrs. Matthews was particularly concerned about a group of students with problems with behavior and homework completion. The school psychologist arranged an initial meeting between Mrs. Matthews and me. Mrs. Matthews was vaguely familiar with the consultation process before we began our work together, although she had never referred a case.

Relationships

The consultee, Mrs. Matthews, was a white, female teacher in her twenties. The client was a group of fourth-grade students from various ethnic groups and both genders in her class. I was the consultant—a white female in my twenties, pursuing a doctorate degree in school psychology at a nearby university. I received weekly supervision from an advanced graduate student (white, female) who was regularly supervised by the course professor.

The history of the teacher's concerns played a role in the working relationship between Mrs. Matthews and me during this case. When we began working together, the teacher seemed extremely grateful for my support. Mrs. Matthews needed someone with whom she could share her thoughts, feelings, and concerns in a non-evaluative setting. School administrators had been involved as needed when student disciplinary issues arose, but the process had not resulted in a long-term resolution for the grade-wide behavior problem. The consultee-centered nature of the consultation model that I was implementing seemed more fulfilling and helpful for this teacher. Our work together gave Mrs. Matthews a chance to express her frustrations and delve into some of the issues she was facing in her classroom. After we built a solid working relationship, I encouraged Mrs. Matthews to consider alternative perspectives to her current view of the problem and to think about some of her personal beliefs about "fairness" in the classroom.

Communication Skills

During supervision, I was encouraged to make use of paraphrasing to help me stay with the teacher and, most importantly, for the teacher to hear herself. I found paraphrasing to be the most effective communication tool that I used in working with this teacher. I also tried "bond and move," a strategy that we learned in our consultation class (Rosenfield class notes, Spring 2009). The strategy involves being empathetic to the teacher's concern (bond) before moving the discussion along, allowing the teacher to feel heard. In this instance, I found that simply bonding with Mrs. Matthews allowed her to move on herself. The following transcript illustrates how providing support in a collaborative relationship helped the teacher make progress:

Teacher: Parents don't seem to really care how [students] do on their report cards. A lot of the parents struggled in school and feel … it's everybody else's fault, it's not my fault, there's nothing I can do.

Consultant: Sounds like working with the parents has been really frustrating for you.

Teacher: Yeah, but I still try everyday. I try to call them, meet with them, I met with three of them this week … anyway …

In this transcript, Mrs. Matthews recognizes that she is frustrated with parents but she also expresses that she still wants to do what she can at school to get parents involved. I think that my use of a perception check and paraphrase in this instance helped the teacher think past her frustrations and focus on what she can continue to do to improve parent involvement.

Problem-Solving Stages

We used an instructional consultation problem-solving process that involved six steps: contracting, problem identification, intervention design, intervention implementation, evaluation, and closure. The problem-solving process took place over 10 sessions spanning three months.

Contracting

In the first session, we completed contracting, which involved explaining the consultation process and how our case would focus on the teacher's classroom-wide concern. Mrs. Matthews began to discuss her referral concerns during this session, but we did not officially begin problem identification. I used active listening skills and provided support as the teacher expressed her frustrations about the issues in her classroom.

When asked for her expectations for our work together, the teacher simply said, "I just wish the kids would just all start doing their homework." Mrs. Matthews expressed concern about how her students would succeed in middle school, and she felt that a harsher discipline system would force them back on track. From the first session, it was clear that Mrs. Matthews was very frustrated with students not completing their homework and with her many failed attempts to help them. Mrs. Matthews had run out of ideas and patience.

At the end of the session, the teacher asked me a tough question:

> Is this something you think we can actually get to work when it's so hard to motivate them, that there are so many things that they just don't care about like homework and grades and other things? I mean, what do you think? Is this something we can do?

Although I could not promise Mrs. Matthews that we would find a solution, I told her that we would work through the issues together, she would have my support, and we would share ownership of the concern.

At the end of the session, Mrs. Matthews verbally agreed to work with me and we set up our next meeting. Since there was no clear solution to the problems she faced in the classroom, getting Mrs. Matthews' initial buy-in to the consultation process was critical. Although at times during the first session I was concerned by Mrs. Matthews' negativity and harsh approach toward students, I used basic helping skills to express empathy and show that I was listening to her—even when I disagreed with her take on the issue. As a result, Mrs. Matthews seemed to feel supported and was willing to continue meeting with me.

In hindsight, it may have been beneficial to talk to Mrs. Matthews about the "instructional" nature of the consultation process, rather than assuming that she understood the focus of this type of consultation from her prior experiences. The instructional consultation process emphasizes intervention in areas that are under the teacher's control to meet the needs and skills of students in the class. For a novice consultant, it can be challenging and uncomfortable to discuss the teacher's need to change in the beginning of the consultation process.

Problem Identification

During the second session, Mrs. Matthews and I started to write down her concerns on the Student Documentation Form (SDF; Rosenfield & Gravois, 1996; see Introduction, this volume), a form designed for this purpose. Mrs. Matthews listed students' homework completion, motivation, ownership, and behavior in school as the primary problems. Mrs. Matthews felt that all of the concerns were interrelated, but we wrote each separately in order to keep track of everything she mentioned.

Mrs. Matthews was forthright about the reason that she believed that her students did not complete homework. She thought that they didn't care about school and neither did their parents. I encouraged Mrs. Matthews to think of other possibilities—why else might a student not turn in homework? For example, I asked Mrs. Matthews to describe the types of assignments that students were required to complete, and she told me that homework was the exact same set of assignments for reading and spelling every night. Although I did not raise this issue, I began to wonder if students were not doing homework because it was busy work and had no direct link to what was worked on in class. Because our work together was still in the beginning stages, I did not directly challenge Mrs. Matthews' reasoning, but instead encouraged her to think more broadly about the problem. In my own reflections, I started to develop alternative hypotheses to Mrs. Matthews' theory that students had no motivation. While I intended to work more with Mrs. Matthews on developing homework that was tailored to students' learning needs, our work together did not go in that direction. As an instructional consultant, I should have revisited the topic of the homework itself once my relationship with Mrs. Matthews was more established.

Designing the Survey

In the third session, I brought up the idea of conducting a classroom survey about homework to gain the students' perspective. The following brief transcript shows how Mrs. Matthews initially reacted to the homework survey idea.

> Consultant: So I was wondering what you thought about maybe doing a short survey with the class? … Give them a lot of options just to see what their reasons were.
> Teacher: Ok, they won't be honest.
> Consultant: You don't think they'll be honest?
> Teacher: The ones that don't do it won't be honest, it's always everyone else's fault—never theirs.
> Consultant: Even if they don't have to put their name on it?
> Teacher: Yeah I still don't think they'll be honest … but we can try it. I'm willing to try it … Well, I think it's a great idea but next week would probably be a better time.

Since Mrs. Matthews was feeling overwhelmed by the daily report cards and upcoming parent conferences, we decided to revisit the topic the following week. I was surprised that she felt so strongly that the students would lie on an anonymous survey.

In the next session, we revisited the idea of conducting a survey about homework completion with the class and brainstormed items for the survey. Mrs. Matthews and I had different ideas about the design and purpose of the survey. Mrs. Matthews expressed curiosity about what the students would say and whether or not they would take responsibility. I viewed the survey as a way to gather additional explanations for the problem, expand Mrs. Matthews' perspective on why the students were struggling with homework completion, and involve the students in the process.

In creating the survey, we struggled with deciding between keeping questions open-ended or providing response options. Mrs. Matthews was adamant that students would use the survey to deny their responsibility, saying that providing response choices would result in students "circl[ing] all of them or ... whichever one makes them look least responsible." She thought that an open-ended survey given to students who didn't complete their homework might be "torture for them to do the writing and maybe that would actually encourage them to do their homework more." I suggested that the survey would be "a way to get information from the class on kids that do their homework and don't do their homework." Mrs. Matthews liked the idea of asking students why they did complete their homework, and she began to add some more positive questions to the survey (e.g., what homework do you enjoy doing the most? Why do you think you complete your homework in this area or areas?). Hearing my perspective on the purpose of the survey seemed to open the teacher to broadening her perspective and to think of the survey as an information-gathering process and way to engage students. This change was seen in Mrs. Matthews' suggestions to add more positive questions geared toward students who regularly completed homework, which indicated that she was willing to try a slightly different approach and hear what the students had to say.

In the following session, we discussed revisions to the homework survey. I suggested that we change the multiple choice response options that listed reasons for not completing homework so that each response started with "I ..." (e.g., "I didn't bring home the materials"). The teacher really liked this revision because it made the students take responsibility for the excuse and also showed that I had listened to her initial concerns about the survey giving students an outlet to deny their responsibility. The final survey (see Appendix A) that was administered to students had four questions:

1. What homework assignments were turned in today?
2. If homework wasn't turned in, check reasons that apply—I didn't bring home the materials, I didn't feel like doing it, I didn't like the homework, I don't think homework is important, I thought it was too hard, I thought it was too boring, I couldn't concentrate at home, I didn't turn it in, I didn't have enough time.
3. What helps to complete and turn in homework?
4. What homework is most enjoyable?

We revisited the purpose of the survey and also how the teacher would present the survey to the class. We decided that Mrs. Matthews should try to administer the survey as soon as possible because homework during the next two weeks would be different than usual because of state testing.

Analyzing the Survey Responses

In the next session, we discussed the results of the survey that had been given to students the week prior. I compiled the results of the survey into an Excel table so that each row showed a student's responses and each column showed responses to each question. We looked through the results and talked about why the students struggling with homework completion were having trouble either doing the homework or doing the homework and turning it in. The teacher was surprised to see that almost every student put down an assignment that they enjoyed. Overall, we felt like there were many different reasons that the students did and did not do their homework, and that many seemed related to motivation.

The teacher thought that students who did their homework seemed to have a lot more support at home compared to students who did not complete their homework.

Consultant: So it sounds like you feel like the kids that have the home support are the ones getting the homework done?

Teacher: That's very true.

Consultant: So the group of 10 that either are disorganized or are not motivated to do it are not having consequences at home …

Teacher: It's not as important to their family. Grades aren't. The parents seem to talk a big game … but they don't seem to follow through …

Consultant: So it sounds like you've been trying a lot to get the parents involved and that's not really working.

This conversation was helpful because it started to turn the teacher toward the idea of providing extra support for the students without home support.

Intervention Design

We started to discuss possible intervention strategies, and we considered building off the daily report card that Mrs. Matthews was already using with students. In the third session, I had learned about an intervention design that she was working on—a daily report card on which student's behavior was rated throughout the day. Mrs. Matthews was attempting to implement the daily report card with 10 students in her class, but she was feeling very overwhelmed by the time required for her to fill out the chart for each student throughout the day.

Mrs. Matthews brought up her personal struggle with providing rewards for students who were having difficulty, a perception that many teachers share:

Teacher: The hardest thing is trying to determine with my chart here, well what do I do? I don't want to reward what they should be doing cause the other kids don't get rewarded for doing their homework necessarily … I can't make them want to care about it and I don't feel like I should reward the ones who are doing it because they finally started doing homework. I don't know, it's a hard situation.

Consultant: So, you're saying that the ones that are already doing their homework …

Teacher: They don't get a reward everyday for doing it.
Consultant: From you …
Teacher: Right, right.
Consultant: But you know, their parents support it and with parents involved they probably get rewarded a lot for everything in school.
Teacher: That's true.
Consultant: You know, going home, doing their homework. With all that parental support, they probably are getting reinforced for their behavior.
Teacher: Yeah, that's true.
Consultant: So it sounds like one thing that you're struggling with is how do you make this most effective without … creating an unfair reward system in your classroom?
Teacher: Right.

During this discussion, I worked hard to help the teacher take a different perspective about positive reinforcement.

In supervision, we discussed that when I had previously brought up the importance of positive reinforcement, the teacher had been very resistant. My supervisor and I talked about the importance of working on my relationship with Mrs. Matthews before trying to address the subject again. This time, Mrs. Matthews broached the topic herself, suggesting that our relationship had advanced to the point where we could discuss her belief system and possible alternatives to her current viewpoint. Mrs. Matthews acknowledged that she felt conflicted because it was unfair to reward some students but not others for doing what they "should be doing." I used a combination of helping skills, including providing information, paraphrasing, and clarifying, to discuss positive reinforcement with Mrs. Matthews.

In our next session, Mrs. Matthews and I talked about how to implement some of the ideas we had discussed earlier for increasing homework completion. We decided to use the daily report card that the teacher was already using to collect data on behavior and homework for 10 students who were having difficulties in these areas. This system included a seven-point scale to measure the student's homework completion, in addition to other behavioral measures. The teacher's task was to score each student's homework points on the daily report card every morning.

We decided to build off this system that was already in place, since the teacher felt like she was spending a lot of time on this pre-existing intervention. We decided to have each student set goals for the number of homework points they wanted to earn out of seven and then graph their progress each day. Together, we drew out what the graph would look like and then I created an electronic version for the teacher to print and copy.

Implementation

During the next session, Mrs. Matthews and I talked about the implementation of the intervention. We also talked about some changes to our plan that the teacher had made when she introduced the homework graphs to students. For example, Mrs. Matthews had decided to fill out the graphs herself and did not set specific goals with the students. She felt that students were already setting overall goals for the daily report card, and that for homework, competing with each other for the most points was enough motivation. Mrs. Matthews felt more comfortable marking the graphs for the students (instead of the students completing this part) and then letting the students color in their graphs at the end of the week.

I was pleased that Mrs. Matthews felt comfortable making some changes to the intervention because it showed that she was adapting the intervention to meet her needs in the classroom—and that she thought the intervention might be helpful. I did not necessarily agree with all of the changes she made (e.g., making it an informal competition instead of setting goals, limiting the student's involvement), but took the position that the teacher had to decide what she thought was best since it was her classroom.

Evaluation

After two days, Mrs. Matthews felt pleased with the results of the intervention. We talked about how the intervention would continue to look and offering some possible rewards for the students who improved. A week later, the teacher expressed some problems and frustrations with the intervention. This is not uncommon as most interventions need tweaking and obstacles to implementation are expected, especially in the beginning.

Mrs. Matthews felt that the intervention was very successful for some students but not for others. We talked through what was going on with the students and how we might adapt the intervention implementation to fit the current needs in her classroom. It sounded like a lot of students had checked out for the year and the teacher was struggling with motivating them now more than ever. I made a few suggestions to help the teacher manage the intervention since she was feeling very stressed. For example, I asked her if she might reconsider letting the students fill out the graphs so she did not have this added task. Before the session ended, I asked the teacher what else she wanted to get out of our work together. We decided to meet the following week to check in on how things were going and possibly close the case then.

Mrs. Matthews told me that she planned to proactively use the homework graphs for her class next year. This was a big step for her, since when we first met, Mrs. Matthews felt that she had just gotten a bad group of kids. She had reframed the homework problem and taken some ownership for what she could do differently in the future. This discussion was important for me as well, as I recognized that a major goal of our consultee-centered consultation had been met.

Closure

Our last session was very brief because Mrs. Matthews was feeling very overwhelmed by school ending. We discussed how the intervention was going, what she was using the charts for, and how the rest of the school year was winding down and homework would be changing. Mrs. Matthews was using the homework charts to send home to parents with the interim report. She thanked me for working with her, and we wrapped things up.

On my last day at the school a couple of weeks later, I brought the teacher a small gift and thank you card for working with me. She seemed very appreciative and even said, "I should have gotten you a gift instead of you bringing me one!"

Lessons Learned

In this case, I learned the value of *consultee*-centered consultation. I realized early on that the issues going on with the students in this class were larger than a simple problem with homework completion. Although I sought to help the teacher improve students' homework completion, my primary focus in this case was the teacher. Because of the nature of this case and because of lessons learned from previous cases, I prioritized goals for the teacher rather than goals for her class. This case really showed me that the consultant has to work in collaboration with the teacher in order to make classroom-wide changes.

Loss of Objectivity

Following the consultee-centered case model described by Caplan (1995), I identified this as a problem of loss of objectivity. My initial goal for Mrs. Matthews was to help her regain objectivity regarding the students with behavioral and homework problems in her classroom. Loss of objectivity not only impacted Mrs. Matthews' relationship with students, but also distorted her judgment and interfered with her ability to effectively use her own skills and knowledge in the classroom (Caplan, 1995). I was struck by her negativity toward students and their families at the onset of the case, and I realized that the most logical place for us to start our work was to help her see the issue from other perspectives and think through her beliefs and attitudes toward the students.

Importance of Relationships

I think that this case was an important opportunity for me to work on building a relationship with a teacher who had attitudes and practices about teaching that did not align with my own belief system. With support from my supervisor, I was able to think of ways to help the teacher expand her perspective and challenge her own assumptions. The process of creating the homework survey was especially important in giving us a tangible task during which we could brainstorm ideas that went beyond the teacher's assumptions for why the students failed to complete homework. Results of the homework survey helped Mrs. Matthews regain objectivity and identify some positives about students who had been difficult. Facilitating this process was valuable for me in that I learned how working collaboratively on a task could be an intervention for that teacher (Schein, 1999).

Instructional Match

In reflecting on the instructional consultation process, I realize that an important skill area for the teacher was left unaddressed. I had intended to revisit the importance of the homework assignment and its match to the students' needs and skills. Since Mrs. Matthews wanted to work on student motivation, we spent most of our time on interventions designed to understand and increase motivation. As an instructional consultant, it is critical to help the teacher understand the relationship between instructional variables, such as the crucial link between homework level and student performance. As a novice consultant, it was difficult for me to encourage the teacher to challenge existing norms, such as the standard homework that each teacher in her grade level assigned.

We did not conduct any instructional assessments as she and I would likely have done with an individual case. However, more experienced instructional consultants also do assessments on group cases as well. In reflection, I see that exploring the match between the homework assignments and the students' skill level, especially for the more at-risk students, was equally as important in this class level case as it would have been in an individual case. In learning this critical but challenging part of the instructional consultant's role, supportive supervision of novice consultants is crucial.

Student Engagement

The interventions used in this case served the important purpose of engaging students in the classroom in the process. Including students in decision-making, giving students opportunities to make suggestions, and asking students to set goals are research-based strategies shown to improve motivation, achievement, productivity, and behavior (School Mental Health Project, 2011). The classroom-wide survey opened communication between the teacher and students about the homework problem in an objective way. Students lacking motivation and having difficulty in school had the opportunity to express their opinions and perceptions of the problem without criticism from the teacher. Further, the goal setting and graphing of progress interventions were designed to improve student engagement. Student involvement in goal setting has been shown to improve performance and increase student feelings of commitment to the goals (School Mental Health Project, 2011). Unfortunately,

Mrs. Matthews did not directly implement this aspect of the intervention with the students. Overall, I think our work together benefitted the teacher and that she will use some of the strategies we discussed with her future students.

Difficulty in Collecting Data

It is less clear if our work produced outcomes for students currently in Mrs. Matthews' class. I attempted to collect baseline data retrospectively so that I could compare homework completion during the intervention to before the case started, but I found that the teacher's records were unreliable. For example, students seemed to only turn in copies of their daily report cards when they had done well. There were many students with data missing from the teacher's files, making it pretty much impossible for us to track student progress.

Need to Support Intervention

The daily report card intervention that was already in place was clearly a large burden on the teacher and she was thus not able to implement it consistently. Most teachers are open to using daily report cards with individual students or with the whole classroom and use this strategy for a variety of purposes (Chafouleas, Riley-Tillman, & Sassu, 2006). In some cases, however, teachers might need more support for selecting a tool and deciding how to use it (e.g., who completes the ratings, how often, what are the consequences). Especially when multiple students are involved, consultants should work with the teacher to consider the time commitment, feasibility, and possible alternatives before deciding to use daily report cards.

Teacher Change

In hindsight, I think the homework survey was the most effective intervention for the teacher in this case. The survey not only engaged students in the process, but it also provided insight for the teacher and directed the rest of our collaborative work. Mrs. Matthews was adamant about trying to use the intervention from the start of the next school year. From the following statement and other comments made during our final sessions, it was clear to me that Mrs. Matthews had a more positive attitude toward her students than when we started working together:

> Teacher: But I appreciate your help because a kid like this with such a hard life … a kid that doesn't get a lot of support … to see him doing his homework, I think that's pretty good … To see him finally doing his homework, that's great. So even if we only have one or two successes I think that's a good thing because, you know, there's only but so much we can do. I've come to that point in realizing that. And I think your ideas have been really great, I'm going to start implementing a lot of them at the beginning of the year next year, the charts and the graphing with

some of my more at-risk students. So I think a lot of it has been really good …

While Mrs. Matthews did not come away from our work together thinking that she could change every student's academic course, she recognized that she played a role in supporting students, especially students who may not receive much support elsewhere. This was in stark contrast to the Mrs. Matthews I met at the beginning of the case, who believed that being fair meant no one received anything extra. Regaining objectivity toward her students not only made Mrs. Matthews more empathetic and supportive, but it also gave her a chance to feel more self-efficacious about her teaching and to effectively use her knowledge and skills.

Questions for Reflection

1. **It would have been helpful for me to work with Mrs. Matthews on her use of the daily report card and methods for data collection. How could we have developed a better plan to collect data on students' homework completion from the beginning of the case?**
2. **How else might I have measured success in this case? How do you measure success in your consultation cases?**
3. **If I continued in the same school as Mrs. Matthews next year, how could I follow up on our work together?**

References

Caplan, G. (1995). Types of mental health consultation. *Journal of Educational and Psychological Consultation, 6*, 7–21.

Chafouleas, S., Riley-Tillman, T., & Sassu, K. (2006). Acceptability and reported use of daily behavior report cards among teachers. *Journal of Positive Behavior Interventions, 8*, 174–182.

Rosenfield, S., & Gravois, T.A. (1996). *Instructional consultation teams: Collaborating for change*. New York: Guilford Press.

Schein, E. (1999). *Process consultation revisited: Building the helping relationship*. Reading, MA: Addison-Wesley Publishing Company.

School Mental Health Project. (2011, Winter). School engagement, disengagement, learning supports, and school climate. *Center for Mental Health in Schools, 16*.

APPENDIX A

Sample Homework Survey

1. Please list all of the homework assignments that you turned in today:
2. If you didn't turn in all of your homework, what kept you from turning it in?

    ___ I didn't bring home the materials last night

___ I didn't feel like doing it
___ I didn't like the homework
___ I don't think homework is important
___ I thought it was too hard
___ I thought it was too boring
___ I couldn't concentrate at home
___ I did my homework but didn't turn it in because:
___ I didn't have enough time because I was doing:
___ Other reason:

3. What helps you complete your homework or remember to turn it in?
4. What homework do you enjoy doing the most?

10
A Teacher's Concern for One Student Reveals a Classroom-Wide Bullying Concern

Megan Vaganek

Advance Organizer Questions

- **How does classroom level consultation differ from consultation around an individual concern?**
- **How can problem identification act as an intervention?**
- **How can a consultant's feelings, beliefs, and insecurities affect a case?**

My first cases as a student of consultation provided opportunities for me to work with teachers who had concerns about individual students in their classrooms. My experience with a classroom-level case also began as a teacher's concern about one particular fourth-grade student, who was frequently bullied by other students in her classroom. As we worked through the stages of the problem-solving process, it quickly became clear that bullying was prevalent throughout the classroom. Eventually we learned that there was a school-level problem with bullying. The teacher, Mrs. James, and I saw a great opportunity to collaborate on a concern with the potential to reach an entire classroom of students. This chapter describes my case through discussions of problem-solving, influences of school culture, my consultation relationship with the teacher, and my communication skills.

Progress through Problem-Solving Stages

Referral

The site-based supervisor and I discussed ideas for a case that involved more than one teacher or student, a course requirement. After this initial discussion, the supervisor learned about a bullying concern that a fourth-grade teacher had in her classroom. She asked Mrs. James if she was interested in working with me on her bullying concern. The supervisor introduced us and we chose a time to meet about the case.

Contracting

In our first session, I met with the teacher to start contracting. I began the session by telling the teacher a little bit about myself and the consultation course that I was taking. Because my introduction revolved primarily around an explanation of the consultation course and pursuit of a degree in school psychology, the academic nature of my introduction may have influenced her view of our relationship (i.e., my role as a student was salient). Mrs. James told me that she had worked with another consultation student in the past, so she was familiar and comfortable with the audiotaping procedure.

I felt a little uncomfortable in contracting, as I believe this was one of my weakest skill sets. This teacher was familiar with the process; I spent some time using the triangle diagram and the list of stages to explain how we would work together, but I need more practice explaining the ways in which cases that target more than one consultee or client differ from traditional case management that focuses on one teacher/one student. The referring teacher had previously done a more limited case management with the school's early intervention team. It seemed especially important for me to try and explain some of the similarities and differences between a case at the classroom level and an individual case. I emphasized that the team would still be available as a resource if we needed support. We decided that the teacher would be the primary consultee, but we would revisit the possibility of including other teachers or staff in our meetings if necessary. The teacher agreed to work with me and we scheduled a regular weekly meeting time.

Problem Identification

Our problem identification stage involved an evolving set of concerns, which was difficult for me as a novice consultant, although common in consultation cases. In the first session, the teacher shared her concerns about bullying in her classroom. Her initial concern focused on a particular girl, Lisa, in her class who was being bullied by a group of other girls. Mrs. James reported that the student had an IEP and received several services. As a result, she was not concerned about the student's academic progress, but wanted to focus on the student's social skills. Thus, the concern initially revolved around one student: her need for a friend, social skills, and her struggles with bullying at the hands of her peers.

However, as we talked about the students who picked on Lisa and excluded her from the group, the teacher shared more information about the extent of the bullying behaviors in her classroom and school-wide, such as the playground and cafeteria. I mentioned that we could bring in other teachers or staff to work with us on this concern, as it appeared to be larger than we first thought. Mrs. James did not express interest in this suggestion, but indicated that consulting other adults might be an option later.

I asked several relevant questions in this first session. I felt as if I needed more contextual information about the classroom environment to understand the bullying behaviors. I wanted to know: Were there other targets of the bullying? Were there moments where things went well socially for Lisa?

At this point, the teacher described a long list of bullying behaviors, such as purposely excluding kids from activities, eye rolling and facial expressions, laughing at the target student, as well as many others. The next step was to narrow and clarify the specific bullying behaviors about which the teacher was concerned.

In our next session, we discussed the various bullying behaviors present in the classroom. Mrs. James also talked a little bit about the social hierarchy in the classroom, with some girls functioning as ringleaders and some girls as followers. Other students acted as bystanders, not participating in the bullying, but not speaking out against it. The teacher also noted that several boys in the classroom were civil to or even nice and helpful to the target child, offering to show her what she missed while out of the classroom or working with her on assignments.

In addition, we talked about the interventions Mrs. James had tried. Bullying and treating one another with respect had been a concern in her classroom for a long time, and she spent a lot of time and energy trying to address it. She said that bullying was a topic of discussion in her classroom on a daily basis; they talked about being respectful to each other in morning meetings (whole class); they had small discussion groups about bullying and respect; and the teacher pulled out students who were not behaving up to her expectations for lunch bunches, where the focus of the conversation was bullying and respect. In parent–teacher conferences, Mrs. James spoke to all parents about bullying and respect issues. She discussed the problem in more depth with the parents of the most flagrant offenders, but felt these efforts were largely unsuccessful. The teacher expressed frustration that some children received mixed messages from home and school; behavior that might be acceptable or encouraged at home was not acceptable in the classroom. Mrs. James also tried class-wide incentives, where the class could earn playground time, or some other reward, if they earned each letter in the word PLAYGROUND for being good during the week. When the class's behavior was especially disappointing, the teacher would take away letters they had already earned. But, even the loss of an incentive did not seem to motivate the students to behave more respectfully to one another.

Although the teacher had tried several ways to address the problem, she was growing increasingly frustrated with the way her students were treating one another, especially Lisa. Mrs. James also told me that she felt that her interventions could not compete with the many reward programs in the school. Her class was constantly rewarded for good behavior in other environments and the students could act appropriately in environments that were rewarding. The students received regular accolades for their behavior on the bus and for other activities. In addition to compliments, the students also frequently received the school's tokens for their behavior. The tokens are part of a school-wide incentive program, and can be turned in for prizes. The more tokens that a student accumulates, the greater the prize they can choose, such as bringing a toy to school, sitting at a teacher's chair, or choosing a prize.

At this point, we attempted to identify bullying behaviors in observable and measurable terms. Mrs. James and I discussed a wide variety of actions that she considered to be bullying. We concluded that it was not the action per se that qualified as bullying, but the intention behind it. A student might pass a note in class, which is not allowed. But if the student writes a note that is intended to make fun of or hurt the feelings of another student, it is a bullying issue. The teacher saw all of the different behaviors as a manifestation of the same concern. For example she did not feel that name-calling and laughing at another student should be treated as separate concerns because the meaning behind both behaviors was related. After struggling to narrow down which bullying behaviors we could address, Mrs. James and I agreed that we would narrow our concerns down to verbal and non-verbal bullying, an easier way to categorize behaviors. We also shared our concerns about how to collect data on such subtle behaviors and capture the intention behind them. I offered to consult some literature on bullying in search of possible data collection methods.

By now, the teacher's frustration with the concern and the bullies was apparent. Mrs. James was disappointed that young girls she once viewed as well behaved and nice were treating other children poorly. I used several perception checks to let her know that I heard her frustration. She started to open up more about how emotionally affected she was by the case. I also shared the teacher's lack of objectivity. I met one of the bullying "ringleaders" in a lunch bunch with the school psychologist. I realized how difficult it was for me to think about anything other than the hurtful words and acts she committed against another student, even though she was well-behaved during lunch. This experience gave me an opportunity to understand the teacher's perspective a little bit better. I found it difficult to reconcile my opinion of the student, based on our case, with her behavior at lunch. It also was an opportunity to become more aware of how context and other environmental factors affected the student's behavior instead of interpreting the bullying behaviors as evidence of the student's stable personality traits. The teacher echoed this issue; she told me that she believes that her students are good people at heart, but that belief is challenged when she sees them hurt one another, despite all her efforts to teach them the importance of caring and respect.

The teacher was also frustrated because Lisa did not always understand that the other girls were making fun of her. It was not until the child went home and talked to her mother about her interactions with the other girls that she realized that the others were not laughing with her, but at her. The student's mother then contacted the teacher. Unfortunately, by the time some of the bullying came to the teacher's attention, so much time had passed that intervening seemed irrelevant. We talked about the possibility of an observation, but the teacher discouraged me from doing that, insisting that the students could control their behavior in the presence of observers. She claimed that they are even fairly successful at hiding it from her; she is able to catch them only when the students think she is not looking.

In our next meeting, Mrs. James told me that she was also concerned that Lisa did not have any friends in school. She felt that a friendship might buffer some of the negative effects of the bullying she experienced in the classroom. Since the student was involved with the school psychologist and counselor in social skills groups and lunch bunches, we decided that this concern was being adequately addressed. Also, during the spring semester, the teacher noticed that the "mean girls" allowed Lisa to play with them a little bit more. While Mrs. James did not believe they were truly friends with the student, she could accept that they played with her because the teacher made it clear that excluding others was not right. This conversation highlighted another issue that the teacher and I both faced in this case. Mrs. James' goal was to have the students treat each other with respect and internalize those behaviors. We agreed that all we could really control was the external behaviors that the students presented rather than "true beliefs." The teacher and I joked that we would have to "fake it 'til we make it" and worry about the external behaviors first.

After working through problem identification in a few sessions, we realized that we needed more information on bullying before we could move forward. I supplied the teacher with the county's bullying curriculum and shared a few studies on bullying interventions. We realized that the students would be in the best position to provide information about their experiences with bullying.

THE BULLYING SURVEY

As a part of problem identification, we decided to create a survey to get more information about bullying in the classroom from the students. We realized that we needed a better understanding of the students' perspectives on bullying in their classroom and brainstormed the least threatening ways to help the students open up about the topic. We used the book *Bully Proofing Your School* (Garrity, Jens, Porter, Sager, & Short-Camilli, 2004), to give us ideas to create items about specific bullying behaviors and environments. We decided that the survey should be anonymous and that I should collect the papers and compile the data so students knew their handwriting could not be identified. We drafted our survey questions together and then I typed them. I emailed them to the teacher for revisions and we agreed to present this final draft of the survey to the students. I came into the classroom when the teacher presented the survey to the students. I collected the surveys in an envelope and calculated the results.

I brought a summary of the results to our next meeting and asked the teacher for her impressions. The survey asked students to share whether or not they bullied other children. I was surprised that nine out of 20 students self-reported that they bully. Before sharing my impressions, I asked the teacher how she felt about that particular question. She anticipated about half of the class saying they were bullies and was not surprised. We also asked the class to define bullying. The students listed unexpected bullying behaviors and environments that Mrs. James and I never considered, such as the bus stop, at home, and in their neighborhoods. Many students confirmed bullying in environments that we listed, such as bullying on the playground, in the cafeteria, and on the bus. Out of 20 students, 18 stated that bullying happened in their classroom. The teacher was not surprised about the names that the students listed as bullies, but the survey results did confirm that the concern existed in other contexts. We originally talked about a group of bullying girls in her fourth-grade classroom, but the issue extended to boys, other classes, and other places at school and beyond.

Mrs. James later shared that her students asked several times about the results and what we would do with them. She noticed that after we administered the survey, her perception was that behavior in her classroom had improved. The survey seemed to open up discussion about bullying; instead of hearing a lecture, the students were invited to participate in the discussion. After we discussed the results, the teacher questioned how concerned she felt about bullying at that point. It seemed that the survey acted as an intervention in and of itself. Gathering more information about the concern changed the teacher's understanding and perception, and also seemed to have an additional effect on the students themselves. One of the most valuable lessons from this case was that, as Schein (1999) says, everything the consultant does serves as an intervention. The bullying survey that we created, based on *Bully Proofing Your School* (Garrity et al., 2004), provided us with surprising information about the depth and breadth of bullying in this classroom and brought the students into the discussion.

Intervention Design

At our next meeting, we moved forward with intervention design. We decided to use the existing classroom rules, which are based on the school's code of conduct, as the rules for the Good Behavior Game (GBG; Barrish, Saunders, & Wolf, 1969), an evidence-based intervention. The students had created the rules as a class (with some teacher guidance) at the beginning of the year. The rules are:

1. Be kind to others with your actions and words.
2. Everyone has the right to make a mistake without being laughed at.
3. Keep yourself to yourself. Be in control.
4. Walk, don't run, both in and out of the classroom.
5. Don't talk while the teacher or another student is talking.
6. Time is spent on productive learning.

We planned to introduce the GBG to the students, with an emphasis on cooperation with teammates. The teacher said she would discuss the survey with the students in the context of the rules, outlining which bullying behaviors were in conflict with which rules. Mrs. James and I wanted to emphasize positive reinforcement for appropriate behaviors instead of punishment for bullying. Using the GBG game and the existing classroom rules gave us an opportunity to encourage the students to engage in behaviors that were incompatible with bullying. The reward for the team who best followed the rules was the choice between a lunch bunch with the teacher or a free homework pass.

We decided to collect baseline for the GBG by tallying the times that students in the whole class demonstrated examples of the rules and times when students broke the rules. In the problem identification phase, we explored bullying behaviors. In an attempt to track positive outcomes, we decided to base our intervention on appropriate behavior. We tracked data on a class-wide basis. The teacher collected baseline data on all six rules for three days during the afternoon math and content period (1.5 hours). We subtracted the number of tallies earned for unsuccessful behaviors from the tally of successful behaviors. On days 1, 2, and 3 the class earned -20, -4 and 2 points respectively. We noted that the baseline was increasing and discussed collecting a few more days of baseline data. Because of absences and other scheduling issues, Mrs. James was unable to collect additional days and we decided to start the intervention on the following Monday, in spite of the increasing baseline data.

The teacher and I also decided to reduce the number of rules that we would track for the game. We felt that the rules "walk" and "being in control" were related to "keeping self-to-self" and that "allowing everyone the freedom to make mistakes" could be combined with "being kind through actions and words." We also combined the ideas of "spending time on productive learning" with "not talking when the teacher or another student is talking." Mrs. James felt that these rules could be less repetitive (certain interactions or behaviors were qualifying as multiple rules when she collected baseline) and easier for her to track. Looking back, we should have repeated baseline data collection with our new criteria.

Implementation

The teacher split up the class into two teams based on their field day teams (a grade-level event that was recently held at school). The teacher also included field day in her explanation of the game, saying that the game would help them work together in the classroom and in their field day activities. Mrs. James had already changed the students' seats to reflect their team membership. The class had a discussion about the Good Behavior Game, including the way it was played, the rules the teacher was looking for, and the reward for the winning team. At the end of the game each day, the teacher told the class how they did. The class played the game for five days (see Table 10.1 for points after five days). At the end of the week the red team had 76 positive behaviors and 37 negative behaviors for a total of 39. The blue team had 70 positive behaviors and 24 negatives for a total of 46. Overall, both teams performed exceptionally better than the baseline.

Table 10.1 GBG Points Over Five Days

Red Team			Blue Team		
Positives	*Negatives*	*Total Score*	*Positives*	*Negatives*	*Total Score*
76	37	39	70	24	46

Intervention Evaluation and Closure

In our final meeting, we graphed data from the GBG and closed the case. The teacher and I discussed ways in which we could have improved the data collection process so it was easier on the teacher. As the teacher implemented the intervention, she found it difficult to observe everyone for the entire hour and a half. She also had some concerns with tracking the data in terms of groups of students versus individuals. When an entire table was following a rule, their team got a point. But if one student was following a rule, the teams also got one point. If she used the GBG again, she said she would have to think more about this issue, so that all students would need to participate and be held accountable for their table. We also talked about structuring the game so that the teams competed against a pre-set criterion instead of each other. We noted that the way we calculated the data might have influenced the winner. If we only collected instances of rule following, the red team would have won. The teacher felt that it was important to look at positive and negative behaviors together.

I asked Mrs. James for her thoughts on the intervention and outcome. The teacher was happy with the students' performance during the Good Behavior Game. From what she told me initially, I heard that she was happy with the progress but I wanted to hear it explicitly:

> Consultant: That's good. How do you feel about the whole thing?
>
> Teacher: I like the idea of the game. I think I would need to manage collecting the data a little better. I almost think they could have collected it themselves. I kinda feel like there was some generalizing. Sometimes I would catch kids doing good things but they could have been doing good things all along and I could have missed it. At some point there we crossed a line, or I said this whole group is doing a good job.

In addition to the large improvement from baseline in rule following, the teacher saw a noticeable reduction in instances of unsuccessful behaviors (rule-breaking) when she observed her class. She found that the same students were usually responsible for inappropriate behavior. Students seemed to be more accountable for their behaviors and they encouraged each other to behave appropriately. Mrs. James was also pleased that the students did not gang up on each other or treat each other poorly when a student caused the team to lose a point. Despite some concerns about data collection, the teacher said she would use the GBG again in the future.

Consultee Evaluation of the Process

After discussing the outcome of the case, I asked Mrs. James for feedback on the consultation process and on me as a case manager. The teacher thought that we worked together collaboratively but she wished that we had time to be more thorough. She called herself a "data-person," saying that she would have liked to have implemented the game again and been able to better track the data better. Mrs. James thanked me for my flexibility with her hectic schedule. The teacher also told me that she would change very little about the case if she could. We both agreed that we learned a lot while working on this case.

At the school level, the survey informed us that the bullying concern extended far beyond the girls in her classroom. However, even after Mrs. James expressed greater concern about bullying on the playground and in the lunchroom, she did not want to set up a meeting with other relevant school personnel to address the issue. At the end of the school year, the principal was interested in the results of our case, but no formal problem-solving process was underway at a higher systems-level when I left at the end of the school year.

The Effect of School Culture

The culture of a school is affected by the demographics of the teachers and the community that it serves, district policies and curriculum, and other environmental factors. But other more subtle cultural factors also come into play. In my case the cultural issues with the greatest influence related to the educational philosophy and beliefs of the administration and personnel.

Positive Reinforcement

The most influential school culture issue that impacted this case was, oddly enough, the school's emphasis on positive reinforcement. The school staff were proud of the fact that they have no discipline referrals; students are not sent to the principal's office for rule violations. The goal is to empower teachers with the skills to handle problems within their classrooms. This philosophy is in line with the school's strong support of problem-solving teams.

While the referring teacher and I both agreed that positive reinforcement is an incredibly powerful way to change behavior, and in line with our personal beliefs, we struggled with how to align those beliefs with the students' responses. We wondered if too much positive reinforcement and a lack of meaningful consequences fueled the fire of our bullying concern. Often, Mrs. James alluded to her perception about the students' attitude about reinforcement: if they weren't rewarded today, they would probably be rewarded tomorrow. The teacher eventually shared that she felt students had so many opportunities for rewards that the loss of a reward was not meaningful.

Sarason (1996) suggests that the school culture and its norms have an impact on behavior. In this case, the teacher felt that the children were too frequently rewarded. The teacher's concern about the limited effectiveness of any positive reinforcement intervention we might have created is an illustration of an impact of the school environment on a single teacher's perception of her classroom. The school- and class-wide reinforcement programs are not faded over time. Students who work with several teachers and specialists are often exposed to multiple rewards and reinforcement systems. The teacher and I worried that if the environment suggests that the students will always receive a reward, students may feel entitled or may not be affected if a reward is lost because another one will soon become available.

In addition to the strong emphasis on positive reinforcement, the lack of meaningful consequences for unacceptable behavior was another issue Mrs. James and I discussed. We both expressed frustration that there were some behaviors that might call for disciplinary action and loss of reinforcers, but such consequence did not have much of an impact, given how easy it was to earn reinforcers back. Mrs. James often implied that her freedom for instituting consequences was limited by the administration and social pressure in the school. It was unclear if the school policies or environment truly limited the rules and consequences that the teacher could implement in her classroom; as a consultant, I chose to focus on understanding the teacher's concern and designing an intervention with which she was comfortable. Before our work together, the teacher noted that she did occasionally take away incentives and has children call their parents to explain their unacceptable bullying behavior, but those were the only alternatives she felt able to use when we discussed "consequences."

Mrs. James and I both had strong emotional reactions to the bullying behavior. In reflecting on those feelings, I wondered if we might have wanted the children who were being hurtful to others to experience a negative consequence. The teacher had also tried several ways to address the problem and some form of punishment or discipline may have looked like an attractive alternative. In the end, we agreed that positive reinforcement was in-line with our beliefs. We found a way to implement an intervention that used reward as a motivator. It is important for new consultants to reflect on how they can help teachers maintain objectivity, support teachers' feelings, and enable teachers to develop appropriate interventions in light of unacceptable student behavior.

Consultation Relationship

This I consistently felt that Mrs. James and I were building a functional working relationship. By our second meeting, we both used "we" language regularly. This was evidence that the teacher took ownership of the case. She shared with me her emotional reactions and her frustrations, conveying the deep concern she felt about the case. We made every effort to draft materials in the meetings, but we both offered to do work outside the sessions as needed. Mrs. James followed through in most cases when we assigned tasks, such as collecting data and communicating with her class and administration.

However, our working relationship was not free of concerns. Mrs. James always expressed her willingness to meet, but did not consistently follow through. This became frustrating for me. There were times where she had to cancel meetings, leave early or start late because of other appointments or impromptu issues that came up due to her other responsibilities in the school. Early in our relationship, we established a norm that allowed interruptions from other adults. Almost weekly, someone would come into the room to get coffee, drop off papers, ask questions about sub plans or just stop by and say hello as they passed her room. Mrs. James always apologized for the interruptions, but they continued for the entirety of our case.

For example, in the sixth meeting, her classroom instructional assistant came in during our meeting. Mrs. James and I continued our meeting but the teacher asked the instructional assistant for information or impressions. The next time we met, I asked Mrs. James if we should include the instructional assistant in our meetings as another consultee. She did not feel this was necessary. I suggested that we could bring her into the case when we planned the intervention if necessary. I later came to wonder if this event set the tone for later interruptions.

The interruptions led me to question the teacher's investment in our work together. My confidence as a consultant was affected; I began to question the progress and effectiveness of the case and my skills. I wondered if the teacher agreed to work with me as a favor to a graduate student rather than out of a genuine desire to work on a concern in her classroom. As I spent more time waiting in the hallway or sitting awkwardly while another meeting happened in front of me, my worries escalated. Through supervision and reflection I was able to refocus and consider ways to improve the working relationship, including openly discussing the interruptions and adapting the meeting times.

I never felt comfortable explicitly stating my frustration with the interruptions and I convinced myself that as long as we continued to work well together, the interruptions could continue. Instead, I often suggested meeting 15 minutes earlier than our usual time, so we could have more time to work. Overall, I do not believe that the interruptions or canceled meetings had a *major* impact on the outcome of our case, but I did come to understand through supervision that these issues must be addressed when they begin. Had we discussed interruptions right away, we may have avoided creating these habits and made further or faster progress. At least I might have felt less frustrated by addressing these issues head-on rather than stewing in silence.

On a few occasions, the teacher referred to the case as "your study." This was one of her only deviations from "we" language. As described below, in our first meeting I introduced myself but talked mainly about the consultation course as the reason I was in the school and working on cases. The teacher may have concluded that she was helping me with a school project, in addition to receiving support for a concern in her classroom. Even when she no longer indicated that her main concern was in the classroom, Mrs. James wanted to continue the intervention as planned. It is possible that she did not want to negatively affect my "study" or experience in any way by making changes.

Communication Skills

Over the course of the case, my evaluation of my communication skills changed multiple times. During the problem identification stage, I was aware that I asked more relevant questions about the classroom environment and specific bullying behaviors than I would have liked. Relevant questions were also more frequent when the teacher and I were discussing information that I shared.

Relying on relevant questions served a few purposes for me. Admittedly, using relevant questions was easier for me, especially when I felt nervous. Bullying is also an interesting topic and I wanted to know as much as I could, as quickly as I could, about the landscape of the classroom. My heavy-handed use of relevant questions may have also been a way to rely on the teacher for content information about the general subject of bullying, when I could have better prepared for bullying cases with a brief literature review. A more effective and collaborative approach would have been to use paraphrases and clarifying questions to explore each of the teacher's concerns and descriptions. The other necessary information would have evolved from there.

At the suggestion of my school psychologist site supervisor, I read *Bully Proofing Your School* (Garrity et al., 2004). This book stimulated me to ask additional relevant questions about bystanders and bullying behaviors. After these topics were on the table, it was again crucial to return to other communication skills in order to learn about the teacher's perceptions of these issues. Reading about the concern we were facing helped me as a novice consultant to consider the wider classroom environment and focus our discussions on the classroom rather than individual "bullies" or "victims." It was important for this type of concern for us to maintain a focus on the system as whole rather than the individuals who make up the classroom system.

I also struggled with learning how to interrupt the teacher less often. On the tape, I heard myself interrupting too much, but as I tried to work on this area, I stopped interrupting when it would have been productive. Finding a balance between speaking and listening was a struggle for me in this case.

Lessons Learned

This case provided me with valuable experience as a new consultant. Every case provides opportunities for growth in the areas of communication skills and knowledge about the problem-solving process. This case gave me an opportunity to identify several skills that I developed. I strengthened my skills in implementing a class-wide intervention and using a survey to collect class-wide information. I also developed communication skills and confidence as a consultant.

Confidence as a Novice Consultant

Building confidence as a novice consultant is a challenge. Around the time of our first few meetings, I started to work on decreasing my use of filler words, such as "yeah," "right," and "ok," which did not add anything to the discussion. Focusing on this goal did decrease the use of these words, but increased my self-consciousness about my communication skills. I started to notice the words in my speech in other contexts and had trouble balancing necessary evaluation of my speech with a hypercritical focus on aspects that I found less effective. As a novice consultant, it is important to honestly evaluate yourself and look for ways to improve. However, it is also important to be compassionate with yourself as you learn, make mistakes, and build skills. An emphasis solely on the mistakes deflated my confidence. Through supervision, I worked to acknowledge areas that needed improvement while also highlighting skills that improved. When I was asked to bring a short list of examples of things I did well in my sessions, I was better prepared to work on other skill areas with confidence.

Doubting my ability to communicate effectively and collaboratively coincided with a general loss of objectivity about my role as a consultant. I questioned what I had to offer the teachers with whom I worked. In supervision I worked on acknowledging the positive things I brought to the case, such as support for the teacher, a place to share and narrow her concerns, and data collection and analysis. It is easy for a novice consultant to feel inadequate, especially when you feel that the process is not going well; supervision is a great support in these situations.

In our last few sessions, I felt more confident and positive about my skills in this case. Hearing the teacher thank me for the progress we were making during intervention design and again during closure reassured me. I think my lack of confidence as a consultant and insecurities about my communication skills raised my anxiety level in my sessions and probably impeded my effectiveness as a consultant to some degree. Supervision helped me to consider the objectivity of my negative self-evaluations, practice skills, and celebrate successes. The experience gave me an opportunity to recognize the need to balance constructive criticism of myself with acknowledgment of my strengths.

Defining Behaviors and Setting Goals

Working on a class-wide bullying concern helped me gain skills in the problem identification stage. In this case we had difficulty narrowing concerns. Instead of focusing on a few specific behaviors on our long list, we reached the conclusion that the concern was really about treating others with respect and following the classroom rules (e.g., there were several specific behaviors that fit into these areas, such as name calling, excluding others). As a novice consultant it was difficult for me to break out of a structured approach to problem identification, in which each observable behavior is considered a new and different concern. Reading a few studies and practical guides on bullying prevention helped me to see bullying as a big picture concern rather than a list of specific behaviors. I would encourage novice consultants to conduct brief literature reviews to familiarize themselves with a new topic, but not to forget to focus on the teacher's perception of the concern.

Unfortunately, we did not set goals to guide our evaluation. After implementing the Good Behavior Game intervention for a week, I saw how we might have set goals for the GBG. The teacher and I could have set a criterion (e.g., points earned) for the students to meet in order to earn a reward and we could have raised the criterion for intermediate and long-term goals. We could have focused just on successful rule-following behaviors or continued to subtract unsuccessful behaviors from the successful ones. With goals set, we also would have known when to fade out the intervention, if we implemented it for a longer period of time. As cases progress and we start to feel more comfortable as consultants, it is important for beginning consultants to refer back to the basic steps in the problem-solving process.

Using a Survey as an Assessment Tool

This case also gave me an experience with class-wide data collection using a survey. The survey helped the teacher and me in problem identification by providing information about specific bullying behaviors, environments, and the students' perceptions of bullying in their class, grade, and school. The survey helped us generate some discussions as well as add new information. Based on some of the changes in the class's behavior after the survey, I can see how I might continue to use surveys as a mini intervention. The survey seemed to have acted as an intervention in and of itself by opening up a forum for the students to share their experiences. Not long after conducting the survey, the teacher told me that she felt that the bullying issue decreased in the classroom. Students also frequently asked her about the results of the survey. Reflecting on their behavior and bullying in general may have influenced some behavior change by the students or changed the teacher's perception of the behaviors. Eliciting feedback from the teacher and students is a good way for novice consultants to evaluate their skills, as well as open their eyes to unexpected effects of their work.

After conducting the survey, the teacher and I thought of changes we could make if we administered another bullying survey. This experience will help me in creating classroom data collection methods in the future. I was able to practice the first steps in intervention evaluation in this case by identifying possible changes we could make to the intervention and data collection method.

Unfortunately, the teacher and I did not have time in the school year to implement the game with our proposed changes. I would encourage novice consultants to follow-up with their consultees and schools after their practicum work officially ends, as a way to provide any final support (e.g., documents, impressions, suggestions, etc.) to the professionals who provided a valuable training opportunity and to collect data as a scientist-practitioner.

Loss of Objectivity

The use of communication skills, especially when the teacher has lost some objectivity, is especially important. The bullying concern was a very emotionally loaded issue for the teacher. She was frustrated by the bullying itself, the ineffective interventions she tried, and the constant reinforcement of the students in other environments. I had several opportunities to show the teacher that I heard her frustration and I often shared her feelings. I tried to give the teacher a space to talk about her concerns, but at the same time move the process forward and avoid storytelling. I think I helped the teacher feel validated; she had told me that it seemed like she was the only one talking to these students about the bullying problem and she felt that having another adult involved lent credibility about the concern in the students' eyes. I think it also helped the teacher feel as if her concern was credible as well. Maintaining objectivity is not only a concern for consultees. I also needed to work on maintaining objectivity. It is difficult to help a teacher to see things objectively when my own opinions clouded my judgment of the concern. It is important for novice consultants to be aware of how the content of a case and the relationship with the consultee may permeate one's own personal biases and emotional reactions.

Communication and Relationship Skills

This case specifically helped me to overcome obstacles in my communication skills, as I worked with a verbal teacher with a similar communication style. In a way, she provided a mirror for my own communication behavior in terms of interrupting and speed. At the end of the consultation relationship, I regretted that I had not addressed certain issues in our relationship as they first happened, such as interruptions and late/canceled meetings. These minor issues grew to be considerable areas of frustration for me as a new consultant. It is important for consultants, even when they are students in training, to face these uncomfortable conversations upfront to prevent erosion of the consultation relationship.

Systems Thinking

This case gave me a special opportunity to see a concern about one student evolve to address a classroom-wide concern. We considered bullying to be a systems-level issue and that feels like a more powerful way to affect many more students. Instead of applying an intervention designed for one individual and later sharing it with other students, we thought of the classroom as the unit as we identified the problem, designed an intervention, tracked progress, and evaluated the intervention.

Systems-level cases provide a unique opportunity to invite more consultees into the relationship than in traditional individual cases. The logistics of such a relationship is a potential roadblock for systems cases. Not only will the consultant face conflicting schedules, but also consultees may not be interested in collaborating with other school staff. Despite the teacher's concern about bullying in the lunchroom and at recess, she was reluctant to extend our relationship to include other teachers, cafeteria staff or other school personnel. In the end, our intervention was limited to the classroom. School staff, including the principal, took note of our interesting case during team meetings. As a new consultant with only a few months to spend in that school, I can only hope that this case inspired teachers and administration to think about bullying from the classroom, grade level and, maybe, even the entire school level.

Questions for Reflection

1. **Think about an uncomfortable issue you are dealing with in your consultation relationship. What is preventing you from addressing it? Why might it be important in the long run to have a conversation with the consultee about this issue and what can you do in your next session to bring it up?**
2. **How does being a student impact your relationship with your consultees?**
3. **How would you approach an issue of too many positive reinforcement programs, each with different requirements, tokens, and rewards? What changes might you suggest? Whom would you approach about it and what would your goals be for your consultee(s)?**
4. **How could the consultant have encouraged the school to consider a systems-level case that considered bullying as a school-wide issue? What resources would have been necessary?**

References

Barrish, H., Saunders, M., & Wolf, M. (1969). Good behavior game: Effects of individual contingencies for group consequences on disruptive behaviors in the classroom. *Journal of Applied Behavior Analysis*, 2, 119–124.

Garrity, C., Jens, K., Porter, W., Sager. N., & Short-Camilli, C. (2004). *Bully proofing your school: Elementary edition*. Frederick, CO: Sopris West.

Sarason, S. (1996). *Revisiting "The culture of the school and the problem of change."* New York: Teachers College Press.

Schein, E.H. (1999). *Process consultation revisited: Building the helping relationship*. Reading, MA: Addison-Wesley.

Part V
Consulting with Special Education Teachers

The role of consultee-centered consultation in the special education classroom is well documented in these two chapters. Elise Pas demonstrates how careful attention to problem identification can challenge assumptions about the function of behavior in a student with autism, and lead to a more productive outcome for student and teacher alike. Elizabeth Tsakiris takes the consultee-centered consultation process into the domain occupied by teachers of classes for students with more severe disabilities, and examines its role in that complex context.

11
Case Metamorphosis through Consultation

Elise T. Pas

Introduction

In this chapter, a school consultation case completed with an elementary special education teacher to address the behaviors of a student diagnosed with autism will be summarized. The target behavior in this case was that the student stood too close (i.e., within six inches) to others (i.e., teachers and sometimes students) when communicating. Occasionally, the student also tapped on the other individual's forehead. The purpose of presenting this case example is to address three important questions.

Advance Organizer Questions

- **How does a consultant in training apply consultation skills typically used with general education teachers when working with a special educator?**
- **Why is it especially important to establish a collaborative relationship during contracting when working with a special education teacher?**
- **Why is following all of the steps in the problem-solving process essential?**

Culture of the School

The school in which this case was completed is a mid-sized elementary school with a high percentage (i.e., over 90%) of ethnic minorities. The school psychologist on site was a multi-talented psychologist who engaged in a plethora of activities including:

1. active involvement on the school's pre-referral problem-solving team (which used the Instructional Support Team approach; Kovaleski, 2002);
2. classroom-based assessment and interventions;
3. counseling activities; and
4. psychological assessments.

The school psychologist was only based in this elementary school for two days a week. Despite the psychologist's broad ability and knowledge base, the psychologist was very busy and often needed to respond reactively to urgent problems.

The problem-solving model in the school reflected the IST model, which follows a team-based expert approach. Typically, teachers came to the team with a concern that was already severe and causing the teacher a high level of stress. Experts around the table (i.e., the instructional support teacher/facilitator, school psychologist, and administrators) assigned tasks (such as data collection) and shared advice on interventions for the teacher to conduct. The expectation was that the teacher would go back to her/his classroom, complete the assigned tasks, and come back to the team with results. Teachers sometimes had difficulty implementing these recommendations because of the lack of time that the instructional support teacher had to help the referring teacher understand and execute these processes. As a result, many meetings conducted were without assessment data or data on implementation fidelity. In general, the problem identification stage was largely missing from the process and interventions were either not implemented or not successful (i.e., because they were not well-matched to the problem or because the problem had not been clearly identified); in turn, the teacher and the team often experienced frustration with the outcomes.

This process is in contrast to one that I tried to achieve in this case example. Instead of working with a team, the teacher and I met one-on-one. The one-on-one nature of the work done was not practiced elsewhere in the school building. In addition, teachers generally (and this consultee specifically) were not accustomed to being actively involved in the problem-solving process. Special educators were also not often involved in this type of problem solving because the school-level team process was a "pre-referral" process used for students not yet evaluated for or placed into special education. Given this culture, clarifying the expectations for this one-on-one consultation process was extremely important. Despite being starkly different from the typical experience in this school, the consultee was excited to work one-on-one to problem-solve for this student and issues of resistance, which can often arise when a consultant works against the culture of the school, were not an issue. The consultee welcomed this opportunity but was not fully equipped with the knowledge of how this process would or should proceed.

Relationship with the Consultee

During this case, I was a third-year school psychology doctoral student and had already completed a full year of training, practicum cases, and supervision in consultation. Prior to graduate school, I had gained extensive experience in functional behavior assessment and analysis while working as a teacher's aide for students with autism. As a result, I had been waived out of the applied behavior analysis course requirement in the graduate program and actually served as a teaching assistant for the course. As part of this teaching assistant position, I supervised others in behavior modification, including the process of functional behavioral assessment, data collection and interpretation, and intervention development and evaluation. Thus, I was easily able to focus on the consultation aspects as I had considerable knowledge of applied behavior analysis.

The consultee was a special education teacher who taught in a small class (i.e., about six students) of students with autism. The teacher was an early career professional with a few years of teaching experience and was well-respected in the school as an effective and extremely dedicated teacher. Both of us identified as Caucasian females. The target student was an ethnic minority.

The relationship actually began with this teacher in the fall of the school year, when she contacted me regarding a different student with challenging behaviors. Shortly after our work began, this other student changed educational settings. Therefore, my work regarding this student was terminated. The special education teacher and I then began working together with a new student, who became the target student in this case example. We began to discuss the target student's case as I had conducted a re-evaluation assessment for his Individualized Education Plan (IEP) as part of my fieldwork. At the conclusion of testing and following the re-evaluation meeting, we began working together in a consultative dyad to address some concerns which arose in the testing and meeting. While this was a great opportunity to blend formal assessment and intervention, this made setting a collaborative relationship more difficult than in prior consultation work completed. As a school psychologist practicum student, having completed a formal diagnostic evaluation, I functioned and came to be seen as an "expert" by the teacher, which made it difficult to transition to a collaborative consultation role. In addition, I was assigned this assessment case because of extensive work completed in applied behavior analysis prior to graduate training and for my ability to focus on measurable and objective IEP goals.

In short, resulting partially from the preceding evaluation as well as the larger school context and culture, it was difficult to develop a collaborative working dynamic with this teacher. For example, I often dominated the relationship by speaking more than the consultee, failed to reflect and process what she said, and asked close-ended questions that directed the process. While the teacher was extremely motivated to address the student's concern, she was unfamiliar with a collaborative problem-solving approach and required a clear conversation as well as modeling of the collaborative relationship. As will be discussed later, this failure to establish a collaborative relationship had implications for the path of problem solving and started with the contracting stage. Fortunately, through supervision, this concern was identified and addressed. This case example will demonstrate the importance and value of thorough supervision meetings, which in this case involved taped recordings of each session and written consultant process notes.

Communication Skills

In the first two sessions, I did a lot of talking for our dyad, which included providing information and asking close-ended, directive questions. For example, I asked questions like "Would you say you see this behavior with other students or just adults?" or "So it seems that both you and his mother are concerned about this?" This did not allow the teacher to provide information to me or to expand on her own ideas about the problem and I inadvertently established a dynamic in which I communicated that I was an "expert" and knew what to do to solve this problem. As a result, the teacher frequently agreed with my thoughts and suggestions, asked for my opinion about what we should do, and did not tend to contribute her own ideas to our problem solving. Though I was aware of these dynamics, I struggled in the first two sessions to refocus our communication process to help the teacher make contributions and feel empowered. After the second session, the supervisor for this case (my campus course instructor) asked me to go back and listen to the tape and write a process log reflecting again on this session. In response, I wrote:

> During the session and both times that I listened to the tape [the teacher's] questions struck me. There seems to be an element of collaboration between us, but it is clear that she regards my opinion and decisions as important (i.e., she does not feel autonomous to say what should or should not be a part of the [intervention] without my approval). When I divert her questions to me, and ask what she thinks, she will tell me. One way to enhance the collaboration between us is to continue reflecting her questions back to her instead of answering them for her.

Listening to the tape again also helped me think about content concerns in our case such as the need for data and the types of questions one asks, as is demonstrated from this process note:

> Once we were talking about the best setting to take data in, I asked a lot of questions. I could have done this with more open-ended questions like "Tell me more about how he behaves in [a particular] setting." This is also where a functional behavioral assessment could come in.

Despite my expertise in functional behavior assessment, I enabled us to spend most of the time in these two sessions focusing on the information we knew and our preconceived assessment of the problem, rather than thinking about how the data should enhance our understanding of the problem. By the end of the session, we had agreed on data for the teacher to collect, but again, this idea and decision was not made in a collaborative way.

During the third session, the teacher apologized a lot for not collecting data and this re-emphasized to me that there was not shared ownership in this case. Her apologies likely stemmed from the fact that I had stated at the end of the second session "if you could get three data points this week …" As a result, the teacher felt that she had been assigned a task and was apologetic for not completing it. Instead, during the previous session, I could have said, "Let's discuss how we would like to collect the data." After reflecting on these issues between the second and third session, I decided to reset the expectations regarding the working relationship, which I will describe below. We spent the rest of our time together in the next session talking about our relationship, how this consultation process differs from other consultation in the school, and where this fits with the IEP process. In process logs, I noted:

> Once I got past trying to transition to [the] topic [of our roles], I felt that we finally had a dialogue about consultation; something we should have done during contracting. I think this went better than my first try and hope this helps us move forward in problem identification.

In subsequent sessions, I switched to using more open-ended questions (e.g., "Tell me what happens before, during, and after the behavior occurs"), paraphrases and clarifications (e.g., "Your examples of the behavior all seem to involve adults; would you say this behavior is occurring most often with adults or does he display it with other students as well?"), to help the teacher reflect on her points made and for her to draw her own conclusions. Most importantly, even when I knew the answers to my question, the use of clarifying questions assisted the teacher in drawing the conclusions, established a more collaborative working relationship and empowered the teacher to answer her own questions. For me, this required patience and wait time; this largely differed from my earlier approach, where I freely offered advice and solutions. I needed to be cognizant of and purposefully use my communication skills differently.

Due to this shift in communication skills used, a new dynamic was established where the teacher equally contributed to the process as an expert in teaching as well as the student's needs. My main role was to keep our dyad focused on the problem identification process, and to accurately reflect and clarify the teacher's ideas. In reality, the teacher had all of the solutions to this problem, but just needed someone to help her think them through. In response to this need, I deliberately used clarifications for the teacher to expand on the antecedents and consequences of the behavior. This was in contrast to the earlier used close-ended questions, which forced the teacher to describe the problem as I believed it existed. An important thing to note was not only did my former approach fail to establish a collaborative working relationship, but my initial assessment of the problem was inaccurate and therefore would not have led to an adequate intervention. In only asking close-ended questions, I worked to verify my own "truth" of the problem and failed to recognize immediately that my conceptualization was wrong. It was only after changing the dynamic of our working relationship that the teacher and I figured out the true function of the student's behavior.

Following the changed approach to this consultation case, the teacher and I spent a lot of time reflecting on how the environment was eliciting and enabling this student's behavior (i.e., thinking about what the adults were doing) and how to shift the environment to elicit a different behavior from the student. Through reflective paraphrases and clarifications, as well as more focused effort on data collection, the problem was more efficiently and correctly identified. As a result, the entire conceptualization of the problem changed and, subsequently, so did the intervention ideas. Toward the end of the consultation work, the teacher expressed satisfaction that we had time to reflect on her own and the teacher aides' behavior, and verbalized that this was the most helpful part about our meeting. She also mentioned having "learned so much," which was an indicator of the success in not just addressing the student's needs, but in building her skills.

Problem-Solving Stages

Contracting

This case was referred as an outgrowth of a formal psychological assessment completed for the student's IEP renewal. The teacher and I began work on another case prior to this case; however, this was ended when the student transferred from this school. Because we had gone through contracting previously, I started by saying, "You may remember the last time we started a case, we started out with contracting where we talked about what the process is going to look like?" To this, the teacher responded, "yes" and I said, "We can just quickly go through that. What can you remember about last time about what this will look like and what we will do?" The teacher responded by saying "Oh my gosh … I've got a bad memory" and then continued reviewing the specifics of the previous case, mentioning collaboration and reviewing the academic goals for that other student. I focused on how the consultation process involves targeting academic goals and related it to the current potential targeted "off-task behaviors." Then, I *briefly* walked through the stages of problem solving and elicited agreement on the collaborative process, "shared ownership," and weekly meetings. In actuality it is likely that I did not do a comprehensive contracting in the first case, and when this became apparent in the second case, I failed to revisit it adequately. The missed opportunity at this point was that I did not elaborate on the "collaboration" that the teacher referred to and I ended the contracting stage prematurely. This "trap" of ending contracting prematurely arose from several factors, which are reviewed below.

After the first session, I noted in the supervision process notes:

> I went through the contracting quickly because we had worked together before and time was running low. In retrospect, it may have been better to work through this more slowly and elicit her to provide more information about the process. In general, I have struggled with making contracting interactive, but because I had worked with her before it felt even weirder to go through this really slowly. This is an issue I have seen in all of my contracting.

As identified here, I, like many novice consultants, struggled with contracting, feeling that it was awkward and unnecessary. In this case, the fact that there was a prior relationship with this teacher led me to assume a collaborative working relationship existed, which made me feel uncomfortable re-presenting the contracting process. Also, the fact that the teacher was a special (not general) educator led me to make assumptions about her prior knowledge of problem solving and made me want to avoid talking about something (i.e., the process) that the teacher already knew about. However, by rushing through the contracting stage, probably in both cases, I failed to set the tone for a collaborative working relationship. As a result, these issues re-surfaced in the third session, when I, as well as my supervisor, felt that both the teacher and I were operating in a non-collaborative manner and, as a result, were also not successful in identifying the problem. Therefore, in our third session, the teacher and I revisited contracting as well as the dynamic between us. Due to state assessments and spring break, this session actually occurred over a month after the first session. Below is a partial transcript of my statements to the teacher during the third session on this issue:

> This is actually a good opportunity to revisit some of the stuff that we talked about in the first week. I hear you apologizing to me and feeling badly about [not collecting data] and I am wondering if we can kind of go back to where we quickly skimmed through the process and talk a little bit about our relationship. You don't have to feel bad about this; a really essential part about the type of consultation that I would like to do is a little different from what I understand the IST [Instructional Support Team] process may be like. I don't want this to be an expert mode, like "I'm the boss" and that I will come in and say "this is what you should to do" and if you don't do it that I will [think or say] "That bad teacher didn't collect data." I really want to work—I guess a good phrase is shoulder to shoulder (Gravois, Gickling, & Rosenfield, 2007)—with you about this concern.

The lesson I learned from this case was the importance of establishing the roles of the consultant and consultee and a shared understanding of the process early on. Also, contracting is an opportunity to practice and model the interactive nature of the problem-solving process. By engaging in an interactive contracting session, a consultant can set the stage for a dynamic in which consultant and consultee have a back-and-forth conversation about concerns. As the consultant in this case, I struggled with how to make the contracting interactive and therefore either talked *at* the consultee or avoided it altogether. As a result, much of the initial problem identification meetings that followed were not productive.

Problem Identification

Similarly to the contracting stage, there were two iterations of problem identification in this case. Both are highlighted here to demonstrate what an inadequate problem identification process and effective problem identification look like, as well as the outcomes of both processes. It is important to note that problem solving is a dynamic process and that just because the consultant addresses a stage, does not mean that the work of that stage is finished. If the dyad moves through a stage inadequately, it is essential to come back to it, as the teacher and I did in this case. Supervision played a major role in achieving this realization, as it was through a supervisor's prompting that I saw that problem identification was inadequate and needed to be restarted.

There was considerable background information on the target student, who was diagnosed with autism and visual impairment. Despite these difficulties, according to the teacher, the student was on grade level in many areas; he decoded and read fluently at his grade level and mastered anything he could memorize (e.g., grade level math facts, spelling tasks). As a result of these strengths, he received reading and math instruction partially in a general education classroom with the assistance of an aide. He had significant difficulties with expressive communication and socialization and struggled with applied skills (e.g., reading comprehension, math word problems, and applying spelling rules to new words). Like many students with autism, the student did not generalize skills; rather, he needed to be explicitly assisted to generalize the skills he knew in isolation. To address these needs, the student received this instruction in the special education setting.

Based on the preceding psychological assessment, which I had conducted as part of my fieldwork placement, two possible concerns were identified:

1. increasing the student's standing distance during social interactions (e.g., standing at a distance of one foot or greater from other's when interacting) as he often stood in close proximity when speaking to others; and
2. increasing the student's *active* on-task behaviors (e.g., raising his hand to participate and providing responses) since his passive on-task behaviors (e.g., sitting and attending) were adequate.

The student's mother was extremely concerned about the former, given implications for quality of life. There was an open line of communication with the student's parents, who were very knowledgeable about his disability and highly involved in his education.

Problem Identification, Take One

Two concerns were identified as part of the IEP re-evaluation process and were a starting point for discussion in our first consultation session. The teacher expressed concern with the student's interactions with peers, and described this as a "quality of life" issue. More specifically, the student often stood within six inches of others and tapped on their foreheads. These behaviors did not lead to appropriate social interactions with peers or adults. Initially, the teacher expressed the desire to begin by addressing social distance only during recess, as recess is a social setting. I followed up by asking whether this was the only place the behavior occurred. At this point, the teacher mentioned that the student engaged in it often and that it could be related to his poor vision. We then began to discuss the student's mother's perspective on this concern, as the mother identified this as a priority during the psychological evaluation. The mother felt that the student's vision was adequate with his glasses, the student engaged in this behavior to achieve social connectedness, and that there may have been a sensory component (e.g., visual stimulation and touching others) to this behavior. The teacher and I prioritized another concern, "active on-task behaviors," as secondary and one that would not be addressed during this consultation.

At the start of the problem identification, we spent a lot of time discussing multiple case details (i.e., those outlined above). As a result, the teacher and I became lost in the wide array of information available to us about this student. Further, I missed opportunities to clarify important information that would have led to more efficient problem identification (e.g., settings and whether this occurred with adults only, peers only, or both). Later on in the problem solving, the teacher provided more pertinent information that I could have elicited earlier, such as the fact that "when redirected" (i.e., a relevant consequence to the behavior), the student made a verbal want request. Also, the teacher stated that the student engaged in this behavior mostly with adults, but that she was concerned that it made him stand out among peers. Instead of focusing in on the behavior as occurring with adults (i.e., beginning to assess the setting of the behavior), I led our problem solving to focus on where to intervene (i.e., pointing out that we should not just focus on recess).

From there, the conversation turned to previously attempted interventions. This is an example of jumping too far ahead and failing to recognize that the majority of work needed in a consultation case is the identification of the *problem*, *not* the identification of a *solution*. Without the former, the latter is impossible. In summary, I resorted to using the process I commonly saw practiced in the school—jumping to give advice and intervention ideas—without focusing enough time on data collection and problem identification.

At the end of the first session, *I* decided that we should collect data on how far the student stood from others (which had been established already during the psychological assessment as no further than six inches) and that we could start by prompting the student not to touch others' foreheads. The behavior was well defined at this point (which was a positive step towards problem identification), but in retrospect, we should have been focused on data to determine the function of the behavior by assessing settings in which the behavior occurred (e.g., recess, with adults) and the antecedents and consequences to the behavior (e.g., being prompted and then asking for something he wanted).

In the second session, the focus of conversation continued to be intervention focused, including how to teach the student to stand further away from others.

Our data collection was related to the outcome (distance from others) rather than assessing why this behavior occurred. The teacher and I operated under the assumption that the behavior occurred because he did not understand social distance pragmatics, which we believed to be a symptom of his autism. This illustrates the easy trap for consultants, which is to focus on *assumptions* about behaviors instead of focusing on *data* to determine why behaviors occur. This also highlights a diversity issue; when working with students of diverse backgrounds or circumstances (in this case, a student with disabilities), it is even more important to guard against falling into the trap of making assumptions about a group (e.g., students with autism lack skills with social pragmatics, and therefore any inappropriate "social" behavior must be the result of the disability). At the early stages of this case, I automatically made assumptions, rather than relying on the problem identification process, in guiding our approach. It was only with the prompting of my supervisor that I realized what I did.

In these two sessions, consultant-driven conversation focused on the intervention, which resulted in a delay identifying the true cause of the behavior. I knew that to establish an observable and measurable definition of the behavior, one should establish when the behavior does and does not occur, what occurs before the behavior, and what occurs after the behavior. Despite this knowledge, I enabled us to skip over the step of collecting data on these elements. In some ways, our combined expertise on autism led us to see this as a symptom of autism (i.e., lack of understanding of social pragmatics) without thinking more broadly about the problem and trying to define it.

Problem Identification, Take Two

After some reflection about the first two sessions, listening to audiotapes of our first two case sessions, composing reflective logs, and discussing the case with the supervisor, I realized that our dyad needed to restart the problem-solving process. As indicated earlier, we revisited the contracting stage and then started a new conversation about problem identification. In listening to the tapes of the first sessions again, it became clear that a functional behavioral assessment was needed and that data on the antecedents, behavior, and consequences would help to determine the function of the behavior.

To start, we collected data about settings in which the behavior (i.e., standing within one foot of another person and tapping their forehead with his finger or fingers) did and did not occur and how far the student was from the adult when it did occur. In the fourth session, we reviewed the data and made some hypotheses of possible functions, based on patterns in the settings identified in the data. The teacher and I decided to collect more data regarding the settings throughout the next week. In the fifth session, the new data were reviewed and it was apparent that the student only stood too close to others and tapped their forehead when in the bathroom, where he received toileting assistance, and also when he wanted something (e.g., he wanted to make a request for access to a tangible item or time with the teacher). The teacher noted a trend that each time the student engaged in the standing too close and tapping behavior, he started a sentence saying, "I want" (twice) and then got close to the teacher's face and sometimes touched the teacher's forehead. We agreed to collect more data on this behavior, this time emphasizing the consequences rather than the settings or distance he stood from others.

The data made it clear that the student engaged in this behavior when he wanted something, and that the consequence was that the adult often guessed what he wanted, in order to redirect him. Therefore, we collected data on his appropriate requesting what he wanted (i.e., when he said "I want the [item]"). In the seventh session, we reviewed the data and found that he only appropriately asked for his blue ball and vanilla wafers. When he stood too close and tapped the teacher's forehead, he was asked what he wanted (i.e., she would list items and ask him "Do you want [item]?"). It turned out that each time he indicated either wanting time at the computer, to listen to a CD, or time with the teacher. The teacher communicated that the student was successful in asking for the ball and wafers because he requested them most frequently and the teachers had been working on this request with him for the longest amount of time. We determined that the function of the standing too close and tapping behavior was to receive prompting to make a request for a desired item. Therefore, we decided that the intervention needed to teach him a replacement behavior for getting his needs met.

Implementation Planning

Once it was determined that the student needed to be taught how to ask for other desired items, I asked the teacher to discuss how she taught the student to say the sentence "I want the blue ball." This question empowered the teacher to design the intervention and helped build our collaboration. Partly, it seemed that the student had mastered the sentence "I want the blue ball" because:

1. it was a highly desired item;
2. the teacher had made the blue ball constantly available for the student (i.e., whenever he asked for it, he could get it); and
3. the teacher had visual prompts for the ball all over the room.

On the other hand, the student was not always permitted time at the computer, to listen to the CD, or time with the teacher when he had asked in the past. In addition, visual prompts were absent for these reinforcer items.

The teacher stated that she and the teacher's aides relied more on verbal than visual prompting with these other items. In fact, previously, the student had a communication book with pictures of desired items that he could remove and hand to an adult, but it was no longer used. I then prompted the teacher to recall the shaping steps she used to teach asking for the blue ball, to see if the same steps could be used to teach him to say "I want the (computer, CD, teacher time, etc)." Again, this empowered the teacher by making her realize that she knew how to address this concern and had successfully done so in the past. We agreed that the first step was to allow him to use visual prompts (pointing to a picture of what he wants), then just name what he wanted (i.e., the item name), and by the end of the intervention he would be able to use a sentence ("I want the _______"), similar to the steps used to teach him to request the ball and wafers. The teacher expressed a fear of giving the answers too quickly, so we discussed how to ensure adults did not just give him the answer by pointing to or naming the item for him. The teacher and I agreed that the adults could hand the student the communication book as he approached them (before he could touch an adult or get too close), so that he could find a picture of what he wanted.

Implementation

The teacher worked with the two teacher aides in the classroom to ensure that everyone used the communication book with this student. Due to the small class size and individualized education that each student received, implementation fidelity was high. As soon as we decided that the student needed to be taught to ask for the desired items, all adults used the book regularly.

Evaluation

To keep the data collection simple, we agreed to collect frequency data of how many times a day the student stood within one foot of an adult and tapped their forehead. After the first week, we reviewed the data and found that the student only stood too close and touched someone's forehead one time, on only one day, whereas he had engaged in this behavior multiple times per day during the baseline phase of data collection. See Figure 11.1 for graph of behavior during baseline and intervention data collection.

We reviewed the baseline data to determine the number of times the student had appropriately requested an item prior to the intervention. At the most, he

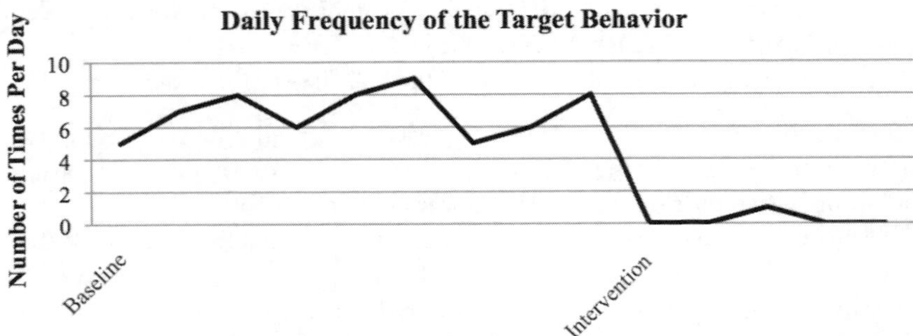

Figure 11.1 Daily Frequency of the Target Behavior.

had appropriately asked for something three times in one day. The teacher decided to collect data on frequency of appropriate requesting and the "too close" behavior data in the next week. Typically, the intervention evaluation process would have continued for a few more weeks, but since this meeting occurred in the second to last week of school, it was our final meeting.

Closure

The teacher and I worked together to summarize the case and the student's progress in a closure memo to be put in the student's file for summer school and next year's teacher. This was helpful in providing both the teacher and me the opportunity to reflect on the case, review what had been done, and get closure for the case. Having the opportunity to summarize the progress we made was helpful for the teacher. Finally, we discussed the beneficial elements of this process, in order to clarify the areas of growth she had experienced.

She talked about benefiting in two major ways:

1. the ability to think about and design new ways to collect data; and
2. the opportunity to "bounce ideas back and forth and hypothesizing," in a "structured way," so that she could see the behavior of concern in a new way.

The teacher stated that she felt that all teams should work like we did, on a weekly basis to improve practice. She stated feeling grateful that even when she "went off on tangents," that I was "able to pull [her] back in." The teacher noted that she would apply these new skills in the future.

Lessons Learned

In reference to the introductory questions, there were a few major lessons learned from this case.

1. Though the focus of my training was in working with general education teachers, all of the same elements were helpful and necessary in working with a special educator. By working with a special educator with a small class size and the assistance of aides, issues of implementation fidelity and resistance to individualizing an intervention for one student were absent. This enhanced the success of the intervention in this case. On the other hand, assuming that a special educator would be well versed in problem solving led me astray and resulted in a delay of problem identification.
2. The school context and culture around problem solving is an important element to consider. Though I clearly saw the school process and was able to identify how I wanted to proceed differently, I still fell into a role that largely mirrored the problem solving at the school. A consultant should always keep the broader context in mind.

3. The contracting stage is essential in setting the stage for the problem-solving process. By skimming past this as a consultant, the important opportunity for defining the working relationship is missed, the communication skills used are impacted and, as a result, the problem identification process is derailed. It is important to take time in both contracting and problem identification, even when the consultant feels sure that the consultant and consultee have a shared understanding of the process and problem. The bulk of the work of problem solving needs to be done up front during the contracting and problem identification stages.
4. Having extensive content knowledge can be helpful when working with teachers, though it can also cause you to lose sight of the process. By having an expertise in autism and behavioral analysis, I easily switched from a collaborative consultant into an expert. This led me to impose my own assumptions onto the problem, rather than staying true to the collaborative problem-solving approach. In the end, the process and not my content knowledge is what allowed us to successfully meet this student's needs.
5. Communication skills are an integral part of the consultation process and, for me, the use of the appropriate skills (e.g., reflection of questions rather than providing answers) required patience and wait time.
6. Finally, without a reflective supervision process, none of the above lessons would have been learned. Having tapes of the sessions allowed my supervisor to identify exactly where I went wrong in the process; without those tapes, the supervisor only would have known what I shared. The tapes also served as a tool in supervision; once the supervisor realized the problem, she referred me back to the tape with some prompting rather than simply telling me the problem and solution. This allowed the supervisor to model the communication and problem-solving skills I needed to use with the teacher.

Questions for Reflection

Based on the experience of this novice consultant in this case, consider these thought questions:

1. **How will you balance bringing expertise to the consultation process while promoting a collaborative working relationship that empowers teachers to find solutions to student concerns and to grow professionally?**
2. **Are there consultation skills that I identified as challenging that you can foresee yourself struggling with? What can you do to ensure that you enhance these specific skills during your training?**
3. **In what ways does working with special versus general educators change the problem-solving process?**
4. **The relationship between the consultee and me was friendly at first. Why do you think friendliness did not translate automatically to collaboration during this process?**

5. **Do you think the shared gender and race between us contributed to the relationship? If so, explain how. Similarly, from a multicultural consultation perspective, what could I have learned and done differently had the cultural incongruence of the student with the consultant and consultee been explored?**

References

Gravois, T.A., Gickling, E.E., & Rosenfield, S. (2007). *IC Teams: Training in instructional consultation, assessment, and teaming.* Books 1 & 2. Catonsville, MD: ICAT Publishing.

Kovaleski, J.F. (2002). Best practices in operating prereferral intervention teams. In A. Thomas & J. Grimes (Eds.), *Best practices in school psychology IV* (pp. 645–656). Washington, DC: National Association of School Psychologists.

12

Leaving No Teacher Behind: Widening the View and Changing the Perspective

Elizabeth Tsakiris

Introduction

Currently, the literature on Instructional Consultation (Rosenfield, Silva, & Gravois, 2008) and many other consultation models that focus on teacher support do not discuss or explore the use of this model within special education programs. Indeed, often one of the goals of this type of model is to limit special education placements and referrals. While not explicitly stated in theory, many practitioners operate under the assumption that once a child is referred for special education services, consultation services end. Consultation practica in school psychology programs, for example, are not typically conducted with special education teachers, particularly those teachers with students who have severe and multiple challenges compounded with intellectual disabilities.

The above omission, regardless of whether or not it is intentional, fosters the belief that special education is the "answer" for the teacher and the child, and even more erroneously that the special education teacher and her team have or should have all of the answers. For students with relatively few hours of special education services, some aspects of the collaborative consultation problem-solving model may remain intact, especially for the classroom teacher. However, most of consultee-centered consultation services of the school psychologist are still reserved for the regular education teacher, not the special education teacher or other specialists.

To provide a "backdrop" context for the case described in this chapter, I interviewed 20 teachers of children with severe challenges in one mid-Atlantic school district with self-contained classrooms. The students received intensive services a maximum of 40 hours per week. Of these teachers, 15 had classrooms in regular education settings, and some of the students had access to participation with regular education students at times. Five of the teachers worked in special education centers, whose students had no access to typical peers. *None* of the special education teachers reported having access to the support systems of the consultation problem-solving model (i.e., the problem-solving school team) in their building, even when their classes and programs were located within the same public school. Most of the staff members on the school teams did not interact professionally with these special education teachers. As a general rule, in looking across the continuum of student need, there were fewer if any consultation services available to the special education teachers from the school's problem-solving team and/or the school psychologist when the students they served had more severe intellectual disabilities and/or behavioral challenges.

While the five center-based teachers and six of the special education classroom teachers reported having team meetings with speech-language, occupational, and physical therapy related service providers to problem-solve, none of these team meetings followed a collaborative process. Rather, a return to the medical model of seeking expert advice was the default process. When crises arose, specialists usually were called in to support the teacher. They provided suggestions for classroom restructuring and behavior plans over several visits. However, the teachers reported seeing them more as stepping stones to help get a student removed from their classroom and placed in another program—although this removal seldom occurred. The analysis and identification of the problem did not focus on the entire system in great detail, but upon the child's performance and behavior *in isolation*. In all cases, this was without exploring the possibility of a "mismatch" between instruction/environment and the child (Rosenfield, 2008).

Applying Instructional Consultation (IC) to a Special Education Teacher's Concern

The following case study is an attempt to apply the IC model with Lynn, a special education teacher serving a classroom of six students with severe behavioral and cognitive challenges, and her student, Marjory. Marjory was 17 years of age with a long history of intractable aggressive behaviors that included biting and injuring staff and students. This study explores the need for an IC model for teachers of these students as well as their school systems at large. It illustrates the potential benefits IC can offer to support teachers within this unique and challenging special education population.

Advance Organizing Questions

- **What roadblocks do special education teachers of severely challenged students face in seeking help to improve the performance and behaviors of their students?**
- **How can collaboration be promoted when the special education program is completely separate from the larger school culture?**
- **Can the IC model be effective to provide this support? If so, what would need to be changed/adapted for it to become a part of the school culture?**
- **What additional skills must a consultant master when working with a special educator?**

Culture of the School

Marcetti School serves over 500 elementary school students from kindergarten through fifth grade. The majority of students are in the middle to upper-middle class socioeconomic status. But at least one-fourth receive Free and Reduced Lunch and Breakfast, indicating that a lower socioeconomic group is also a part of the student body. The minority population is 25% with 15% of this group of Hispanic descent. The school is located in a middle class suburban neighborhood, near local grocery and retail stores in strip malls and county recreation facilities.

In addition, a program called Pathways had two classrooms in the building—one for elementary aged students and one for students ages 12–18. These classrooms were for students with severe behavioral challenges and intellectual disabilities/autism. At times these were compounded by physical/orthopedic challenges, although these were never the prime disability. The program was moved from a self-contained center to this public school location, in an effort to be more inclusive. The Marcetti PTA did not want the Pathways program to have the same name as the school, and voted that the program keep its name of Pathways. They added "Pathways" under the name Marcetti School on the sign in front of the building and on all stationery.

While there is a principal of Marcetti, there is also a coordinator of the Pathways program. Administrative responsibilities are assigned accordingly. The Pathways program coordinator served three other schools where other Pathways classrooms were located, and was in Marcetti usually two days a week. In matters of crisis, the principal of Marcetti has the final authority in decision-making, but in the day-to-day operations of the program, the coordinator is in charge of Pathways.

The Pathways and Marcetti students have separate libraries and playgrounds. A separate school psychologist was assigned to serve the Marcetti students in the building, but not Pathways. However, speech language and occupational therapists worked with both student populations. I was assigned as the school psychologist to the Pathways program on the first day the students arrived as a part of my caseload.

The multi-layered administration and staff appeared to be "collaborative." (See Figure 12.1.) However, like the sign in front of the school, there was a distinct separation between dealing with problems for Marcetti and Pathways. The reality for the Pathways' special education classes was that the problem-solving process was done by individual decision makers at any given point, with an outward appearance of collaboration. (See Figure 12.2.)

Time was never allotted in the school day for the Pathway teachers to meet with each other. All such meetings took place on a "catch as catch can" basis, with before and after school time reserved for the administration to give information to teachers. Para-educators were not paid to be a part of class planning, and therefore came to the building when the students arrived and left when the

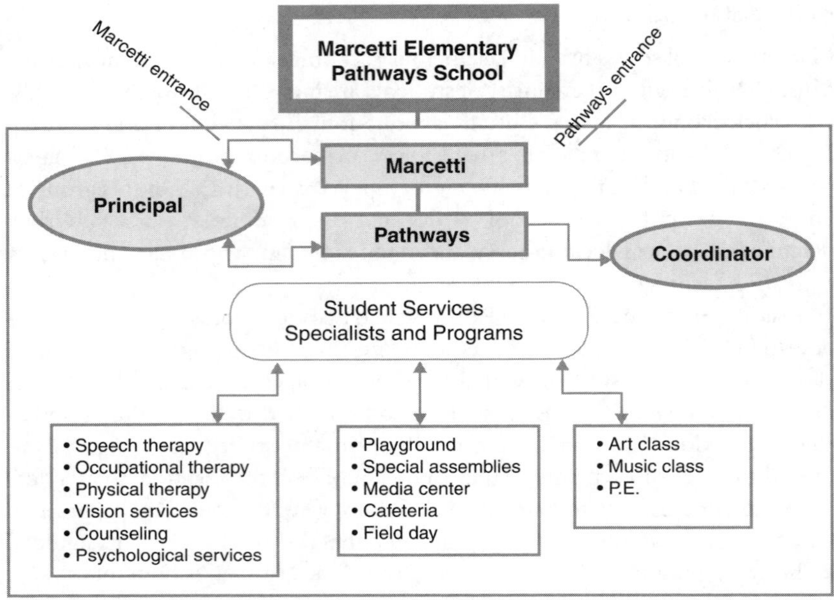

Figure 12.1 The Illusion of Collaboration and Inclusion.

students departed. Students in the Pathways' classes ate lunch in their classrooms, not in the lunchrooms with the other students in the building. Given the severity of the student challenges, trained assistants and/or teachers had to be with them during this time period. This meant the teachers ate their lunch with the students. The staff rotated this responsibility so that each staff member could eat lunch one to two days a week outside of the classroom. Throughout the rest of the building, Marcetti teachers ate lunch in the teacher lounges. In this regard, I soon learned that the Pathways program was a "sub-culture" of the building and had a different set of "rules" to be followed. By default, I was soon to become a member of this "sub-culture"—only learning the rules on the job.

Reflection One

The cultural dynamics of Pathways at Marcetti were very different from the other schools in my caseload over the years. At the time, I was serving six other schools that also housed special education students with intensive needs. My work with school staff during the past six years, while not clearly defined as an IC model, was team based. Decisions about student programming were made collaboratively, not always by the same team players in each school, but always within a team decision-making process.

I failed to look closely at the individual cultures of Pathways and Marcetti as well as the school culture of the Pathway/Marcetti unit—assuming they were

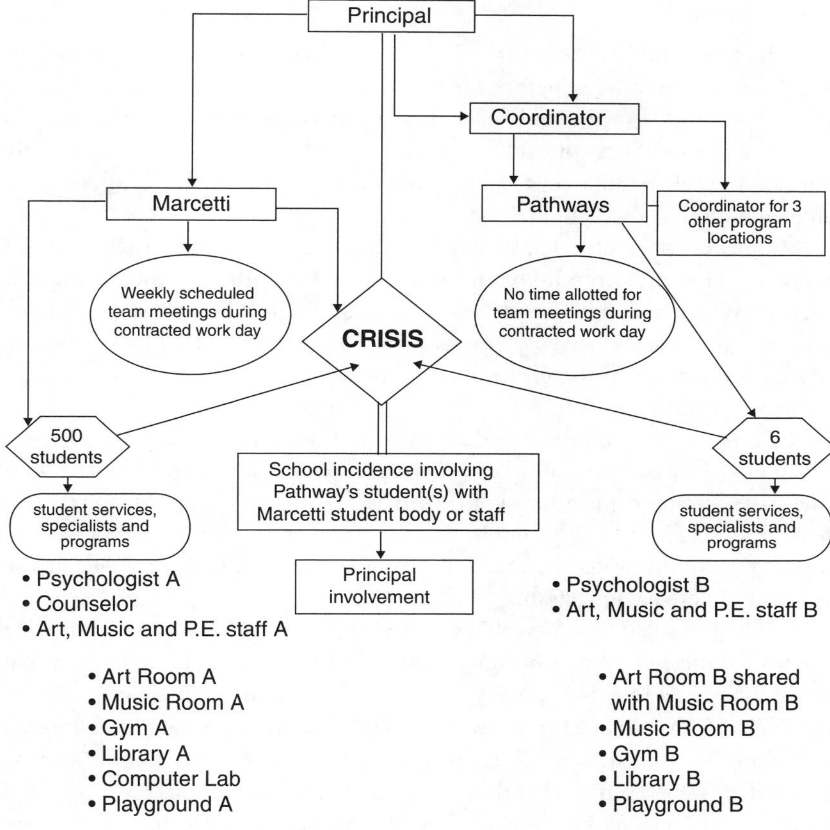

Figure 12.2 The Reality of Separation.

the same. Instead, I operated by default, assuming the same behavioral regularities (Sarason, 1996) of my other programs. For example, I neither paid attention to the obvious information provided by the school sign outside the building, nor ever asked for an administrative flow chart. Not doing so left me vulnerable to pre-judge the dynamics of both programs, as opposed to understanding them. In my IC coursework I learned to look for more of the "hidden" complexities of school cultures as opposed to making any assumptions. My IC supervisor suggested activities that I could have been done before actually meeting with the teacher so I would have a better understanding of not just the school procedures she had to work within, but also the dynamics within these procedures. Activities like eating lunch in the staff room, looking at school newsletters, as well as observing student/teacher movement during the day could have helped lead to an understanding of the " unspoken" aspects of the Marcetti/Pathway cultures.

Relationships

Lynn had been hired as a special education teacher for the 12–18-year-olds at Pathways only one week before the school year began. However, she was no stranger to working with students with complex challenges. She had a master's degree in special education and five prior years of teaching students with severe autism at the elementary level using applied behavior analysis strategies closely aligned with the Lovaas model.

My professional experiences began as a special education teacher for 13 years, working in both self-contained and inclusive settings with regular and special education students of all ages and disabilities. I had returned to graduate school to become a school psychologist, earned certification, and was working on my doctorate. Enrollment in consultation courses at the university was a part of this trajectory, and the practicum requirements involved consultation in the schools. My employer had assigned me to serve Pathways as a school psychologist in addition to other job assignments. The referral to assist with Marjory's teacher came after the first semester of the consultation course had been completed, and I had completed other practicum experiences with the IC model. I was motivated to see if IC could be effective for teachers in the specialized Pathways program.

Building a relationship with Lynn required negotiating a path between acknowledging her feelings of frustration and educating her about the potential of the IC model to provide her support. Neither occurred in isolation of the other. A major challenge for me in this project was not to get caught in the trap of "admiring the problem," even when many variables which could not be controlled were continually thwarting intervention efforts. This required maintaining a balance between allowing the teacher to express her frustrations with the "system," but not letting this release of feelings interfere with focusing on the student and her identified goal. At times, drawing the line in this regard was not received positively by the teacher. As a former special education teacher, I empathized with her concerns and had to pay close attention to setting boundaries. I had learned in the IC classes that "sharing the reality" (Higgins, 1999) of the frustrations which the teacher incurred in dealing with a problem may actually limit/bias one's ability to understand and evaluate the problem effectively.

Communication Skills

An assessment of my own communication skills in this project correlates with the progress of the consultation process described below. In the IC model, key communication skills are paraphrasing, perception checking, requesting clarification, asking relevant questions, and offering information (Rosenfield, 1987). My initial communications with Lynn emphasized paraphrasing and perception checking. My choice of what information to paraphrase during our initial sessions was critical to the momentum and productivity of the sessions.

At first I made the mistake of perception checking Lynn's frustrations too often without structuring the interview to focus on student behavior and her goals. This bogged the process down and made it sound more like a therapy session. After two such sessions, and advice from the IC supervisor, the sessions slowly began to involve much more requesting clarification through statements and questions designed to help clarify the problem identified. I made a subtle shift to spend more time paraphrasing Lynn's behavioral descriptions and goals than her feelings and frustrations. I also began to ask clarifying questions that required more specificity and details on Lynn's part regarding her concerns about Marjory's behaviors. I learned by the fourth session how to recognize when the session was getting off target just by paying attention to the amount of perception checking I was doing, and noting how often this could get us off track.

In the category of offering information, I had to guard against offering solutions to the problem, as opposed to just sharing relevant information or research. The IC supervisor taught me to first tell the teacher that I had some experience/knowledge about the problem, and then ASK her if she would be interested in hearing about it. A variation of this was to tell her I had some information in regard to the problem, and letting her know she could ask me about it anytime (the present or future sessions). This technique bought me time to think before responding with my own expertise/experience. This helped to maintain the teacher's power of choice, as well as her ownership of the problem for which she had requested consultation.

The combination of my expertise in the field and the intensity and frequency of Marjory's aggression to herself and others made holding back my own ideas for intervention strategies very difficult for me; but when I took the time to do so, the resulting interventions were much more successful. However, there were times that I had to move to direct service provision, when the problems, both physical and emotional, needed immediate attention on the same day. This "hands-on" time paid off, as staff and Lynn knew that I understood what it was like to "be in their shoes" more than any of my past descriptions of my experiences could tell them. They needed to see me doing what they did in order to trust me and perhaps more importantly trust themselves, their own skills, and be open to more constructive feedback. However, when such situations occurred, I had to make the boundaries clear with Lynn immediately after the crisis. The best way to do this was for me to respond to the crisis outside of the consultation model, and as quickly as possible (even on the same day) return to the teacher-centered IC model to focus, change, or modify our interventions. This combination of direct and indirect service delivery was essential in this case.

Reflection Two

I learned a tremendous amount about my own communication skills, as well as how to monitor and expand them to meet consultation outcomes. I learned that my skills in perception checking and requesting clarification were well established because of my other coursework and clinical and educational experience, but that there needed to be balance. The lack of balance was nullifying the positive effects these communications could provide! But I was frequently conflicted between my desire to get the task done versus being empathic and helping the teacher feel better. Getting lost in either state would detour the process. In this regard, the clear structure of the IC process helped me become aware of which path I was taking at any given time, where previously I would not even know I had switched directions. The IC model kept me on task to the point where the teacher could harness her creativity to develop and deliver effective interventions to maximize instructional availability for her student.

Problem-Solving Stages

Referral and Entry

In my previous experiences with other schools and programs, referrals were made for my services at team meetings, usually with my participation/presence. This case was referred for my services from the program coordinator of Pathways. He stated that the Pathways program needed help with Marjory's violent behaviors. This small change in procedure was another red flag that Pathways did not operate with the same cultural regularities as my other schools as well as the broader one of the school system itself. In hindsight, I should have switched gears at this point and attempted to learn about and understand this separate culture before I entered the consultation relationship further. Requesting clarification regarding Pathways' practices and procedures that staff utilized to plan and implement effective strategies would have given me better information with which to proceed.

Unfortunately, I continued to operate under the false assumption that Pathways had similar culture procedures to my other programs, and inquired about when a team meeting would be held to determine which services were needed for this teacher and student. The coordinator's response was that I was being ordered to do something because the teacher was emotionally upset, the principal was worried about the safety of students in the building, and the student was becoming more dangerous to herself and others. Even as the so-called "expert" in dealing with such problem behaviors, I was not accustomed to referrals made in this manner, and particularly without having the teacher present. I soon learned this crisis response model was the norm for other programs in the district for students with severe intellectual and behavioral challenges. A more collaborative process was the norm for the other students in Marcetti, as well as for other school buildings that did not provide services for children with complex special needs.

I informed the coordinator that I would present the consultation format and process to Marjory's teacher, and would get back to him regarding whether or not she was in agreement with the process and willing to work with me. I soon learned that even this first step would not be easy. When I contacted Lynn to set up a meeting to see if she wanted my services, she told me to come and meet with her anytime in the morning. I suggested 9 a.m. and came to her room.

I did not know that I was to meet with this teacher while her students and para-educators were in the room. The teacher was required to be in her classroom at all times, given the severity of the behaviors of her students and the potential harm that could happen to the students and staff. School administration subsequently informed me there were no allotted times during the teaching day that she could meet outside of the classroom. One possible exception was her lunch time, *if and only if* there were enough staff in the room to be with the students should a safety issue occur in her absence. When I stated that I could not conduct consultation services in this manner, administration reiterated that this was the way things were done in this program, and that's the way I had to work. My school psychology district supervisor told me to abide by the school administration's policies. I proceeded to start the contract process with Lynn in her room, with five interruptions from her staff when they truly needed her assistance.

Over time, Lynn and I carved out 30-minute time intervals before her school day started for which neither of us was paid. She stated she really felt she needed to try this process so she could better serve her students, and did not want to abandon it because of the time constraints. She also did not want to cause any friction with school administration by requesting additional time allotments because it was her first year in the system.

I soon found the practice of meeting at non-contractual times to be common among the other special education classes in Pathways' programs at other school sites. There was almost a clandestine nature to this practice, as the program coordinator usually was unable to attend such meetings, despite invitations offered to fit his schedule. At the same time, school administration would not go on record saying they "approved" these meeting times because it implied they were asking staff to report on non-duty hours. Many of the Pathways' teachers' meetings with classroom staff (when they couldn't get together on off-duty hours) occurred randomly throughout the day whenever anyone had a moment—in the hallway, while taking students to the restroom, and while students were going to other classes, such as gym. Because the larger school culture of Marcetti failed to provide an arena for problem solving at Pathways, let alone collegiality and sharing, the special education teachers of Pathways had created it themselves whenever and wherever they needed it. This unmet need for team meetings contributed to the creation of a sub-culture, where the Pathways staff made their own procedures to meet their needs. The unintentional, but ultimate, effect of this practice was to take away Pathways' staff time from direct instruction with students, in order to ensure all classroom team members were kept in the loop of information/problem solving about their students.

Reflection Three

A consultative/collaboration model was not in place in the school at the time the case was assigned to me. Establishment of such a model is a critical facilitator for effective consultation. Since the teacher had not made the referral, I might have said I wouldn't conduct a consultation unless this culture was first in place. I was familiar with Marjory's behaviors in other school programs where I worked, and I wanted to experiment with consultation with teachers of severely challenged students, so I elected to proceed. However, I recognized the challenge of doing so in this context.

Contracting

Lynn was not surprised when I called her by phone to set up a meeting time. She indicated the program coordinator had told her I would be contacting her. I made it clear that unlike her relationship with the program coordinator, the consultation with me would be voluntary, not supervisory. Her initial response was "Whatever … Nobody here cares about what happens anyway in my class, no matter how much I ask for help."

At our introductory meeting I explained the consultation process using the triangle and graphic illustration (Gravois, Rosenfield, & Gickling, 2002). At least five times in the 10-minute presentation, Lynn stated, "I just want to know how to make Marjory stop hurting people AND not get hurt myself." The intensity of her efforts to get this point across caused me to switch gears from contracting to communicating, so I commented, "She is really hurting people in your classroom and this is so scary. You must feel that no one has been listening to you and getting you the help you need." Lynn became quiet and began to cry. She spoke of how she had been asking for help for over a month, and only when Marjory bit the finger of one her teaching assistants who had to go the emergency room, did she feel as if the school administration was finally paying attention to her. She also added that she would "do whatever you tell me to make her stop, I promise!"

At this first formal IC session, I struggled with challenges within the consultation relationship with Lynn that would continue to evolve over time. These issues centered around how to keep moving forward in the action steps of formal contracting and eventually problem identification in the IC model while still making sure Lynn felt she was being heard and validated. If the latter were not accounted for, Lynn's motivation to "stick with the process" would wane. If it were overemphasized, the process would stagnate.

Explaining to Lynn that I would not be telling her what to do and that we would be engaged in a voluntary, collaborative relationship confused her, but she did begin to listen. When I told her the relationship would be confidential, she indicated she was happy to know this.

Our initial session ended with Lynn having an illustration of the consultation process to review and a handwritten contract to consider (note: written contracts are not typically part of the contracting stage, but seemed to make sense to me in this situation). She wanted to sign it immediately, but I was wary of her need to "rush to solve the problem" (Rosenfield, 1987) versus understanding and making the commitment to the process. I told her to take it home, read it again, and we set up our next meeting time. Lynn called me the next day at my other school and asked me where she could fax the signed contract. The call came in at 7:10 a.m. on the messaging machine, before any staff at this different school were even in the building.

At a later point in the IC process Lynn and I chose to return to the contracting stage and revise the consultation contract formally. This occurred when she wanted more time to talk about her feelings and requested to be able to get "some of this off her back for a few minutes." The IC process was flexible enough to allow us to return to contracting for revision. In our revision, we agreed on limits in regards to how, when, and for how long "getting stuff off her back" would occur as a compromise position rather than interfering with the problem solving/intervention stages, or ending the IC relationship.

Problem Identification and Analysis

From my work with other teachers, I assumed that problem identification would require more time than it did with this case. As a well-trained and competent special educator, Lynn was very skilled in looking at antecedents and consequences, and had already kept daily data regarding the behaviors of Marjory and her other students. Lynn had not allowed her frustrations and emotions to impact her expertise in this skill area. Indeed, she had operational definitions for targeted behaviors of each of her students that had been determined and agreed upon with all of her classroom staff. I was able to also observe the behavior and pick it out based on these definitions. Baseline data were available for all of Marjory's problem behaviors: biting, dropping to the floor, scratching and kicking others, and destroying property. Discussing the topography of behaviors could still easily slip into "complaining" about them for both teacher and consultant. Given my history with Marjory over several years and first-hand knowledge of many failed interventions, I was vulnerable to negative judgments and giving opinions based on past frustrations. Continuous self-monitoring of my own behaviors and communication skills was required.

We decided to look at which behaviors occurred in isolation, or occurred in sequential chains together. Lynn was readily able to identify the dropping to the floor as the initial behavior that would always escalate into one or more of the others. The more we talked, with only minimal clarification questions from me,

Lynn was able to see that there was a progression in tone and volume with Marjory's vocalizing before she dropped to the floor. She suggested that maybe if we could work toward a goal of decreasing the vocalizing, we could interrupt the chain. With such complex behaviors, forming the definition of desired performance required discrete analysis that accounted for multiple variables: Marjory will drop to the floor and require physical intervention to stand no more than twice a day. (The present rate was close to 40 incidents a week.) Although best practice is to write goals in the affirmative (what Marjory would be doing instead of floor-dropping), Lynn was adamant that the only way she would know if progress was being made was if both the dropping decreased AND Marjory got herself up from the floor after she dropped. She noted that even on days when less than 10 incidents of floor-dropping occurred, the time staff had to spend physically moving/lifting Marjory was extensive and impacted instructional time for other students. Marjory weighed 190 lbs. and was close to six feet in height, so moving her from the floor required three individuals. Lynn agreed to indicate the desired performance goals behaviorally for Marjory as long as she could measure a decrease in the problem behavior and the physical intervention required to deal with them.

Marjory's records showed a history of these behaviors and various interventions to attempt to decrease them. However, the most salient information in the records over the last six years was that Marjory's aggression and floor-dropping had been relatively intractable. There were periods of less frequent episodes of the behavior. These usually correlated with hospitalizations and intensive behavioral programs in a special center, as well as medication changes. Given this history, Lynn's willingness to work with these behaviors, as opposed to just throwing up her hands given their long history, was impressive. She did not set out to be a miracle worker, but at the same time was determined to give Marjory the best chance to make it in her classroom and increase the time she was actually available to and involved in direct instruction.

Lynn's own data showed that when floor-dropping was ignored (sometimes for as long as two hours, for which she would scream and try to crawl and aggress at anyone near her) and staff stayed nearby but just out of reach, Marjory would eventually get up and walk by herself to the next task/activity. Indeed, this was the most successful intervention in the special center three years ago, before two residential programs had determined they were not able to work with her. In the special center, however, the variables of other typical student classrooms, hall activity, and such were not present, let alone concern for the safety issues for other students.

The initial problems we identified were screaming and floor-dropping (with precise duration, volume levels, parts of body on floor, etc. to define each). This was because Lynn felt these affected Marjory's availability to instruction the most, as well as her ability to have enough staff to teach the other students in the class. Baseline data were taken rapidly over a two-week time period by staff, and graphed on the Student Documentation Form (SDF).

Reflection Four

Recognizing and allowing Lynn to demonstrate her competence in the above skill areas was important for both of us. She was able to gain back a sense of power and self-efficacy that had suffered under the stress of the challenges in her room and building. It had not only dealt a blow to her self-confidence, but also had caused her to lose objectivity (Caplan, 1970), and this process increased her motivation and drive. It also humbled me, as I was able to avoid seeing myself as an expert or a therapist—and indeed made it impossible to fall into these traps.

I also found myself having to set an example for the teacher when actually I shared her frustrations based on my own history with this student in "real time." This confluence of emotions regarding one student over time had not occurred before in my career, and required continuous self-monitoring of my thoughts and emotions simultaneously. The definitive nature of the IC model with its "map" of steps and boundaries was critical for me to keep focused on the task at hand. I don't think this would have been possible within a less defined methodology.

Intervention Design Stage

A two-tiered intervention was designed. Despite Lynn's invitations and my requests, the Marcetti school principal and coordinator of Pathways both declined to attend the meetings to plan the interventions. They did however, request copies of our plan for their approval. The first tier involved immediately redirecting/distracting Marjory when pre-cursor vocalizations started, as well as staff clearing proximal areas from students. The second required moving away from physical contact and from anyone giving verbal/facial attention. Staff members were positioned in three different location points in the area surrounding Marjory. Only a verbal request paired with basic sign language to "Get up. Let's go to ______," was delivered every three minutes. When Marjory responded positively, she was guided without praise to the activity, and praised later after five minutes of on-task behavior. Previous data showed if praised for getting up, she would drop down again. If her response was negative, physical, verbal, and nonverbal contact was again withdrawn.

Administration and staff agreed to the plan. We designated three people every hour that would be Marjory's guards when she dropped to the floor and clear the area of other students. The intervention was started. Various activity stations were set up, including the one she may have initially avoided with her behavior, as distracters from precursor vocalizations.

Reflection Five

I was careful not to underestimate the time and effort that would be involved in such a program, and that if we began it, we would likely see an initial sharp increased intensity and frequency of floor-dropping. The task would be to hold the course over the next week or two to judge the effectiveness of the intervention. I expressed my opinion that this should not be initiated unless there was a commitment from everyone to do this, for at least three weeks. I knew from experience that doing it for a brief time and then changing the intervention significantly would cause us to have a much bigger problem than we started with. Offering this information was essential.

Intervention Stage: Take One

The first two days went as expected—three incidents on the floor lasting two-and-a-half hours each—most of the school day. However, when Marjory stood up, she did so without being physically forced to by the staff. Days four and five had one incident each of one hour and two more of 10 minutes, suggesting progress was being made. All staff knew how to collect the data, as well as conduct the intervention. All regular education teachers were notified of what would be happening in the halls and how to divert their students if given the directions to do so by Lynn's staff.

Before the second week began, both the school principal and the program coordinator announced that the intervention was too disruptive to other students in the hallway, and said that at no time could Marjory ever be in any hallway in the school building any more. This meant she would have to stay in the classroom with five other severely disabled youngsters, eat there, use the bathroom there, as well as not attend art, music, and PE with her own classmates. She would not even be allowed to walk to her classroom off the bus down the hallway, and instead have to be walked outside to her back classroom door.

Reflection Six

Looking back, I should have asked questions about what types of disruption, as well as at what intensity levels, could be tolerated by the school administration and student body of Marcetti. This was an important aspect of the school culture that I had neglected to examine at the onset of the IC process, let alone request it to be defined for me. Given the types of behaviors many Pathways students demonstrated in general, it was critical to know what intensity levels of which behaviors the school could or could not tolerate, and where and under what conditions in the school building. Whether defined explicitly or not, such limit setting is present in all school cultures. The easy way out, when it was as ill-defined at Marcetti/Pathways, was to place blame on school administration for not being more actively involved in the original intervention design for Marjory.

The more responsible action to have taken would have been to schedule a meeting with the school administration on my own and describe Marjory's behaviors, estimate levels of their intensity/duration and "play out" various scenarios of potential impact to Marcetti from a building, staff, and student perspective. The fact that I had been "assigned" to this case (as opposed to a teacher requesting my assistance), warranted such action within this school culture. This was particularly true because the culture at large and "sub-culture" of Pathways had never really been integrated. Such a meeting may have fostered more administration involvement in the intervention design in the first place, and at the very least provided them with a more realistic base to evaluate proposed intervention.

Problem Identification Stage: Take Two

We also found we needed to return to the problem-solving process, as we discovered we had new problems. When Marjory would drop to the floor, unless it was art or PE time, other students in the room would show escalations in their maladaptive behaviors, including head banging and scratching in a more self-abusive manner. Lynn had frequency data of all her students' behaviors and at what time they occurred, and it was easy to see that their highest frequency of maladaptive behaviors correlated with the same time periods as Marjory's floor-drops.

Intervention Stage: Take Two

In an attempt to revise the strategy but keep its integrity, the rest of the class (five students) was moved out to take a hall walk any time Marjory would engage in a floor-drop, while the same procedures were followed. However, given the change in environmental factors and break in consistency for Marjory, the frequency and intensity and duration of her tantrums (again back up to two to three hours) did not make moving the other kids out of the room feasible. The principal and program coordinator stated there was no other location they would approve to move the other youngsters to, even until Marjory's behaviors were more stable. Fortunately, we didn't have this intervention in place for more than a day before the school principal stated we could not implement it. We returned to the model and problem solving.

Intervention Stage: Take Three

In the end, we decided to implement another intervention that involved moving her within the classroom to a small room.

This was not ideal, but could ensure the most consistency for Marjory. This was difficult to set up, because Lynn's data showed that moving Marjory to a quiet room (alternative structure room) in the classroom escalated her behaviors, and indeed served as a reward because she had to be physically moved by three staff to this location in the room. This physical interaction was more rewarding to Marjory than being in the room, which was aversive to her. We opted to proactively set up several areas for direct one-to-one instruction in the room, separated by large vertical mat dividers. Break times and praise were always rewarding for Marjory, so we made work times short, in different locations. When floor-drops did occur, staff would divide up to retain proximity, and other staff would move the other class members to a different area of the room, or else model ignoring Marjory to the other youngsters. This in turn resulted in designing another program for another student to learn to request help instead of scratching when she needed to be away from Marjory.

Evaluation of Intervention

The data on the SDF form showed much variation in the rate and frequency of Marjory's behavior under all three interventions. When looked at on a weekly basis over the two-month time period (with three different intervention plans), it was clear that the first plan was most effective. However, when the data from all three interventions were viewed graphically on a linear level, there was a small, but definitive slope indicating a decrease in the behavior. There was a zigzag pattern between days with over 20 incidents of floor-dropping, to days with eight or under, but after a month, the 20 incident high points were decreasing to 15 and even one 10-incident high point. In this regard, the intervention, while not meeting the desired outcome, did show a modest improvement, but at a slow rate that was complicated by the frequent intervention changes.

However, from a consultee-centered perspective, the effect on the teacher was impressive. It was not possible to move this student to a different placement for a number of systems related issues, but it was possible to support Lynn in her work with Marjory. In contrast to the small change in student outcomes, there was a successful teacher outcome in this case. It occurred in the changes made for Lynn. She learned that she could turn her frustration into positive intervention energy—not just for the sake of changing Marjory's behavior—but because of her own intrinsic motivation to be an effective teacher. She saw that these changes in attitude, even in the face of questionable results, changed the attitude and competencies of the rest of her classroom staff. The process of change became as important as Marjory's outcome, due to the consultee-centered focus of the consultation. And yet, even the limited amount of success that occurred with Marjory could never have happened without it. Lynn noted that the process had taught her she was a good teacher, and that she could still be a good teacher regardless of the level of administration support, because she was an excellent teacher to start with. With all the challenges, she had forgotten that. Finally she added with a grin, "I guess I needed Marjory to teach me this—didn't I? Funny how things work out that way."

Lessons Learned

The inconsistency of resources and facilities required me to monitor my own feelings constantly and keep myself looking at what the teacher wanted to achieve for herself and her student. I had to be focused on not bemoaning what was or wasn't available in terms of time, training, staff, or materials on any given day. For example, designation of an alternative structure room for individual instruction to prevent property destruction (as opposed to consequent it) was made by program staff, and two days later was no longer available because administration wanted it used for other tasks. Showing the data of change, even for these two days, did not change the administrators' decision, nor did I gain their help in accessing another location. These are clearly systems issues that need to be addressed, probably at the district level.

I quickly learned that expressing my own anger at the school and passing judgment (even nonverbally) on such comments as "undermining staff efforts at student success," or "setting the student up to fail," would not help Lynn with Marjory at the present moment in her teaching day. Indeed, it got us both off task too easily. Such issues needed to be dealt with in a different forum. I also realized that I was serving as a role model for productive, professional, and student-focused behavior. Only by establishing the boundaries for myself could I provide them for the teacher. I had to give up the luxury of complaining, not just within the project, but in all of my interactions with colleagues in the building, who for years had engaged in this with me. I knew, however, that I could not effectively support a teacher in how to do this or expect such professional behavior unless I could do it for myself. This also involved me openly telling Lynn about how I had seen that my own behaviors were not productive for our relationship, as well as prevented a focus on the student. Changing and acknowledging my behavior in this regard was a significant factor that contributed to the success of this consultation relationship, and changed the direction it was heading.

As noted previously, Lynn initially resented the drawing of these boundaries, but did accept and work with them once she had input into the format of our sessions. While giving her a brief respite for emotional expression could be helpful at times, it could also backfire into an unending cycle of complaining versus action. There were also hints that the consultation relationship might end too abruptly if there was not a transition period in changing these boundaries. Eventually, the length of this venting time decreased in proportion to Lynn's success with interventions, and her own ability to see this success rather than focus on variables that she could not control.

Recording the specifics of how we would be working together was critical in this consultation for Lynn. It laid the foundations for her to determine, design, and implement strategies that would enable her to teach her student. Over time, the written documentation served not only as a means to document the student's progress, but enabled Lynn to see her own competencies. Seeing these words in writing and using the visual charts helped change the thought process from "what was wrong with Marjory" to what do we need to help you teach and manage her behavior more effectively. It was more efficient and effective in achieving this paradigm shift than any verbal discussion using words alone.

The visual focus secured her attention and kept her from being overloaded with her emotions and frustrations. It also prevented me from turning into a counselor as opposed to an instructional consultant. Despite several qualitative differences between IC models within regular and special education, this aspect of using the "visual map" and changing the focus from the student to what the teacher needs to do to help her was remarkably similar to what I had observed occur in IC in regular education programs.

Helping Lynn to own her power to design and experience what she could accomplish successfully in teaching Marjory on any given day was a complex task. It required flexibility, including working with her and her classroom staff to develop back-up interventions when resources were not available, as well as the continual tweaking of interventions so they would be the least dependent on the variables that were the most inconsistent, as opposed to just complaining about them. It also required adjusting goals to sometimes less ambitious ones to ensure success, as opposed to talking about what couldn't be done because "we lost this or that, didn't have money/staff for this or that."

Lynn had to get this power for herself within a school culture that would not acknowledge her success or provide consistent support to make this possible. Constantly telling myself that I could not solve her problem or take care of her became a frequent meditation for me during this project. Supporting and encouraging her own creativity and resourcefulness, as opposed to just giving her my own expertise in this situation, required much restraint on my part.

Getting in touch with my own need to be the expert and chief problem-solver was the second most important factor in the progress of this consultation relationship. I had to learn to ask if she wanted to hear my thoughts/ideas when I could sense that the expert side of me resurfaced in its arrogance. When her response was affirmative, the next task for me was to present only minimal/skeletal pieces of information, constantly asking her opinions, and eliciting her expansion/association process to take such information and integrate it within her own classroom framework. The temptation, given the serious nature of many of the behaviors, was to jump into the expert role. My resistance to this tendency showed Lynn that she could indeed determine and monitor interventions that were successful, as well as identify the variables that limited success for her.

Finally, the consultation process seemed to show her that she could become flexible in the face of inconsistent administration/staff support. This meant not denying her feelings, but instead re-channeling and using this energy to keep the focus on her student and her goals. Indeed, we both learned this, even though our roles in the process were different.

Closing Thoughts

A Call for Systems-Level Consultation

Only the public education agency has a legal mandate for service provision for students with such severe problems. With the onset of budget cuts at the national level, few agencies have enough extra financial resources to help provide for students like Marjory—especially when they are not legally bound to do so. Their funding is earmarked for those they are legally required to serve. Indeed, when Marjory's services from education end at age 21, she will be eligible for adult services, and educational monies will drop out.

School systems must first acknowledge this dilemma they face when serving students like Marjory. School psychologists consulting with classrooms like Lynn's need to recognize when reasonably successful outcomes cannot be achieved because broader system issues stand in the way. Just like teachers, systems are prone to get stuck in "blaming the student" without fully analyzing and attempting to solve the problem. Consultation at the system level is necessary to address these issues and shed light on the fiscal and personal safety consequences that occur when they are dealt with on an ad hoc basis or ignored.

Redefining Success

So what really is a successful outcome that teachers with students like Marjory can strive for? For a number of systems related issues, it was not possible to move this student to another placement in a timely way. Outcomes for such students need to focus on the most critical behaviors that pose a risk to safety and prevent availability to instruction in the foreground. In the background, attention to determining essential behaviors necessary for the student to access and even be able to function in adult programs is essential. The two will often intersect, as behaviors necessary to be available to instruction are often the same as those necessary to function more independently in an adult services program. Defining the environmental variables that impact/exacerbate these behaviors (e.g., the hallways at Marcetti) that can and cannot be controlled is critical to help determine the facilities to house classrooms for these students.

A successful outcome in this case must also start small enough so that a teacher can see progress. For example, a possible successful outcome for Marjory might be defined as the ability to walk down an empty hallway (which cannot be accessed by other individuals) with two escorts to a teacher-determined destination for four continuous minutes without aggression or floor-dropping. This leads to the logical question: "What environmental, building, safety and staff resources do we need/have to make achieving this goal possible?" School psychologists are well suited to develop such goals and define the environmental variables necessary to achieve them with precision. They can also provide the objectivity to serve as a go-between for emotionally exhausted front line personnel and budget-strapped system level administration.

Widening the View so no Teacher (or student) is Left Behind

WHAT THE INSTRUCTIONAL CONSULTATION MODEL CAN OFFER

For the school psychologist who chooses to serve such populations and teachers, IC offers a model for collaboration and expertise in a dynamic forum.

IC has the elements of structure and flexibility that are essential to serving students whose complex challenges are not easily understood. Like Marjory, many have behaviors that make them a danger to themselves and others, and that have been resistant to other interventions over time. The structure of the IC model provides a potential safety net, allowing the school psychologist to give stability and organization in a situation fraught with emotional overload. This overload drains the objectivity, cognitive resources, and motivation these teachers need to make maximum use of their skills and creativity to help such students become more consistently available for instruction as the first step in teaching them. The communication skills of paraphrasing and perception checking helps teachers feel supported, while requesting clarification and defining the problem keeps them on task. The communication skill of offering information could be expanded to obtaining information that can come from current research with such students across the fields of neurology, medicine, psychiatry as well as education, a role uniquely suited to the school psychologist.

But for an IC model to be truly effective for such unique student populations and their teachers, it must start at the top in the form of a systems-level consultation. Administration well above the school level need to be made aware that although the number of students like Marjory in special education programs is small, the cost to school staff, school buildings, materials, and other students is high not just financially, but also in terms of safety for staff and other students in the building. The stakes become even higher when housed in inclusive settings like Marcetti; and as in this particular case, there are limits placed on implementation of the behavior and learning strategies that have the most potential to be effective. Behaviors of significantly complex students that have a history of resistance to intervention require more, not less, flexibility in school environment adaptation as well as staff allocation and planning time. The school psychologist who is familiar with such students and staff at the "front line" level is in a unique position to frame the impact of these students in the context of the culture of each school building, as well as the system itself.

The school psychologist has the skills to report the impact of such students not just in individual classrooms, but in and across the school buildings where they are served with both quantitative and qualitative data. Consultation to the systems that design and deliver such programs by school psychologists can facilitate more accurate appraisal of the cost/benefit ratio of public as opposed to non-public options for serving such students.

In contrast to responding to the crises that will inevitably occur with such students, proactive planning at a systems level could not only lessen the impact, but also mediate and possibly prevent their occurrence. Once again, this issue is not one of blame, but of the need for open acknowledgement of this dilemma to determine how to deal with it. School psychologists can use the IC model at a systems level to help both school and system level administration look at the issues of risk and resources objectively and facilitate active as opposed to reactive problem solving for these teachers and their students. Such consultation could promote a cultural norm where no student or teacher is left behind—or unsafe.

Questions for Reflection

1. **What issues in this case are common to those in more traditional Instructional Consultation cases?**
2. **Would there be value in having all students in Instructional Consultations participate in a case like this one, with close assistance? Why or why not?**
3. **Is use of the IC model even appropriate for teachers of significantly challenged students? Why or why not?**
4. **What would it take to establish an IC model in a school district for teachers and classrooms for severely challenged students?**
5. **How could the role of school psychologist who serves similar populations be expanded to include consultation at the systems level? What levels of stakeholders in the system should be involved in such consultation?**

References

Caplan, G. (1970). *The theory and practice of mental health consultation.* New York: Basic Books.

Gravois, T.A., Rosenfield, S., & Gickling, E. (2002). A multi-dimensional framework for evaluation of instructional consultation teams. *Journal of Applied School Psychology, 19*, 5–30.

Higgins, E.T. (1999). "Saying is believing" effects. In L.L. Thompson, J.M. Levine, & D.M. Messick (Eds.). *Shared cognition in organizations* (pp. 33–48). Mahwah, NJ: Lawrence Erlbaum Associates.

Rosenfield, S. (1987). *Instructional consultation.* Hillsdale, NJ: Lawrence Erlbaum Associates.

Rosenfield, S. (2008). Best practices in instructional consultation. In A. Thomas & J. Grimes (Eds.). *Best practices in school psychology V* (pp. 1645–1660). Washington, DC: National Association of School Psychologists.

Rosenfield, S., Silva, A., & Gravois, T. (2008). Bringing instructional consultation to scale: Research and development of IC and IC teams. In W.P. Erchul & S.M. Sheridan (Eds.). *Handbook of research in school consultation: Empirical foundations for the field* (pp. 203–223). Hillsdale, NJ: Lawrence Erlbaum Associates.

Sarason, S. (1996). *Revisiting "The culture of the school and the problem of change."* New York: Teachers College Press.

Index